Women

and the

Vatican

To Roman Catholic Women

Simply put, one cannot, or at least should not, claim to have the perspective, but can only present a perspective, and hope it will lead to thoughtful consideration and an open dialogue with those who see things differently.

—Mary Aquin O'Neill

WOMEN

AND THE

VATICAN

An Exploration
of Official
Documents

IVY A. HELMAN

ORBIS BOOKS

Maryknoll, New York 10545

Founded in 1970, Orbis Books endeavors to publish works that enlighten the mind, nourish the spirit, and challenge the conscience. The publishing arm of the Maryknoll Fathers and Brothers, Orbis seeks to explore the global dimensions of the Christian faith and mission, to invite dialogue with diverse cultures and religious traditions, and to serve the cause of reconciliation and peace. The books published reflect the views of their authors and do not represent the official position of the Maryknoll Society. To learn more about Maryknoll and Orbis Books, please visit our website at www. maryknollsociety.org.

Copyright © 2012 by Ivy A. Helman.

Published by Orbis Books, Maryknoll, New York 10545–0302.

Manufactured in the United States of America.
Manuscript editing and typesetting by Joan Weber Laflamme.

Grateful acknowledgment is made to Libreria Editrice Vaticana (© Libreria Editrice Vaticana) for permission to reprint sections of the Vatican documents included herein.

Queries regarding rights and permissions should be addressed to: Orbis Books, P.O. Box 302, Maryknoll, New York 10545–0302.

Library of Congress Cataloging-in-Publication Data

Helman, Ivy A.
    Women and the Vatican : an exploration of official documents / Ivy A. Helman.
        p. cm.
    Includes bibliographical references (p.) and index.
    ISBN 978-1-57075-967-3 (pbk.)
    1. Women in the Catholic Church. 2. Women—Religious aspects—Catholic Church. 3. Feminism—Religious aspects—Catholic Church. 4. Catholic Church—Doctrines. I. Title.
    BX2347.8.W6H45 2012
    282.082—dc23

2011032124

Contents

Acknowledgments

Much of the research for this book began during the writing of my dissertation. I am forever grateful to the members of my dissertation committee, Ellen Ott Marshall, Rosemary Radford Ruether, and Karen Jo Torjesen, for their support, guidance, and commitment. Thank you all for continuing to challenge, engage, and inspire me still today.

There are many other people I must thank for their role in putting this book together. Susan Perry, senior editor at Orbis, who took a chance on me by offering me the opportunity to write my first book; none of this would have been possible without you. Thank you.

I would also like to thank Margaret Farley, one of my professors at Yale Divinity School. You showed me the power of faith and commitment and continuously inspire me with your voice that is not afraid to speak up for what you believe is right, fair, and just. Thank you for your years of support, encouragement, and friendship. You inspire much of the work I do.

Lisa Sowle Cahill and Mary Ann Hinsdale, colleagues of mine at Boston College, who met with me early in the planning and proposal stages of this book; thank you for the brainstorming sessions, the resources you shared, and your advice concerning organization and chronology.

I also am indebted to family and friends. Thank you, Margaret Jennings, not only for being a great colleague at Boston College but also a great friend. I really enjoy our chance encounters, catching up on how you are doing and learning the progress of that megalithic three-volume project on which you are spending so much of your time.

My mother, Jean Maiwald; I really do not know where to begin. It is not possible to summarize everything you have done for me and the numerous ways you have supported me and helped me grow throughout my life. I know a thank you is not enough. This book would not have been possible without everything you have done for me, especially now with your support of me as I begin a new chapter of my life.

My father, James Helman, who has always had high academic expectations for me; I hope I can make you proud. I wish we lived closer so when I need a break we could play a round of golf and drink a beer together.

Finally, I am forever indebted to Eileen Ennis. You have been the best friend anyone could ask for, and I am so glad we found each other again after all these years. Who knew you lived in Quincy? Your kindness and generosity are unmatched. There was a lot going on in my life while I was putting this book together, and I do not think I would have had the strength to persevere without you by my side. Thank you also for letting me stay with you for a month while I looked for a new apartment. Words cannot express how happy I am to have you in my life.

Introduction

This book answers questions about women from the perspective of the Roman Catholic Church. It addresses general ones: Who is a woman? What roles should women have? What significance should motherhood have in women's lives? How do women balance careers and family life? Should women work outside the home? How do women find fulfillment? What do women contribute to this world? How do women make this world a better place? It also looks at more focused questions about women and the Roman Catholic Church: What vocations are open to women within the Roman Catholic Church? Can women be priests? What do women contribute to the life and work of the church? What have women done within the history of the church? How did Jesus treat women? What is the theological significance of women as the first observers of the resurrection?

From a theological perspective, these questions cannot be sufficiently answered before the 1960s, even though there are some documents beginning in 1880 that discuss women.[1] Before the 1960s, Roman Catholic theology often addressed women's roles and duties as wives and mothers, only rarely venturing into their lives outside the home. When the documents did, they addressed women's rights as workers. While this separation of women into their own significant theological category began in the late 1880s, it became more focused in the 1930s with *Casti connubii*, only becoming developed fully after 1960. Starting in the 1960s the theological language changed significantly, specifically toward defining womanhood, women's roles in the family and the church, women's interaction with the world, and how women are to find fulfillment.

---

[1] All Vatican documents can be found on the Vatican's official website (http://www.vatican.va). The reader should be aware that this anthology includes selections from many documents but few documents in their entirety, and the endnotes have been dropped during the editing process. Most of the documents on the Vatican website contain the endnotes if the reader is interested. However, one should note that some documents on the Vatican website have in-text references, but the publisher has not supplied the content of the notes at the end of the document. A good resource in this case is http://www.papalencyclicals.net.

One can trace this historical development of a Roman Catholic official theology of womanhood in parallel with another historical development found in the larger society: feminism. This seems to account quite well for the new acknowledgment of women as a distinct group or class within Vatican documents in the late 1800s. It also suggests a new way to understand the plethora of Vatican documents about women after 1960. In fact, it is true that the Roman Catholic Church has been highly influenced by feminism, and as feminism developed and the concept and role of women changed, the church addressed the "woman question." This does not necessarily imply that Roman Catholic leadership was against or for women's movements (and what became known as feminism) per se, but rather that as society (prodded by feminists and others seeking personal, civil, and social rights) began to lay out new understandings of womanhood, the leadership of the church felt the need to define its concept of womanhood as well. To see this point more clearly, one must explore the history of feminism in the United States and beyond.

THE HISTORY OF FEMINISM

In her book *Feminist Politics and Human Nature*, Allison Jaggar explains, "'Feminism' was originally a French word. It referred to what in the nineteenth-century United States was called 'the woman movement.' . . . It was used to refer only to one particular group of women's rights advocates, namely that group which asserted the uniqueness of women, the mystical experience of motherhood and women's special purity."[2] First-wave feminism in the United States evolved out of women's experience in abolition around the 1830s. Many women fought for freedom from slavery only to realize their own second-class status. For example, some women went to Britain for an anti-slavery conference and were refused seating. This occurrence led some women to form separate women-only abolitionist groups. Gradually, many women began to understand the full nature of their situation in society. However, how to address their second-class status was up for debate. As already mentioned, some, probably all white, women argued for the uniqueness of womanhood and its contributions toward building a better society. Women from this group advocated prohibition and won it with the premise that women could run a more moral society than men had been running. Yet, in New York in the 1920s, feminism already had turned a critical eye toward the concepts of patriarchy and sexism.

---

[2] Allison M. Jaggar, *Feminist Politics and Human Nature* (Savage, MD: Rowman and Littlefield Publishers, 1988), 5.

In the United States there was also a strand of first-wave feminism that believed women to be equal to men. This branch of feminism is commonly called liberal feminism. Through these individuals, feminism fought to better the position of women within the existing society. One of the ways they saw fit to do so was to push for recognition within an already established legal system.[3] United States women received the right to vote in 1921.

Liberal feminism was also a global movement in the late 1800s and through the first decades of the 1900s. It saw many groups of women from various countries fight for and gain the right to vote using the same logic of gaining rights within a system, arguing for fair treatment in law. In addition, in the 1920s in the United States, this belief in gender equality as sameness produced the Equal Rights Amendment. U.S. second-wave feminism would fight that battle.

Some first-wave feminists also worked for labor laws that granted women certain privileges based on their biological destiny: motherhood.[4] Women had to be protected from workplace danger and overwork. Likewise, women's education should equip them to be successful mothers. Elizabeth Blackwell was one of the more famous feminists who argued this view.[5] Other feminists argued that women who wished to pursue higher education should have the opportunity. In the United States during first-wave feminism many women argued for the right to work.[6] Many women enjoyed paid employment in what were then considered women's jobs such as nursing, midwifery, and teaching. Birth control was an issue in U.S. first-wave feminism despite its heavy ties to the second wave. The form of the protest each wave took was quite different. During first-wave feminism, women advocated for the right to deny sex when their husbands wanted it. This was one of the few ways women could avoid pregnancy because few contraceptive techniques were available. Women organized to reach as many women as possible with contraceptive information.[7]

Most people think that feminism ceased to exist in the United States in any substantial form between the Nineteenth Amendment and the birth of second-wave feminism in the mid 1960s. Globally, however, many women in non-Western and Western countries fought for the right to vote through the late 1940s but did not receive it. Feminist women around the globe continued to fight for that liberal cause, among many others. Simone de

---

[3] Ibid., 5.

[4] Margaret Forster, *Significant Sisters: The Grassroots of Active Feminism 1839–1939* (New York: Alfred A. Knopf, 1985), 75.

[5] Ibid., chap. 2.

[6] Ibid., 128–29.

[7] Ibid., 245.

Beauvoir's classic feminist book, *The Second Sex*, was published in 1949, during what seemed to be a lull in global feminisms.

Likewise, in the United States, feminism was not dead. Every year or so the Equal Rights Amendment (ERA) made it to the floor in Congress. This time period also saw Eleanor Roosevelt as an outspoken feminist advocate. Women entered the workplace in large numbers due to World War II, and some women even started a professional baseball league. Very few of the women were willing to leave their positions when the men came home from the war. Therefore, the tradition of women holding jobs outside the home continued.

Yet, in the early to mid 1960s something in the United States changed. Many women, especially white women, became enmeshed in organizations fighting for civil rights and the end of nuclear war, among other causes. They were continuously made aware of their second-class status because many men did not consider women's issues as important as the antiwar campaign or other issues.

Many white and black women also worked to end segregation and the Jim Crow laws in the South. Participating in this struggle produced different experiences for white and black women. Black women did not feel that their needs were being addressed. They were there to support their men, or so they were told. In order to ally themselves with black men, they were forced to ignore sexism within their community and the larger United States. White women helped champion an end to segregation and once again participated in a similar second-class experience, as their foremothers had during abolitionist times. The experience was particularly poignant for Southern white women. Once again, while fighting for others' rights (even black women did not have much of an opportunity to champion their own rights within the black civil rights movement) many women, both white and black, experienced oppression.

Slowly, these women began to name their experiences as oppression. Many abandoned leftist organizations that had made it quite clear that they did not care for or take seriously enough women's issues. Most members of second-wave feminism became feminists through consciousness-raising groups. It was in these groups that (mostly) white women (at least initially) shared their experiences, realized that they were not alone in those experiences, and began to name those experiences as oppressive.

Ideologically, compared to first-wave feminism, second-wave feminism in the United States moved onto a broader critique of the social structure of oppression.[8] Struggling for equality was more complex than just struggling for rights in a system and therefore more difficult because the level

---

[8] Jaggar, *Feminist Politics and Human Nature*, 7.

of oppression was understood to be all pervasive. However, even though oppression was everywhere one looked, abortion and control of one's reproductive faculty soon became key issues.[9] This most likely occurred for three reasons. First, technological advances in medicine had made abortion more routine and minimized the threat of death. Technology also birthed the pill. However, the pill was not foolproof, and many women saw the need for a backup plan. Second, and equally important, women were enjoying sex more freely than they had in the past, thanks to the sexual liberation movement. Finally, women asserted that in order to be completely autonomous human beings, they needed to have some control over their bodies and not be constantly worrying about becoming pregnant.

During second-wave feminism the ERA, which pushed the idea of gender equality as sameness, finally passed both houses of Congress.[10] It came up for state ratification yet failed to secure the requisite thirty-eight states to grant ratification; it was three short.[11] To this day the loss of the ERA has for some signaled the death of feminism. For example, Susan Brownmiller, in her book *In Our Time: Memoir of a Revolution*, states that the defeat of the ERA was one more step toward the diminishment of feminism.[12]

Some second-wavers also created and espoused separatist ideals. They produced women's papers and journals, opened women's coffee houses, composed women's music, put on women-born-women music festivals, and so on. For example, the Michigan Womyn's Music Festival still takes place every second week in August. Likewise, many separatists embraced lesbianism as a political as well as sexual identity. Authors like Mary Daly and Valerie Solanas typify the separatist ideals of some second-wavers.

It was not only separatist feminists and lesbians who wrote and published women's journals and papers. Some of the major feminist theories

---

[9] Ibid., 117–18; Angela Gilliam, "Women's Equality and National Liberation," in *Third World Women and the Politics of Feminism*, ed. Chandra Talpade Mohanty, Ann Russo, and Lourdes Torres (Bloomington: University of Indiana Press, 1991), 216. Because of this, much of second-wave feminism has been criticized as elitist and as a movement that does not translate well either internationally or among racial or class minorities in the United States (see Gilliam's chapter in *Third World Women and the Politics of Feminism* for this critique).

[10] Rosemary Radford Ruether, *Contemporary Roman Catholicism: Crises and Challenges* (Kansas City, MO: Sheed and Ward, 1987), 38. Ruether points out that the church was against this movement.

[11] Jane J. Mansbridge, *Why We Lost the ERA* (Chicago: University of Chicago Press, 1986), 1.

[12] Susan Brownmiller, *In Our Time: Memoir of a Revolution* (New York: The Dial Press, 1990), 326–27.

of second-wave feminist thinking, writing, and activism came from small independent gatherings of women known as THE FEMINISTS, Redstockings, *Ain't I a Woman*, and more separatist ones like the Furies and Radicalesbians, to name a few.

In the United States, third-wave feminism "began in the late 1980's by feminists who wanted to make women's diversity—or diversity in general—more central to feminist theory and politics . . . and allow for a multiplicity of feminist goals."[13] We can see the beginnings of such a movement in the critiques that some of second-wave feminism was, even if unintentionally, elitist, classist, and racist tendencies. For example, Dorothy Roberts explains in her book *Killing the Black Body: Race, Reproduction, and the Meaning of Liberty* that while many white women fought to not have children, many black women fought to be able to have the children they wanted.[14] Many women of color, especially Native Americans and poor black women, were routinely sterilized without their knowledge or consent. Third-wave feminism recognizes the fact that not only is there oppression of women, but it is highly significant that not all women are oppressed to the same degree or in the same way. In fact, some women oppress other women, and men of differing racial background also face oppression from dominant peoples.[15]

Third-wave feminism also has a much more global reach within a local perspective. Third-wave feminism critiqued many second-wavers[16] who had criticized cultural practices such as female circumcision (called female genital mutilation by those against it). They saw these critiques as inherently wrong. Not only were the critiques of such practices made by white women and probably racist, but they were also very Western and lacked any real knowledge of the critiqued culture. Most significant, those critiques silenced local women's experiences with various cultural practices and their

---

[13] "Introduction to Part 1," in *Feminist Theory: A Philosophical Anthology*, ed. Ann E. Curd and Robin O. Andreasen (Oxford: Blackwell Publishing, 2005), 7, 8.

[14] Dorothy Roberts, *Killing the Black Body: Race, Reproduction, and the Meaning of Liberty* (New York: Pantheon Books, 1997), chap. 2. For specific information regarding the full extent of the damage done to women of color, see pages 89–91.

[15] Jaggar, *Feminist Politics and Human Nature*, 117–18.

[16] For example, Mary Daly has been criticized by various feminists regarding her arguments against *sati* and FGM. Daly critiques the Hindu practice of *sati* and FGM in her book *Gyn/Ecology* (Mary Daly, *Gyn/ecology: The Meta-ethics of Radical Feminism* [Boston: Beacon Press, 1978]). For critiques of Daly and her discussion on *sati*, see Uma Narayan, *Dislocating Cultures: Identities, Traditions and Third World Feminisms* (New York: Routledge, 1997). For critiques of Daly's writings about FGM, see Ellen Gruenbaum, "Feminist Activism for the Abolition of FGC in Sudan," *Journal of Middle East Women's Studies* 1, no. 2 (April 1, 2005): 89–111, 165.

reasons for or against them. Instead, third-wave feminism has encouraged various local feminisms around the globe. It has looked toward building coalitions among women and has embraced both the common cause of women's oppression and the specific ways in which individual women around the globe experience that oppression.

Three prominent feminist theorists and thinkers of the third-wave are Gloria Anzaldúa, bell hooks, and Audre Lorde. There really are too many to name, but hopefully a brief summary of these three feminists' contributions to third-wave feminism illustrates how this wave constructed, changed, and molded a new kind of feminist theory. These women created a feminism that was conscious of race issues and issues of heritage, ethnicity, and difference. For example, Gloria Anzaldúa wrote about life as a *mestiza*, which was lived somewhere in between the borders of the United States and Mexico, even if not literally. She reawakened native cultural myths and created a unique synthesis between Catholicism and the older religions of Mexico, those of the native peoples. Audre Lorde wrote about the difficulties of being a black lesbian mother, the blurred boundaries, the power of the erotic, and race issues. The famous womanist bell hooks wrote passionately about racism in society and within some feminist theories. Like many third-wave feminists, hooks urged feminism to remember that we are as different from one another as we may be the same, and that ignoring those differences not only hurts women but hurts feminism and its potential to do real good.

By the early 1990s feminism saw yet another wave based initially in the United States. This wave questioned the categories of sex and gender. Fourth-wave feminism posits sex and gender to be social constructions not natural givens. Queer theory joined this critique, noting that even the biological sexing of individuals is a social construction. There is a lot more diversity than the two sex system acknowledges. Anne Fausto-Sterling published an edifying book on this topic called *Sexing the Body: Gender Politics and the Construction of Sexuality*.[17] In addition to the social construction of biological sex, queer theory through the pioneering writing of Judith Butler in *Gender Trouble: Feminism and the Subversion of Identity*, enriched fourth-wave feminism with the suggestion that gender is performative and that to disrupt so-called stable notions regarding gender, one should perform transgressive gender identities.[18]

---

[17] Anne Fausto-Sterling, *Sexing the Body: Gender Politics and the Construction of Sexuality* (New York: BasicBooks, 2000).

[18] Judith Butler, *Gender Trouble: Feminism and the Subversion of Identity* (New York: Routledge, 1990), 173–77.

We have just entered this fourth wave, and its emergence is contested. Quite a few feminist historians, such as Estelle Freedman,[19] see this critique of sex and gender as part of the third wave. In other words, some feminists, like Freedman, do not even posit a fourth wave.[20] However, queer theory and its forms of feminism distinguish this wave from third wave, which is more concerned with diversity and levels of oppression than with distinctly questioning the social construction of sex and gender categories.

To some extent it is a misnomer even to categorize waves of feminism. One does not have to die for another to exist. In fact, most waves intermingle. For example, the ERA was a product of first-wave feminism that continued into the second wave. Even with the arrival of fourth-wave feminism, there are quite a few feminists who embrace what could be called a liberal feminist viewpoint, the viewpoint very popular at the turn of the twentieth century. Likewise, third- and fourth-wave feminisms are occurring simultaneously today.

FEMINISM AND THE VATICAN

This historical development of feminism affected the Roman Catholic Church and sparked the construction of a theology of womanhood. Let us look at two of the most direct examples of the way in which feminism has affected the Roman Catholic Church. Its impact is clear in the language of the documents themselves, although commentary will help the reader flesh out this relationship between feminism and the Roman Catholic Church.

The Sacred Congregation for the Doctrine of the Faith (SCDF) released *Inter insigniores (Declaration on the Question of Admission of Women to the Ministerial Priesthood)* on October 15, 1976. In it, the SCDF addresses the question of whether ordination is a human right. Ordination as a human right is a good example of a liberal feminist argument (equal rights within a given system).

Church leadership concluded:

One cannot see how it is possible to propose the admission of women to the priesthood in virtue of the equality of rights of the human person, an equality which holds good also for Christians. To this end, use is sometimes made of the text quoted above, from the Letter to the Galatians (3:28), which says that in Christ there is no longer any distinction between men and women. But this passage does not

---

[19] Estelle B. Freedman, *No Turning Back: The History of Feminism and the Future of Women* (New York: Ballantine Books, 2002), 203–4.

[20] Ibid., 89–94.

concern ministries: it only affirms the universal calling to divine filiation, which is the same for all. Moreover, and above all, to consider
the ministerial priesthood as a human right would be to misjudge its
nature completely: baptism does not confer any personal title to public
ministry within the Church. The priesthood is not conferred for the
honour or advantage of the recipient, but for the service of God and
the Church; it is the object of a specific and totally gratuitous vocation: "You did not choose me, no, I chose you; and I commissioned
you" (Jn 15:16; Heb 5:4).

For the leadership of the Roman Catholic Church, ordination is not a
human right. Many feminists have approached traditional structures to ask
for membership within that structure on the basis of the gender equality
between men and women. In this manner one can see the way in which
liberal feminist ideas assume that both men and women should have access to the priesthood. Yet, to counter this argument, the church deems it
against the nature of ordination to apply the language of human rights to
the priesthood, which was ordained by God and commissioned by Jesus at
the Last Supper. Women cannot be admitted to the priesthood because of
the tradition of the church, the maleness of Jesus, Jesus' choice of apostles,
and the divine mystery of ordination. According to the document, church
leaders have no authority to change this institution (*Inter insigniores*, intro.).
The language of rights and its modern conception do not apply to divine
mysteries and holy institutions.

Another example of the close relationship between feminism and the
official Vatican theology of womanhood is in Pope John Paul's encyclical
Evangelium vitae, published on March 25, 1995. In the document, John
Paul II asks women to create a "new feminism" (99). It seems as if something must be amiss with feminism as it currently operates, how it envisions
a better world, and the way it tries to achieve that better world. This "new
feminism" should hone the gifts women give the world. He writes:

> In transforming culture so that it supports life, women occupy a place,
> in thought and action, which is unique and decisive. It depends on
> them to promote a "new feminism" which rejects the temptation of
> imitating models of "male domination," in order to acknowledge and
> affirm the true genius of women in every aspect of the life of society,
> and overcome all discrimination, violence and exploitation. (99)

As one will come to see, Pope John Paul II rallies behind the concept
of "the genius of women." After having misunderstood feminism's goals
relating to equality, the pope suggests another route for women, one that

he thinks is more suited to their nature. Women should create a feminism based on their roles as mothers who value life and give of themselves freely and with love. This is the acknowledgment of women's "true genius" that appears in the above quote from *Evangelium vitae*. That call to love and to love in a self-giving manner seems to be what the Vatican and the pope think will change the world.

According to the Vatican, one of the ideas secular versions of feminism seem to get wrong is the idea that women should imitate male roles even if those roles support male dominance. This statement addresses feminism, even though it seems to misunderstand the feminist argument. Feminist women do not want to become men. This was never a goal of feminism. Even liberal feminists (who ask for equal access and opportunity) do not want to keep the status quo of various patriarchal systems. Rather, once women have equal access to an institution based on the idea of gender equality as sameness, that institution can be made into one that is more just, fair, and equitable.

THE PLAN OF THE BOOK

This book argues that the Roman Catholic Church has developed a theological understanding of womanhood out of historical necessity and in response to changing global conditions. More important, it explains what that theology is. It seeks to find some common themes and salient features of womanhood according to the leadership of the Roman Catholic Church within the emerging literature. In order to accomplish this aim, this book summarizes a large number of Vatican documents about women. One cannot hope to mention and summarize all of the Vatican documents written about women, but the ones used are the most significant ones and the ones that best represent the general thrust of all the other documents.

It seems necessary to point out that this book is not the first book to highlight the impact of feminism on the Roman Catholic Church, and it will not be the last. It also is pertinent to add that while this book draws a connection between the construction of a theology of womanhood and the historical events of feminism, it does not "choose a side," as one may be apt to do.[21] This book attempts to present the Roman Catholic theology of womanhood from its source. It relies on primary documents issued by the Vatican about women. In fact, as an anthology it provides readers many pages of these documents so that they can see for themselves the main

---

[21] Many feminists point out the various ways in which the church continues its injustice toward women.

themes and ideas as they are presented within the official documents. The author reserves theological comment as much as possible.

In addition to this Introduction, this book is divided into five chapters and a conclusion. Each of the chapters covers a decade from the 1960s to today. (Given that we have just started the next decade, 2011 is included within the 2000s.) The book ends with a conclusion that draws all of the decades' work together and constructs the larger picture of this theology of womanhood according to the Roman Catholic Church.

In Chapter 1 the 1960s are explored. There are six important documents that address women as a group, but selections from only two of them—Pope Paul VI's "Address to Women" and *Humanae vitae*—are part of this anthology. With the development of second-wave feminism in the 1960s came recognition of the changing position of women in the world within these documents. They agreed that women should be treated with the dignity and respect they deserve as members of the human family, and they acknowledged that women all over the world were fighting to gain this respect and dignity. Yet, in the eyes of the church, whatever their public role, women are called to make family life their priority. Work environments must be flexible to allow this. Finally, the Roman Catholic leadership reiterates its traditional position on sexuality in marriage and the divine necessity of married couples to uphold the finality of the sex act (conception).

One of the most interesting developments of the theology of womanhood in this decade comes in Pope Paul VI's "Address to Women," given on December 8, 1965, the close of Vatican II. This very short document beseeches women to use their special abilities of caring, truth, love, and guidance to help men become more life affirming. In this way women are charged with saving civilization from self-implosion and redirecting humanity to more loving, caring, and responsible ways to live on Planet Earth.

Chapter 2 concerns the 1970s. The theology of womanhood developed in the 1970s begins with abortion rights given by the *Roe v. Wade* decision in 1973 in the United States. Its next significant step was to offer a firm defense of the priesthood as a male-only institution. Along the way, though, it also acknowledged the goodness of feminism(s) that fight for the end of sex/gender discrimination and called on societal institutions to inspire equal respect and dignity of all human persons.

Theological concern over sexual ethics and the burgeoning sexual revolution and its promotion of looser sexual mores across the globe were also exhibited during this decade. Some of the writings condemned birth control, abortion, masturbation, sexual acts outside of marriage, homosexuality, divorce, and remarriage. In this regard the church defended the human right to life and disagreed with feminist claims with regard to abortion rights over the right to life. In the documents the church argued that women who lobby for abortion rights miss the fact that they are dealing with a natural process and that abortions go against both human reason and the divine will. The church also explained how it viewed women who procure abortions as murderers and sinners, and how the church allocated punishment for those sins. The documents assign women certain duties. Finally, the church introduced the concept of gender complementarity in the documents—a highly significant theological concept, even though the documents of the 1970s offered little explanation of what was meant by the term.

Chapter 3 focuses on the 1980s, which is when the Roman Catholic Church provided its most complete understanding of women and a theology of womanhood. In this decade the church recognized that the status of women was improving. At the same time, women were often the first to suffer from a lack of rights and freedoms. It is within this context of change and continued oppression that the church explained its understanding of womanhood.

In this decade the church explained the idea that women interact with the world through a technical term: the *order of love*. The *order of love* means that women prioritize love in their lives by loving, caring for, and supporting others. It is through this care for others that women help make the world a better place. Related to this is the quintessential role of motherhood. Mothering is described as physical and spiritual. Women are physical mothers when they birth, raise, and educate their children. Women are spiritual mothers when they care for the sick, hungry, needy, and imprisoned.

Next, Chapter 4 covers the 1990s. One of the developments of the 1990s was a focus on women as the ones who can help make the world a better place because of the value they give life. In this decade women were also called to create a kind of feminism that centers on women's natural, God-given characteristics: nurturing, caring, relationship-centered, faithful, honest, and loving. A feminism that makes the most of these feminine ideals would make the world a better place, a more humane one tuned into a culture of life rather than death. In addition, if women were only free from societal oppression and discrimination so that they could fully develop the way God created them, then the world would become a better place.

In the 1990s the Roman Catholic Church also addressed the priesthood and the question of whether women could be ordained. The church expressed its position in two documents: *Ordinatio sacerdotalis,* which declared that the church lacks the authority to ordain women and required the full assent of the faithful to this declaration, and *Responsum ad propositum dubium,* which declared that *Ordinatio sacerdotalis* is infallible.

Chapter 5 is concerned with the theology of womanhood produced in the third millennium. Women need health-care services, access to education, equal opportunities, better nutrition, the right to be able to own land (or better access to it if that right already exists), adequate financial resources, and the opportunity to borrow money. In this regard, the world must promote the advancement of women as well as their dignity. Women's dignity cannot be secured if women are denied access to opportunities for advancement.

There are a few key elements of the theology of womanhood developed within the 2000s. First, the church argued for the need to recognize gender complementarity. Women can only become fully human if they recognize the relationship between their biological constitution and their social, political, and cultural life. Ignoring biology hurts women and the larger society. Society too must recognize biological determinism if it is ever going to achieve a just society based on truth. Another key concept of the decade is the explicit definition of femininity. Women were made to live for others. Women excel at caring, being honest, listening, being sensitive, valuing life, and cultivating relationships. In other words, the 2000s revolves around gender complementarity, gender equality, motherhood, women's dignity, opportunity, and access.

The conclusion culminates with a synthesis of all of the decades in order to answer the questions posed at the beginning of this Introduction. It also examines the reception of this theology. There are theologians who support the Roman Catholic Church's theology of womanhood and those who do not. Examples from both sides are given. Finally, the author looks to the future and offers some suggestions as to where this theology may go and how it may develop.

VATICAN DOCUMENTS BEFORE 1960

The rest of this Introduction will look at the years before 1960 as they relate to women in official teachings. Before the early 1960s there is very little evidence that the Roman Catholic Church was interested in women as a separate and distinct group of people. It focused most of its attention on women as wives and mothers. There is one mention of them as workers in paragraph 42 of Pope Leo XIII's *Rerum novarum*. Pope Leo XIII, in his encyclical *Arcanum divinae sapientiae*, promulgated on February 10, 1880, discusses the role of women in marriage.

It is Pope Pius XI's *Casti connubii*, published on December 31, 1930, that provides the best source on women from the time period before 1960. In the document the pope explains women's roles as mothers and wives and even addresses the economic need of some families for women to work outside the house. It argues that women were created by God for the oversight of the domestic life and the birthing and education of children; society should not interfere with their duties as wives and mothers. The document claims that if women's emancipation movements succeed in their wishes for equality with men, the societies that support such change are committing crimes against women, God, and the Christian family.

Pope Pius XII's "Allocution to Midwifes," published on October 29, 1951, also offers a rich source of information concerning women as mothers. While addressing those whose profession is midwifery, the document also says much about women. Following the example of Mary, the perfect virginal mother, women should accept their duties as mothers. Motherhood provides women their opportunity for salvation. The document also voices concern over anything that would threaten the finality of the marriage act.

Arcanum divinae sapientiae

The earliest document in modern times that references women is *Arcanum divinae sapientiae*, promulgated on February 10, 1880, by Pope Leo XIII. This document is often referred to in English as the *Encyclical of Pope Leo XIII on Christian Marriage*. As most Vatican documents do, it begins by addressing errors that have come about as societies progress. The document's acknowledged purpose is to redirect Christians back to more Christlike relationships, namely, marriages.

Divorce, polygamy, and the treatment of women in marriage are the main errors it wishes to address (6–7). While God formed marriage as an indissoluble union between one man and one woman in which the two become united as one flesh and bring forth offspring of the covenant, God's creation has been polluted with errors. The document states that the early followers of God, the Jews, began to follow the customs of the lands they lived in and became polygamous. In addition, Moses erred when he granted Jewish men divorces.

Secular laws, especially among the Gentiles, introduced other errors into the institution of marriage. Heads of states could decide on marriages without the participants' consent. Gentiles too practiced polygamy. Nevertheless, one error was worse than these two: the way in which wives were abused and mistreated by their husbands as if they were property. They could be bought and sold by their fathers or murdered by their fathers or husbands if they dishonored the family. Related to this was the conception of men as lustful beasts given permission to do what they must to satisfy their sexual urges.

Pope Leo XIII counters these modern errors relating to marriage by stressing the way in which Jesus blessed the institution at the wedding ceremony in Cana and spoke often about the sin of adultery. Tradition has also sanctified marriage by making it a sacrament and defining the rights and duties of the institution. Men and women enter the institution as free beings drawn together by mutual love, and with that they add their commitment and their "unfailing and unselfish help" (11) when necessary. The document explains that men are the heads of the households and women must obey them, just as Christ is the head of the church and the church must obey Christ. The document stresses that women are not to be ordered around like slaves but must obey their husbands from the positions of companion (11).

In addition, there are a few provisions to protect women from unjust punishment. No one can kill a woman for adultery (14). Fathers may not exercise too much control over whom their children marry (14). Divorce threatens the dignity of women so that they are seen as something to be used and then discarded (29).

To illustrate the language used in the document to define marriage:

Not only, in strict truth, was marriage instituted for the propagation of the human race, but also that the lives of husbands and wives might be made better and happier. This comes about in many ways: by their lightening each other's burdens through mutual help; by constant and faithful love; by having all their possessions in common; and by the heavenly grace which flows from the sacrament. (26)

Marriage is, in other words, good for humans in that it provides humans with a better life. It offers companionship and mutual support. In addition, marriage affords husbands and wives the opportunity to live holy lives as they raise children together.

Rerum novarum

As already shown, women are addressed as wives and mothers in the documents. They are also addressed as workers. *Rerum novarum,* or the *Encyclical of Pope Leo XIII on Capital and Labor,* was published on May 15, 1891. A document about the need for justice for the working-class people of the world, this document specifically addresses women as a class of workers in paragraph 42. It reads, "Finally, work which is quite suitable for a strong man cannot rightly be required from a woman or a child. . . . Women again are not suited for certain occupations; a woman is by nature fitted for home-work, and it is that which is best adapted at once to preserve her modesty and to promote the good bringing up of children and the well-being of the family" (42). In other words, the church acknowledges that women have entered the workplace and that, for justice and natural reasons, they should be given duties that are in accordance with their nature. By divine design women are most protected and the family is more cared for if women do not work outside of the house.

Casti connubii

We once again return to women as wives and mothers in Pope Pius XI's encyclical *Casti connubii,* the *Encyclical of Pope Pius XI on Christian Marriage,* published on December 31, 1930. Before much is even said in the document, Pope Pius XI takes the time to confirm *Arcanum divinae sapientiae* to be as true and valid in 1930 as it was when Pope Leo XIII promulgated it. *Casti connubii* states that it is going to add additional explanation of certain points congruent with its own times.

As *Arcanum divinae sapientiae* declares that in marriage men and women become one flesh, *Casti connubii* adds that their souls are also united (7). It turns from there to addressing why men and women come together in marriage. This is often referred to, in technical terms, as the "end" of marriage or the "finality" of sexual union, which is something that becomes extremely important after the 1960s as well. The end of marriage is the procreation and education of children. The document quotes Saint Augustine, who wrote, "The Apostle himself is therefore a witness that marriage is for the sake of generation: 'I wish,' he says, 'for young girls to marry.' And, as if someone said to him, 'Why?,' he immediately adds: 'To bear children, to be mothers of families'" (11). Likewise, the document states that children bring a certain amount of joy to mothers, which helps women forget the misery and anguish they were in while giving birth. Later, in paragraph 58, the document adds that women are naturally mothers and it is in motherhood that they will find their most rewarding purpose and fulfill their nature.

As well as mothers, women are also addressed as wives. Women are associated with love and the heart and it seems to be for this reason that women are subject to their husbands. They must obey their husband's every request as long as it is not contrary to their dignity or their right reason. Men, as heads of the household, hold the right to rule, while women, as the hearts of the household, have "the chief place in love" (27).

Like *Arcanum divinae sapientiae,* the document also provides more protections for women as wives and mothers. It declares that men cannot leave their sterile wives in order to have children (36). In addition, the end of sex (which is conception and procreation) cannot be interrupted by any artificial or natural means (54–56). This intervention in the finality of the sex act offends God and is sinful. Likewise, the abortion of a conceived pregnancy is also morally reprehensible, even if the mother's own life is threatened by the pregnancy and/or the birthing process (63–64). Infanticide is also a grave sin (65) as is direct sterilization (71). Marriages between members of different faiths or even other Christian denominations will only lead the Catholic spouse to move away from the Catholic Church and will end in the corruption of the children of that union. For these reasons, it is forbidden (82). Unwed mothers should not be provided with more for their needs and sustenance when this assistance is often denied or meagerly given to married women who are legitimate mothers (122).

Casti connubii also addresses women's emancipation. The idea that women should be freed from motherhood in an effort to be equal to men in politics, in economics, and in social relations is criminal and will only lead women to be treated as slaves and property of men (74–75). A certain inequality between men and women is natural and good for the ordering of society, of the home, and of the family (76). The document declares, "If the social and economic conditions of the married woman must in some way be altered on account of the changes in social intercourse, it is part of the office of the public authority to adapt the civil rights of the wife to modern needs and requirements, keeping in view what the natural disposition and temperament of the female sex, good morality, and the welfare of the family demands" (77). It goes on to suggest that the domestic unit was created by God and therefore cannot be altered. If any changes must be made, they need to preserve and work in accordance with women's role within the family.[22]

Allocution to Midwives

Finally, we come to Pope Pius XII's address to midwives called "Allocution to Midwives." There are three significant sections of the document that pertain to women as wives and mothers. First, through creation, God has ordained women to be mothers. Second, through motherhood, women are offered the gift of salvation. Finally, anything that would prevent conception, whether direct sterilization, some form of birth control, or perversion of the sex act so as to remove its procreative end, is strictly prohibited. This is important because it has a direct effect on women, who are the ones who carry children.

---

[22] Ruether, *Contemporary Roman Catholicism*, 37. Ruether explains that the Roman Catholic Church was against women's right to vote on the basis of male authority but quickly reversed this decision when women gained the right to vote in the United States. Then, these women were appealed to in order to further the Roman Catholic social agenda.

God created women to be the ones to carry on the human race. In fact, motherhood is a duty given to women by God in order to fulfill their biological destiny. In this way women also share in some of the attributes of God, such as God's creative abilities, God's goodness, God's wisdom and omnipotence.

It is through marriage, conception, and ultimately motherhood that women also reach their salvation. The document quotes Saint Paul, who wrote that women are saved through childbearing. While labor is quite painful due to humanity's curse caused by Adam and Eve, midwives should help women overcome that pain to see the joy of God's gift to them: a child, motherhood, and salvation. Midwives also have to help women cultivate love for their children and alleviate any fears they may have, especially with their first child.

Catechism of the Council of Trent

This idea that women are saved through childbearing continues a tradition of the church one can find in the *Catechism of the Council of Trent*.[23] This book, first published during the papacy of Pius V (1566–72), uses the biblical passage 1 Timothy 2:15 as support for this statement. Flowing from that idea, women must be subject to their husbands (1 Pt 3:1–2), be dutiful, be responsible for the education and disciplining of their children, and take care of all household concerns. The catechism goes a step further, stating that women cannot leave their homes without their husband's permission, must love their husbands, and must obey them. The *Catechism of Christian Doctrine no. 1–4* published in 1922 supports the idea that women are under the dominion of their husbands because of the Fall.[24]

Returning to the document on midwifery, the document's final theme focuses on any act that would somehow interrupt the conception of children either by the woman, the man, or the couple together. This act goes against God's plan and is a serious sin. Such things as direct sterilization, limiting sex to infertile periods without grave reason (economic, medical, or acceptable social situations), or any sex act that omits of the possibility of procreation is against the order of creation and offends God as creator. Married people enter into the marriage union to become parents, and they consent to that when they are married. In other words, if either party considering marriage is willing to do whatever it takes in order not to conceive, the couple should not marry.

---

[23] Reverend J. Donovan, trans., *Catechism of the Council of Trent* (New York: Catholic Publication Society, 1890), 233–35.

[24] *Catechism of Christian Doctrine, no. 1–4* (Philadelphia: J. J. McVey, 1922), 29.

Some additional pre-1960 thoughts about the place of women come from Francis Connell's book *Outlines of Moral Theology* published in 1958.[25] He includes much of what has already been discussed in Pius XII's "Allocution to Midwives." He also discusses some ideas that come out of earlier church teaching that one does not necessarily find in the main documents explored here. (To explore every document would be almost impossible, so a secondary source helps here.) Women can own their own dowries as well as property, but they cannot spend more money than their husbands allow.[26] Raped women can douche to try and prevent pregnancy, but if it occurs there is no other recourse.[27] In addition, Connell states that since the gospel says women must be silent in churches, they cannot be ordained into the priesthood.[28] Finally, women can refuse sex only if they could not physically handle giving birth again or their husband is not providing well enough for the family they already have.[29]

Before the 1960s little is said about women outside of their capacity for motherhood and their role as wives. Chapter 1 explores the 1960s and by doing so examines the first decade of the development of a theology of womanhood in the Roman Catholic Church. It also addresses the burgeoning growth of second-wave feminism beginning in the 1960s. As the book continues, the reader will gain a greater understanding of the Roman Catholic theology of womanhood and also be able to see the connections between this development and feminism with more clarity.

---

[25] Francis Connell, *Outlines of Moral Theology* (Milwaukee: Bruce Publishing Co., 1958).

[26] Ibid., 110.

[27] Ibid., 171.

[28] Ibid., 221.

[29] Ibid., 231.

Chapter 1

THE 1960s

In the 1960s the Roman Catholic Church began to develop a more thorough understanding of women, their role in the family, and their rising social, political, and economic status. In no small part a rise in the societal status of women due to the actions of second-wave feminism and the lingering effects of first-wave feminism influenced the church.

Beginning in the 1960s, women began to be addressed as a group in their own right. In fact, Pope Paul VI ended the Second Vatican Council with a speech directed specifically to women. He spoke directly to women as well as to intellectuals, artists, those in poverty, those who were sick, workers, and youth. These were groups he considered to need special consideration,[1] and for the next forty years or so women as a group continued to get special theological attention. They had become their own independent theological category, and the Roman Catholic Church developed a theology of womanhood.

Before moving on to this burgeoning development of a theology of womanhood, it is good to be reminded of where feminism was at this point. Beginning in the early 1950s women and men of many different backgrounds were fighting to end segregation laws in the southern United States. It was here that women (primarily white women, but also black women, who were often considered traitors to their race if they pushed for an improved situation for women within the black movement) began to become aware of their secondary status within the groups. This awareness took on greater significance especially for white women as they joined leftist organizations

---

[1] At the closing speech of the Second Vatican Council, Pope Paul VI said, "You will hear shortly, at the end of this holy Mass, a reading of some messages which, at the conclusion of its work, the ecumenical council is addressing to various categories of persons, intending to consider in them the countless forms in which human life finds expression. And you will also hear the reading of our official decree in which we declare terminated and closed the Second Vatican Ecumenical Council. This is a moment, a brief moment of greetings. Then, our voice will be silent. This council is completely terminated, this immense and extraordinary assembly is disbanded."

and peace movement groups that did not take women's "issues" seriously. Women of all backgrounds and colors began to notice that their oppression was structural and all pervasive. As noted in the Introduction, many men in leftist organizations and peace movements did not consider women's issues connected to their causes. So women began to form their own peace movements, leftist organizations, and small consciousness-raising groups. They began to see the ways in which sexism was built into the structure and foundation of the society. Soon, however, the movement became focused on women's bodies and access to abortion, which made the movement's goals more white and more classist. This was an unfortunate turn within the movement that would be corrected in the early 1980s. Yet, by the end of the 1960s, the movement for abortion rights was in full swing.

Given this development of second-wave feminism, it is not coincidental that Pope Paul VI felt the need to address women as a special group at the close of the Second Vatican Council. In addition, the timing of *Humanae vitae*, which came out in 1968, also fits into these developments within the feminist movement.

It is now time to move to the documents themselves. Six documents addressed women as a category during this decade. Only the two most significant, Pope Paul VI's "Address to Women" and *Humanae vitae*, have been included here as selections for the reader. The other documents will be summarized and their theological significance extracted as they pertain to women.

Mater et magistra

On May 15, 1961, Pope John XXIII released the document *Mater et magistra*. It is often referred to in English as the *Encyclical of Pope John XXIII on Christianity and Social Progress*. It mentions women as a class twice. First, as workers: in paragraph 13, Pope John XXIII argues for humane working conditions for women and children. Second, in paragraph 20, he discusses the duties of the state. One of those duties is to protect its weaker members, and the document classifies women as part of that group.

Pacem in terris

The next significant document to address women as a specific theo-logical group is *Pacem in terris*, or the *Encyclical of Pope John XXIII on Establishing Universal Peace in Truth, Justice, Charity and Liberty*. Pope John XXIII issued this encyclical on April 11, 1963. While it contains two main sections that address women specifically (15–19 and 41–43), the docu-ment as a whole addresses what it means to be human, how humans should be treated, and how they should interact. Pope John XXIII also advocates societal structures that provide basic necessities and promote justice, human rights, respect, equality, and liberty.

Beginning in paragraph 15, Pope John XXIII discusses men and women's right to choose the direction of their lives. If women choose to enter the workforce, their duties as wives and mothers should be respected. In other words, jobs that employ women need to operate in such a way that women can put their families as their first priorities. It should be noted that the Vatican believes that men need to be paid a livable wage that would permit women to stay at home rather than force them to work.

Paragraphs 41–43 acknowledge the feminist movement. In the document Pope John XXIII offers the readers a summary of the movement. "Women are gaining an increasing awareness of their natural dignity. Far from being content with a purely passive role or allowing themselves to be regarded as a kind of instrument, they are demanding both in domestic and in public life the rights and duties which belong to them as human persons" (41). He continues this line of thinking, further documenting changes taking place in society. This section of *Pacem in terris* documents society becoming more equal by its acknowledgment of inequality and its attempt to rid itself of problematic relationships based on categories such as class, social standing, and sex, to name just three.

Two documents from the Second Vatican Council (Vatican II) stand out as important for their contribution on the Roman Catholic Church's developing understanding of womanhood as a theological category. They are *Apostolicam actuositatem* and *Gaudium et spes*, or *Decree on the Apostolate of the Laity* and *The Dogmatic Constitution on the Church in the Modern World*. The *Decree on the Apostolate of the Laity* was officially promulgated on November 18, 1965. *Gaudium et spes* was officially released on December 7, 1965, one day before the official close of Vatican II.

Apostolicam actuositatem

Paragraph 9 of the *Decree on the Apostolate of the Laity* is devoted to women as a special category. Before examining its content specifically, a brief summary of the document is necessary because laity includes women. All people regardless of age are called to live good Christian lives and to spread the word of God to the world in a manner that fits their vocation and status in life. They use Christian values to improve politics, economic relations, and social institutions for the betterment of humanity. In summary, all laity are called to meet the needs of the world and care for all humans by exhibiting faith, hope, and charity (love).

Paragraph 9, which mentions women specifically, recognizes the way in which women's positions in society have been changing. The church, through the document, argues that women too should take a more active role in the lay apostolate. Whether this means an expanded role within the church as an institution is not clear, given that the church does not provide more guidance on this comment. Nevertheless, what does seem quite clear is that as women enter further into public life and in jobs outside the home, Pope Paul VI believes women too must fulfill their role as laity. They too should be beacons of Christianity. Women are called to be founts of love, faith, and hope and should focus their effort on making the world a better place for all. It is incumbent on all Christian men and women that they be good, sincere witnesses for the gospel in the world today.

Gaudium et spes

The other Vatican II document that addresses women as a special theological group is *Gaudium et spes*. Women as a group are addressed in paragraphs 8, 9, 12, 27, 29, 52, 60, and 67. This Vatican II document also considers the changing context of the modern world and the role of the church within it. Defining the modern world and explaining the good and evil within it are just two things this document accomplishes. It also suggests ways in which governments should protect people's basic human and civil rights and offers the church's services to the world to help it discern the best possible path for humanity.

A marked perspective in the document is an acknowledgment of the increasingly public role of women in the modern world. The church acknowledges societal changes in politics and economics as well as the way in which males and females interact (8). While greater equality continues to be fought for by many groups, including women, there are many inequalities that still exist. For one, women are not treated across the globe in a way that aligns with their personal dignity as human beings. Where this does not happen, women continue to fight for that just treatment. In addition, people in poverty cry out for help, and workers seek justice, safety, and equitable pay. The council warns humanity that if the creations of the modern world, like technology and economic forces, are not properly managed by humanity, they will eventually take on a mind of their own, overwhelm humanity, and cause new injuries to those already suffering and those who traditionally do not (9).

Gaudium et spes grounds humanity within God's creation, and it is from this perspective that the council asks for human beings to be partners in the work of the world. Genesis describes this partnership between men and women as part of God's intention for creation. Humans are social beings and need to enter into equitable social relationships. Yet, these relationships between people are not equitable in the modern world. Women risk being bought and sold as mere property or worse as sexual slaves (27). Those and other atrocities occur in modern society even though humans are all created by the same God to work together in partnership.

It is in paragraph 29 that *Gaudium et spes* introduces a new concept regarding the creation and dignity of humanity, especially of women. Women have not been singled out before in this direct way regarding their human dignity. The document states that since humans, both men and women, were created by God, both have the same inherent reasoning capacity, share in the divine mission, and therefore are equal. The church document goes so far as to state that "any kind of social or cultural discrimination in basic personal rights on the grounds of sex, race, color, social conditions, language or religion, must be curbed and eradicated as incompatible with God's design" (29). This equality of human dignity and respect will reappear in other documents. It is an extremely important concept regarding the basic equality of men and women. Its main use will be to say that while they are equal, both have different roles. Yet, to not jump ahead of ourselves, this document calls humanity to end social and cultural discrimination, which society is slow to do.

Feminism and other movements working to secure human rights are acknowledged in paragraphs 41 and 60. In paragraph 41 the council encourages the development and implementation of basic human and civil rights across the globe. In paragraph 60 it says, "It is up to everyone to see to it that women's specific and necessary participation in cultural life be acknowledged and developed." Therefore, not only do various groups of men and women need help to secure their basic human and civil rights, but women as a group need additional help and support.

The document also has extended sections on marriage and the family that address women and their roles as wives and mothers. Paragraph 52 describes some of the duties of motherhood, including the important role women play in the lives of children when they are very young. In this regard, societies need to protect women's roles in the family even as they advance women's standing in society. Mothers who work need to be given special consideration in jobs and life outside the home so that they can still keep their families as their number one priority (67).

Address to Women[2]

At the end of the council Pope Paul VI took special care to address women as a group. The entire text of "Address to Women," first promulgated on

---

[2] The document is very short so all quotations should be easily found. The paragraphs are not numbered.

December 8, 1965, is supplied here for close reading and analysis. While women are presumed to be mothers and wives and to have a larger role in society, the pope also asks more of women. Women are described as the primary educators of their children, and it is through their children that women hold a place in the future of humanity. In addition, women need to influence the world by making "truth sweet, tender and accessible" since it is something they already know how to do.

In addition to this description of women as educators and the ones who can make things easier to swallow for men, women are charged with an almost impossible burden: "Women of the entire universe, whether Christian or non-believing, you to whom life is entrusted at this grave moment in history, it is for you to save the peace of the world." Women are also asked to help the church implement the teachings of Vatican II in their communities. Women are assigned other significant responsibilities that include preventing humanity from falling, teaching men to respect life, and watching over and if necessary stopping men from destroying society itself. These tasks place onto women's backs an amazing amount of responsibility. One could even say the document places upon women an undue pressure to fix society. While there are many women out there trying to do just that, Pope Paul VI seems to be upping the ante. Women, by making "truth sweet, tender and accessible," need to reform the church and also save all humanity, but especially men, from their destructive and death-dealing ways. Women's natural characteristics of tenderness, love, unselfishness, humility, and patience will help them accomplish these tasks. This immense charge for all women across the globe seems to make them responsible for society's failure if they cannot or will not help men be peaceful, just, and respectful of life. The church is placing a heavy and difficult burden on the backs of all women, Christian or not, in this document.

Humanae vitae

Humanae vitae was released by Paul VI on July 25, 1968. The document condemns the use of birth control, abortion, sex outside of marriage, and sex that is not open to procreation. Given that *Roe v. Wade*, which granted women in the United States legal access to abortions in the first trimester as part of a women's right to privacy, passed in 1973, this document relates to developments within feminism as well. In addition, *Humanae vitae* is still controversial today because of its sordid history. John XXIII first convened a committee made up of laity (including married couples and scientists) and clerics during Vatican II. They were to look at issues concerning the family and population control and compile their findings in an effort to advise the pope on those matters. While the committee worked, Pope John XXIII died and a new pope was elected: Paul VI. In the end, the committee favored the use of birth control, but Paul VI ignored the findings of the papal commission and released *Humanae vitae*, which continued traditional church teachings on the subject by condemning the use of birth control. These traditional teachings can be found in earlier documents on procreation and sexuality, specifically in *Casti connubii*, released by Pope Pius XI on December 31, 1930, and *Humani generis*, released by Pope Pius XII on August 12, 1950.

In *Humanae vitae*, Pope Paul VI makes clear that part of the church's office is the teaching of morals and ethics (4–6). This includes sexual morality and teachings on abortion. The leadership is well aware of dissent from the laity. In the face of dissent the leadership considers itself to be "a sign of contradiction" (18). Likewise, church teachings should be respected and obeyed (28). This includes teachings on human anthropology, women's roles, sexuality, abortion, and contraception. Failure to conform to church teachings jeopardizes one's relationship with God, one's faith, and one's salvation, because, often, this refusal to conform is sinful.

In terms of preventing birth, the only context in which Christians should be engaging in sexual relations is in marriage. God made men and women to marry each other. Sexuality in marriage expresses many dimensions of what it means to be human. Likewise, sexuality is both a biological fact and part of the divine plan (16). It is in sex that two become one. Sexuality is an essential part of humans; it is the "physical self-giving" (11) of one spouse to the other. Pope Paul VI continues by saying that all life is a gift from God (9). By using contraception or by procuring abortions married couples disrupt God's plan, debase human sexuality, and fail fully to give themselves in the sex act (12 and 13).

Church teachings do offer married couples an alternative to traditional forms of contraception (16). This alternative is often called the family planning method or the rhythm method. If a family wants to reduce the likelihood of pregnancy, women should pay attention to the cycles of their bodies and engage in sex only during their infertile periods. For example, couples may want to space births in order to better care for the children they already have. Or they may want to prevent conception for financial reasons. This form of natural birth control is acceptable to the leadership of the Roman Catholic Church because it respects the laws of nature. As compared to *Casti connubii*, this document seems to consider spacing births and having sex during infertile periods more acceptable. It does not seem to consider this as morally reprehensible even if the reasons are not necessarily as grave as previously required in *Casti connubii*. Periods of infertility are natural in humanity.

Regarding women specifically, the document gives other reasons why contraception in any form is wrong (17). Contraception leads to devaluing women because men come to see women only as objects of pleasure and not as partners. Men would be self-centered and not provide for the physical and emotional well-being of women. Contraception also leads to adultery and moral laxity.

During the 1960s both Pope John XXIII and Pope Paul VI acknowledged women's changing social status, improvements in the dignity and respect given to women, and their fight for their rights as human beings. Previously, as we saw in the Introduction, the Vatican had been leery of feminism and had warned humanity about the damage it could cause the family. Before, women were to avoid working outside the home if at all possible. Now, women do work outside the home even though their jobs should give priority to motherhood and women's family responsibilities. Women and men also share the same human dignity and respect and should act as each other's partners. The duty of the wife to obey the husband seems not to be emphasized as heavily. Nevertheless, women's primary role and responsibilities still lie in the home, taking care of children and providing for the care, love, and support of their husbands.

Based on their roles as mothers, women seem to be charged with more than this. Women are asked to help save humanity from itself; this was not previously considered a woman's task, even though women were supposed to bring up good, moral Christian children. They are asked to teach men (yes, only men, not humanity) to value life and work for peace. Saving civilization from its self-destruction seems to now be another responsibility for women given their loving, compassionate, humble, and concerned nature. Women also need to be Christian witnesses, active laity, and help the church reform to be more in line with the teachings of Vatican II. This is another novel task for women.

One could argue that it seems that the Vatican is describing women as well as acknowledging and supporting (within reason) their changing status in society. In addition, it is giving women more responsibility for the world (even for the future existence of human civilization). Women are also asked to play a larger role in the church. The idea that women are naturally better at teaching, conveying the truth, helping men focus their minds toward life, creating peace, and saving humanity from itself all seem to be new additions to the official theology of womanhood.

One can see the theology of womanhood growing. One can also see how women's traditional mothering role is expanded to saving humanity from its own destructive, death-dealing tendencies. The development of a theology of womanhood challenges Catholic men and women to make the world a better place.

What follows this summary, contextualization, and commentary is Pope Paul VI's "Address to Women" at the close of the Second Vatican Council. The entire document has been reproduced for the reader. In addition, significant sections of *Humanae vitae* have also been reprinted here so readers can read and familiarize themselves with this document as well. The 1960s mark an important step forward in the Roman Catholic Church's development of a theology of womanhood, and the "Address to Women" and *Humanae vitae* are the two most important documents of the decade.

ADDRESS OF POPE PAUL VI TO WOMEN

8 DECEMBER 1965

And now it is to you that we address ourselves, women of all states—girls, wives, mothers and widows, to you also, consecrated virgins and women living alone—you constitute half of the immense human family. As you know, the Church is proud to have glorified and liberated woman, and in the course of the centuries, in diversity of characters, to have brought into relief her basic equality with man. But the hour is coming, in fact has come, when the vocation of woman is being achieved in its fullness, the hour in which woman acquires in the world an influence, an effect and a power never hitherto achieved. That is why, at this moment when the human race is under-going so deep a transformation, women impregnated with the spirit of the Gospel can do so much to aid mankind in not falling.

You women have always had as your lot the protection of the home, the love of beginnings and an understanding of cradles. You are present in the mystery of a life beginning. You offer consolation in the departure of death. Our technology runs the risk of becoming inhuman. Reconcile men with life and above all, we beseech you, watch carefully over the future of our race. Hold back the hand of man who, in a moment of folly, might attempt to destroy human civilization.

Wives, mothers of families, the first educators of the human race in the intimacy of the family circle, pass on to your sons and your daughters the traditions of your fathers at the same time that you prepare them for an unsearchable future. Always remember that by her children a mother belongs to that future which perhaps she will not see.

And you, women living alone, realize what you can accomplish through your dedicated vocation. Society is appealing to you on all sides. Not even families can live without the help of those who have no families. Especially you, consecrated virgins, in a world where egoism and the search for pleasure would become law, be the guardians of purity, unselfishness and piety. Jesus who has given to conjugal love all its plenitudes, has also exalted the renouncement of human love when this is for the sake of divine love and for the service of all.

Lastly, women in trial, who stand upright at the foot the cross like Mary, you who so often in history have given to men the strength to battle unto the very end and to give witness to the point of martyrdom, aid them now still once more to retain courage in their great undertakings, while at the same time maintaining patience and an esteem for humble beginnings.

Women, you do know how to make truth sweet, tender and accessible; make it your task to bring the spirit of this council into institutions, schools, homes and daily life. Women of the entire universe, whether Christian or non-believing, you to whom life is entrusted at this grave moment in history, it is for you to save the peace of the world.

HUMANAE VITAE

ENCYCLICAL LETTER
OF THE SUPREME PONTIFF
PAUL VI
TO HIS VENERABLE BROTHERS
THE PATRIARCHS, ARCHBISHOPS, BISHOPS
AND OTHER LOCAL ORDINARIES
IN PEACE AND COMMUNION
WITH THE APOSTOLIC SEE, TO THE CLERGY AND
FAITHFUL OF THE WHOLE CATHOLIC WORLD, AND TO ALL
MEN OF GOOD WILL, ON THE REGULATION OF BIRTH

25 JULY 1968

Honored Brothers and Dear Sons,
Health and Apostolic Benediction.

I. PROBLEM AND COMPETENCY OF THE MAGISTERIUM

2. The changes that have taken place are of considerable importance and varied in nature. In the first place there is the rapid increase in population which has made many fear that world population is going to grow faster than available resources, with the consequence that many families and developing countries would be faced with greater hardships. This can easily induce public authorities to be tempted to take even harsher measures to avert this danger. There is also the fact that not only working and housing conditions but the greater demands made both in the economic and educational field pose a living situation in which it is frequently difficult these days to provide properly for a large family.

Also noteworthy is a new understanding of the dignity of woman and her place in society, of the value of conjugal love in marriage and the relationship of conjugal acts to this love.

But the most remarkable development of all is to be seen in man's stupendous progress in the domination and rational organization of the forces of nature to the point that he is endeavoring to extend this control over every aspect of his own life—over his body, over his mind and emotions, over his social life, and even over the laws that regulate the transmission of life. . . .

Special Studies

5. The consciousness of the same responsibility induced Us to confirm and expand the commission set up by Our predecessor Pope John XXIII, of happy memory, in March, 1963. This commission included married couples as well as many experts in the various fields pertinent to these questions. Its task was to examine views and opinions concerning married life, and especially on the correct regulation of births; and it was also to provide the teaching authority of the Church with such evidence as would enable it to give an apt reply in this matter, which not only the faithful but also the rest of the world were waiting for.

When the evidence of the experts had been received, as well as the opinions and advice of a considerable number of Our brethren in the episcopate—some of whom sent their views spontaneously, while others were requested by Us to do so—We were in a position to weigh with more precision all the aspects of this complex subject. Hence We are deeply grateful to all those concerned.

The Magisterium's Reply

6. However, the conclusions arrived at by the commission could not be considered by Us as definitive and absolutely certain, dispensing Us from the duty of examining personally this serious question. This was all the more necessary because, within the commission itself, there was not complete agreement concerning the moral norms to be proposed, and especially because certain approaches and criteria for a solution to this question had emerged which were at variance with the moral doctrine on marriage constantly taught by the magisterium of the Church.

Consequently, now that We have sifted carefully the evidence sent to Us and intently studied the whole matter, as well as prayed constantly to God, We, by virtue of the mandate entrusted to Us by Christ, intend to give Our reply to this series of grave questions.

II. DOCTRINAL PRINCIPLES

7. The question of human procreation, like every other question which touches human life, involves more than the limited aspects specific to such disciplines as biology, psychology, demography or sociology. It is the whole man and the whole mission to which he is called that must be considered: both its natural, earthly aspects and its supernatural, eternal aspects. And since in the attempt to justify artificial methods of birth control many appeal to the demands of married love or of responsible parenthood, these two important realities of married life must be

accurately defined and analyzed. This is what We mean to do, with special reference to what the Second Vatican Council taught with the highest authority in its Pastoral Constitution on the Church in the World of Today.

God's Loving Design

8. Married love particularly reveals its true nature and nobility when we realize that it takes its origin from God, who "is love," the Father "from whom every family in heaven and on earth is named."

Marriage, then, is far from being the effect of chance or the result of the blind evolution of natural forces. It is in reality the wise and provident institution of God the Creator, whose purpose was to effect in man His loving design. As a consequence, husband and wife, through that mutual gift of themselves, which is specific and exclusive to them alone, develop that union of two persons in which they perfect one another, cooperating with God in the generation and rearing of new lives.

The marriage of those who have been baptized is, in addition, invested with the dignity of a sacramental sign of grace, for it represents the union of Christ and His Church.

Married Love

9. In the light of these facts the characteristic features and exigencies of married love are clearly indicated, and it is of the highest importance to evaluate them exactly.

This love is above all fully human, a compound of sense and spirit. It is not, then, merely a question of natural instinct or emotional drive. It is also, and above all, an act of the free will, whose trust is such that it is meant not only to survive the joys and sorrows of daily life, but also to grow, so that husband and wife become in a way one heart and one soul, and together attain their human fulfillment.

It is a love which is total—that very special form of personal friendship in which husband and wife generously share everything, allowing no unreasonable exceptions and not thinking solely of their own convenience. Whoever really loves his partner loves not only for what he receives, but loves that partner for the partner's own sake, content to be able to enrich the other with the gift of himself.

Married love is also faithful and exclusive of all other, and this until death. This is how husband and wife understood it on the day on which, fully aware of what they were doing, they freely vowed themselves to one another in marriage. Though this fidelity of husband and wife sometimes presents difficulties, no one has the right to assert that it is impossible; it is, on the contrary, always honorable and meritorious. The example of countless married couples proves not only that fidelity is in accord with the nature of marriage, but also that it is the source of profound and enduring happiness.

Finally, this love is fecund. It is not confined wholly to the loving interchange of husband and wife; it also contrives to go beyond this to bring new life into being. "Marriage and conjugal love are by their nature ordained toward the procreation and education of children. Children are really the supreme gift of marriage and contribute in the highest degree to their parents' welfare."

Responsible Parenthood

10. Married love, therefore, requires of husband and wife the full awareness of their obligations in the matter of responsible parenthood, which today, rightly enough, is much insisted upon, but which at the same time should be rightly understood. Thus, we do well to consider responsible parenthood in the light of its varied legitimate and inter-related aspects.

With regard to the biological processes, responsible parenthood means an awareness of, and respect for, their proper functions. In the procreative faculty the human mind discerns biological laws that apply to the human person.

With regard to man's innate drives and emotions, responsible parent-hood means that man's reason and will must exert control over them.

With regard to physical, economic, psychological and social conditions, responsible parenthood is exercised by those who prudently and generously decide to have more children, and by those who, for serious reasons and with due respect to moral precepts, decide not to have additional children for either a certain or an indefinite period of time.

Responsible parenthood, as we use the term here, has one further essential aspect of paramount importance. It concerns the objective moral order which was established by God, and of which a right conscience is the true interpreter. In a word, the exercise of responsible parenthood requires that husband and wife, keeping a right order of priorities, recognize their own duties toward God, themselves, their families and human society.

From this it follows that they are not free to act as they choose in the service of transmitting life, as if it were wholly up to them to decide what is the right course to follow. On the contrary, they are bound to ensure that what they do corresponds to the will of God the Creator. The very nature of marriage and its use makes His will clear, while the constant teaching of the Church spells it out (10).

Observing the Natural Law

11. The sexual activity, in which husband and wife are intimately and chastely united with one another, through which human life is transmitted, is, as the recent Council recalled, "noble and worthy." It does not, moreover, cease to be legitimate even when, for reasons independent of their will, it is foreseen to be infertile. For its natural adaptation to the

expression and strengthening of the union of husband and wife is not thereby suppressed. The fact is, as experience shows, that new life is not the result of each and every act of sexual intercourse. God has wisely ordered laws of nature and the incidence of fertility in such a way that successive births are already naturally spaced through the inherent operation of these laws. The Church, nevertheless, in urging men to the observance of the precepts of the natural law, which it interprets by its constant doctrine, teaches that each and every marital act must of necessity retain its intrinsic relationship to the procreation of human life.

Union and Procreation

12. This particular doctrine, often expounded by the magisterium of the Church, is based on the inseparable connection, established by God, which man on his own initiative may not break, between the unitive significance and the procreative significance which are both inherent to the marriage act.

The reason is that the fundamental nature of the marriage act, while uniting husband and wife in the closest intimacy, also renders them capable of generating new life—and this as a result of laws written into the actual nature of man and of woman. And if each of these essential qualities, the unitive and the procreative, is preserved, the use of marriage fully retains its sense of true mutual love and its ordination to the supreme responsibility of parenthood to which man is called. We believe that our contemporaries are particularly capable of seeing that this teaching is in harmony with human reason.

Faithfulness to God's Design

13. Men rightly observe that a conjugal act imposed on one's partner without regard to his or her condition or personal and reasonable wishes in the matter, is no true act of love, and therefore offends the moral order in its particular application to the intimate relationship of husband and wife. If they further reflect, they must also recognize that an act of mutual love which impairs the capacity to transmit life which God the Creator, through specific laws, has built into it, frustrates His design which constitutes the norm of marriage, and contradicts the will of the Author of life. Hence to use this divine gift while depriving it, even if only partially, of its meaning and purpose, is equally repugnant to the nature of man and of woman, and is consequently in opposition to the plan of God and His holy will. But to experience the gift of married love while respecting the laws of conception is to acknowledge that one is not the master of the sources of life but rather the minister of the design established by the Creator. Just as man does not have unlimited dominion over his body in general, so also, and with more particular reason, he has no such dominion over his specifically sexual faculties, for these are

concerned by their very nature with the generation of life, of which God is the source. "Human life is sacred—all men must recognize that fact," Our predecessor Pope John XXIII recalled. "From its very inception it reveals the creating hand of God."

Unlawful Birth Control Methods

14. Therefore We base Our words on the first principles of a human and Christian doctrine of marriage when We are obliged once more to declare that the direct interruption of the generative process already begun and, above all, all direct abortion, even for therapeutic reasons, are to be absolutely excluded as lawful means of regulating the number of children. Equally to be condemned, as the magisterium of the Church has affirmed on many occasions, is direct sterilization, whether of the man or of the woman, whether permanent or temporary.

Similarly excluded is any action which either before, at the moment of, or after sexual intercourse, is specifically intended to prevent pro-creation—whether as an end or as a means.

Neither is it valid to argue, as a justification for sexual intercourse which is deliberately contraceptive, that a lesser evil is to be preferred to a greater one, or that such intercourse would merge with procre-ative acts of past and future to form a single entity, and so be qualified by exactly the same moral goodness as these. Though it is true that sometimes it is lawful to tolerate a lesser moral evil in order to avoid a greater evil or in order to promote a greater good," it is never lawful, even for the gravest reasons, to do evil that good may come of it—in other words, to intend directly something which of its very nature con-tradicts the moral order, and which must therefore be judged unworthy of man, even though the intention is to protect or promote the welfare of an individual, of a family or of society in general. Consequently, it is a serious error to think that a whole married life of otherwise normal relations can justify sexual intercourse which is deliberately contracep-tive and so intrinsically wrong.

Lawful Therapeutic Means

15. On the other hand, the Church does not consider at all illicit the use of those therapeutic means necessary to cure bodily diseases, even if a foreseeable impediment to procreation should result there-from—provided such impediment is not directly intended for any motive whatsoever.

Recourse to Infertile Periods

16. Now as We noted earlier (no. 3), some people today raise the objection against this particular doctrine of the Church concerning the moral laws governing marriage, that human intelligence has both the right and responsibility to control those forces of irrational nature

which come within its ambit and to direct them toward ends beneficial to man. Others ask on the same point whether it is not reasonable in so many cases to use artificial birth control if by so doing the harmony and peace of a family are better served and more suitable conditions are provided for the education of children already born. To this question We must give a clear reply. The Church is the first to praise and commend the application of human intelligence to an activity in which a rational creature such as man is so closely associated with his Creator. But she affirms that this must be done within the limits of the order of reality established by God.

If therefore there are well-grounded reasons for spacing births, arising from the physical or psychological condition of husband or wife, or from external circumstances, the Church teaches that married people may then take advantage of the natural cycles immanent in the reproductive system and engage in marital intercourse only during those times that are infertile, thus controlling birth in a way which does not in the least offend the moral principles which We have just explained.

Neither the Church nor her doctrine is inconsistent when she considers it lawful for married people to take advantage of the infertile period but condemns as always unlawful the use of means which directly prevent conception, even when the reasons given for the later practice may appear to be upright and serious. In reality, these two cases are completely different. In the former the married couple rightly use a faculty provided them by nature. In the later they obstruct the natural development of the generative process. It cannot be denied that in each case the married couple, for acceptable reasons, are both perfectly clear in their intention to avoid children and wish to make sure that none will result. But it is equally true that it is exclusively in the former case that husband and wife are ready to abstain from intercourse during the fertile period as often as for reasonable motives the birth of another child is not desirable. And when the infertile period recurs, they use their married intimacy to express their mutual love and safeguard their fidelity toward one another. In doing this they certainly give proof of a true and authentic love.

Consequences of Artificial Methods

17. Responsible men can become more deeply convinced of the truth of the doctrine laid down by the Church on this issue if they reflect on the consequences of methods and plans for artificial birth control. Let them first consider how easily this course of action could open wide the way for marital infidelity and a general lowering of moral standards. Not much experience is needed to be fully aware of human weakness and to understand that human beings—and especially the young, who are so exposed to temptation—need incentives to keep the moral law, and it is an evil thing to make it easy for them to break that law. Another

effect that gives cause for alarm is that a man who grows accustomed to the use of contraceptive methods may forget the reverence due to a woman, and, disregarding her physical and emotional equilibrium, reduce her to being a mere instrument for the satisfaction of his own desires, no longer considering her as his partner whom he should surround with care and affection.

Finally, careful consideration should be given to the danger of this power passing into the hands of those public authorities who care little for the precepts of the moral law. Who will blame a government which in its attempt to resolve the problems affecting an entire country resorts to the same measures as are regarded as lawful by married people in the solution of a particular family difficulty? Who will prevent public authorities from favoring those contraceptive methods which they consider more effective? Should they regard this as necessary, they may even impose their use on everyone. It could well happen, therefore, that when people, either individually or in family or social life, experience the inherent difficulties of the divine law and are determined to avoid them, they may give into the hands of public authorities the power to intervene in the most personal and intimate responsibility of husband and wife.

Limits to Man's Power

Consequently, unless we are willing that the responsibility of procreating life should be left to the arbitrary decision of men, we must accept that there are certain limits, beyond which it is wrong to go, to the power of man over his own body and its natural functions—limits, let it be said, which no one, whether as a private individual or as a public authority, can lawfully exceed. These limits are expressly imposed because of the reverence due to the whole human organism and its natural functions, in the light of the principles We stated earlier, and in accordance with a correct understanding of the "principle of totality" enunciated by Our predecessor Pope Pius XII.

Concern of the Church

18. It is to be anticipated that perhaps not everyone will easily accept this particular teaching. There is too much clamorous outcry against the voice of the Church, and this is intensified by modern means of communication. But it comes as no surprise to the Church that she, no less than her divine Founder, is destined to be a "sign of contradiction." She does not, because of this, evade the duty imposed on her of proclaiming humbly but firmly the entire moral law, both natural and evangelical.

Since the Church did not make either of these laws, she cannot be their arbiter—only their guardian and interpreter. It could never be right for her to declare lawful what is in fact unlawful, since that, by its very nature, is always opposed to the true good of man.

In preserving intact the whole moral law of marriage, the Church is convinced that she is contributing to the creation of a truly human civilization. She urges man not to betray his personal responsibilities by putting all his faith in technical expedients. In this way she defends the dignity of husband and wife. This course of action shows that the Church, loyal to the example and teaching of the divine Savior, is sincere and unselfish in her regard for men whom she strives to help even now during this earthly pilgrimage "to share God's life as sons of the living God, the Father of all men."

Chapter 2

THE 1970s

In the 1970s there were five main documents that discussed the role of women and continued developing and enriching a theology of womanhood in the Roman Catholic Church. Included in this anthology are key sections of three of those documents: "Declaration on Procured Abortion," *Persona humana,* and *Inter insigniores.* Some new developments in the theology of womanhood include a thorough defense of a male-only priesthood, a more direct response to abortion given the U.S. *Roe v. Wade* decision in 1973, an acknowledgment of misogynistic treatment of women in early church documents, a heightened concern for women's rights in civil society, and a new understanding of personhood in general and womanhood in particular in response to the sexual revolution in the United States and elsewhere in the 1960s and 1970s.

The 1970s also confirm the previous theology developed in the 1960s and before. Women naturally possess certain characteristics that they need to use to help make the world more just, more compassionate and more humane. Women's primary responsibility is the home and the children, and this is where they find their most satisfying fulfillment. Finally, women are equal in dignity and deserve equal respect as human beings, but women and men have different and complementary roles to fulfill in society.

It is now time to examine the following documents in further detail:

- SCDF, "Declaration on Procured Abortion," released on November 18, 1974;
- Pope Paul VI, *Discours de Pape Paul VI au Comité pour L'Année Internationale de la Femme,* promulgated on April 18, 1975;
- SCDF, *Persona humana* or *Declaration on Certain Questions concerning Sexual Ethics*, published on December 29, 1975;
- SCDF, *Inter insigniores* or *On the Question of Admission of Women to the Ministerial Priesthood*, promulgated on October 15, 1976; and
- Pope Paul VI, *Angelus Domini*, address given on January 30, 1977, whose suggested English title in *Ordinatio sacerdotalis* is "The Role of Women in the Plan of Salvation."

DECLARATION ON PROCURED ABORTION

The SCDF approached Pope Paul VI on June 28, 1974—just eighteen months after the United States granted women the legal right to abortion in the historic *Roe v. Wade* Supreme Court case—asking for confirmation of the document entitled "Declaration on Procured Abortion." The pope ordered that it be decreed, which it was when it was released on November 18, 1974. While the entire document is included for the reader to examine, it is also important to draw attention to its important themes and to offer the reader a summary of how this document fits into the other documents of the 1970s.

The "Declaration on Procured Abortion" begins by acknowledging movements to legalize abortion in various countries, saying, "The problem of procured abortion and of its possible legal liberalization has become more or less everywhere the subject of impassioned discussions" (1). In light of this development the church considers helping humanity choose pathways that do not diminish human dignity to be part of its mission. Thus, this document contains a defense of human dignity, urges respect for life, and affirms the right to life.

The document declares that the church continues to espouse the same doctrine about life and conception that it always has (4). Human life must be protected, respected, and cherished as a gift from God: "We understand that human life, even on this earth, is precious" (5). The church argues that this can also be seen in the Ten Commandments, specifically the one prohibiting killing.

Beginning in paragraph 6, the church traces the history of anti-abortion rhetoric in its tradition. The document claims that from the *Didache* and from Tertullian to Saint Thomas Aquinas and Pope Sixtus V, along with various popes and in the Second Vatican Council, the church has always promoted life and recognized abortion as a sin against life and against God, who is the giver of life. Respecting life is part of the duty of Christians, and support for doing so can also be found within humanity's rational capacity. In other words, human reason alone leads one to respect life.

Within church history, the document states, one can see this anti-abortion stance in the punishments given to women who procured abortions. One example is the declaration at the Council of Mainz in 847 "that the most rigourous penance would be imposed 'on women who procure the elimination of the fruit conceived in their womb'" (7). While there was some discussion in the Middle Ages that the penalty for abortions be less strict if the soul had not yet entered the fetus, the church details Pope Innocent XI's condemnation of such a position. This section also explains how most of the church fathers and the early popes condemned abortion because it opposed human reason, natural law, and God's law. The popes of more recent history have also condemned abortion teaching by concluding that life is precious from beginning to end and anything that stops or cuts off life is a crime of utmost gravity (7).

In addition to condemnations of abortion, the document also discusses what life means and specifically what it means to be a human and a creation of God. According to the church, humans are innately free beings and possess immortal souls. Humans are also naturally social beings who live in communities and have certain rights within those communities concerning their livelihood, wellness, and life. Yet, in the end, even with this need for human social interaction, it is only in God that humans find true fulfillment (8–9).

As we have seen in the previous chapter in the discussion of *Humanae vitae*, the church understands its role in the world as enlightening humanity to better ways of living. One of the ways it sees fit to do so within the "Declaration on Procured Abortion" is in its discussion of the right to life. In a direct way church leadership fits the right to life within current social discourse on human rights (10–11) by declaring that the right to life is the basis of all other rights humans possess in society.

The church also uses modern science to make its case. For the church, life begins at conception, and in light of a human's right to life, one must protect all life, even that in women's wombs that is not yet fully formed. In fact, the church cites scientific evidence of the activity of the newly fertilized egg moments after conception as proof that life already exists (12–13). Even at this early stage of development the zygote is human, because one cannot become human if one is not already human to begin with (12).

The document then changes focus and discusses reasons women might seek abortions, including financial situations, birth defects, an already large family, and the threat of childbirth to the woman's health and/or life. The church declares these reasons invalid (14). No matter how dire they may seem, these reasons can never justify taking away the right to life (14).

Many of the above-mentioned arguments have been part of the feminist movement's push to secure abortion rights for women. The church is quite cognizant of this fact. The document, in paragraph 15, focuses its attention on feminism and the movement in feminism for abortion rights. In terms of some feminist goals, church leadership sides with women who struggle with and fight against societal oppression and bias. The church also acknowledges that when it comes to women and their place in society, there is still a lot of progress that needs to be made, depending on the country under discussion.

The church considers the feminist push for abortion rights to obscure the real issue at hand. According to the church, abortion is not about rights but about human life. Any discussion or choice about abortion is about nature, and nature is immutable. Nature is part of humanity and that includes sexuality, its finality, and when applicable, the new life that emerges from sexual relations. When one disrupts nature, one sins against God and threatens to denigrate humanity. One who procures an abortion commits murder because termination of a pregnancy is the end of something natural, something alive, and something very much human, according to the church.

Next, the document addresses technological progress to make abortions easier and the development of birth control. According to the "Declaration on Procured Abortion," all of these have the potential to increase human lack of respect for one another and for life itself. Birth control affects the teleology of the sex act by making conception impossible. These technological advances could also cause more immediate problems. For example, women who have abortions may never be able to have children again or may be sickened and die from the procedure (19).

According to the document, above all these other concerns is the right to life. All human life must be protected no matter what. No government or authority has any right to interfere with this aspect of humanity. Likewise, justice dictates that systems be put into place to handle situations in which a woman cannot take care of her child. Two examples are monetary support and adoption services. Thus, a woman has some recourse other than abortion (23). Likewise, people must work to better society so that women do not feel that abortion is their only option in a given situation (26). In the end, it is the responsibility of the entire church and all its faithful to make the world a place where abortions are unnecessary because all life is respected, cherished, and supported (27).

DISCOURS DU PAPE PAUL VI AU COMITÉ POUR L'ANNÉE INTERNATIONALE DE LA FEMME

Pope Paul VI released *Discours du Pape Paul VI au Comité pour L'Année Internationale de la Femme* on April 18, 1975. The year 1975 marked a special year within the life of the Roman Catholic Church. It was declared a Holy Year by Pope Paul VI. During a Holy Year, the church puts considerably more emphasis on the spiritual aspects and practices of the church. The concept of the Holy Year, first developed in the Middle Ages by the medieval popes, draws from the Old Testament celebration of the Jubilee Year. During the Jubilee Year the land would lie fallow to allow it a chance to rest. People did this to give thanks to the Lord for all that the land had provided. During this year Jews forgave the debts they owed to one another and freed slaves.

While the church declared 1975 a Holy Year, the international community proclaimed it the International Year of the Woman. This was initiated and promoted by the United Nations. The UN resolution pronounces:

> Noting that the United Nations has designated 1975 as International Women's Year
> Aware that the Declaration of Human Rights states that everyone is entitled to all rights and freedoms without distinction of any kind; and "Considering that discrimination against women is incompatible with human dignity and with the welfare of the family and society," the International Humanist & Ethical Union approves and supports the objectives of the International Women's Year as set by the General Assembly:
> > "To promote equality between men and women"
> > "To ensure full integration of women in the total development effort"
> > "To increase the importance of women's contribution to the strengthening of world peace."
> and:
> urges its member organisations in their respective countries to initiate, develop and support programmes of education, and to promote legal, political, and social actions toward achieving these goals of equality, development and peace.[1]

The United Nations planned events to promote and advance the dignity of women in the world. It also worked closely with nations, communities, and peoples to advance the place of women in society.

In mid 1975 we have *Discours du Pape Paul VI au Comité pour L'Année Internationale de la Femme*. In fact, this document mentions both the Holy Year and the International Year of the Woman, which is highly significant because it shows once again the effect of feminism and changing global conditions as being within the scope of the church's purview. Likewise, one can see the way in which feminism and global change affect church theology and how church leadership has taken the International Year of the Woman and the Holy Year, two historical world events, quite seriously in its reflection on women found in this address.

Discours du Pape Paul VI au Comité pour L'Année Internationale de la Femme begins by urging the world to promote the dignity and the participation

---

[1] International Humanist and Ethical Union, "International Women's Year, 1975," IHEU Congress, 1974; http://www.iheu.org/node/2127.

of women in society. It says the issues surrounding women and their rights are delicate because speaking about equality of rights without discussing the situation of women in the world is very problematic. The document urges recognition of the fact that there are many women around the world who do not have basic human rights or even the basic conditions of dignity and respect. Everyone must work to discover, respect, and protect the rights and prerogatives of every woman, whether single or married. In addition, women must be respected in their chosen career path, whether that is academic life, professional life, or staying at home to raise children. In fact, all areas of civil, social, and religious life must secure the rights, respect, and dignity of women. According to the church in this document the International Year of the Woman seeks not only to obtain for women equality of rights; it also seeks to ensure that women are integrated into the world as it continues to develop.

According to the document, women must be able to participate in the life and mission of the church. The church acknowledges that women have and continue to nourish the Catholic faith immensely. For example, some women participate in various parts of church life at the parish and diocesan levels. Yet this is not enough. Women must also be allowed to work within the church's evangelical mission and be incorporated more fully into the life of the Christian community itself.

The document also addresses civic and social life for women. The church believes that part of women's contribution in the world is to reinforce peace between humans. The Congregation declares that this idea should have a lasting resonance with all, particularly during this Holy Year, a year of spiritual renewal. In addition to building up a more peaceful world, women are asked as members of families, as educators, and as participants in all sectors of society to work to build a more just and congenial society. The document declares:

> Yes, Christian Women! The future of civil society and the church community awaits very much the arrival of your sensibility, your capacity to understand, your tenderness, your perseverance, generosity and humility. These virtues are in accordance with a feminine psychology, magnificently espoused in the Virgin Mary, and are also the fruits of the Holy Spirit. This Holy Spirit will surely guide you toward full flowering in the achievement of what you seek—what we all seek.[2]

---

[2] "Oui, femmes chrétiennes, l'avenir de la société civile et de la communauté ecclésiale attend beaucoup de votre sensibilité et votre capacité de comprehension, de votre douceur et de votre perseverance, de votre générosité et de votre humilité. Ces vertus, si bien accordées à la psychologie feminine, et magnifiquement épanouies dans

In other words, the world waits with bated breath for the gifts of women to help make it a better place. Church leadership hoped that this introspective Holy Year would further promote the mission of the UN's International Year of the Woman by highlighting the many ongoing and future contributions of women to the world. Likewise, the church reminded the world that it owes women because of their contributions: respect, full participation, rights, and dignity.

PERSONA HUMANA

The next document, released at the close of the Holy Year by the SCDF, is *Persona humana*, or *Declaration on Certain Questions Concerning Sexual Ethics*. This document describes what it means to be human and gendered and the difference between the genders as well as the use of birth control, consecrated virgins, premarital sexual relations, masturbation, and homosexuality. In addition, it acknowledges the birth of the sexual revolution (as did the "Declaration on Procured Abortion") and seeks to clarify church teachings regarding sexual ethics in light of this flourishing sexual revolution.

The document begins by defining sexuality as one of those forces in life that is part of being human and a very significant part at that. It connects one's biological sex to one's gender, thereby not distinguishing a difference between the two. Therefore, one's sex/gender affects a human's life on biological, psychological, and spiritual levels as well as plays an important role in human development, growth, and maturity. This suggests that one's sex/gender reaches down to the very depths of the individual, to the soul. Each gender experiences life differently because of the all-encompassing nature of how one's sex affects one's life (1).

Also, there are basic differences between the genders (5). For example, women, who biologically support life in their wombs and give birth to new life, are the ones whose duties revolve around this new life and the home. In the United States, for example, society is organized to support these differences by granting women maternity leave, having laws that make it illegal to discriminate in hiring practices if the applicant is pregnant, and providing financial assistance for newborns and other child-rearing concerns.[3]

---

la Vierge Marie, sont aussi des fruits de l'Espirit Saint. Cet Espirit Saint vous guidera sûrement dans le plein épanouissement, dans la promotion que vous cherchez, que nous cherchons tous" (English translation by author).

[3] The document does not lay out these specific examples. They are my illustrations of what the document means.

For the church, this discussion of the human person and the important role one's sex/gender plays in one's life leads naturally to a discussion of sexuality, conception, and birth control. The document begins by stating that sexual acts are permissible only between a married man and woman. Any heterosexual sex outside of marriage—before marriage, through adultery, or on account of remarriage—denies the essential characteristics of how God intended sexuality to be (7). Married heterosexual sex is the only acceptable expression of sexuality, and each sex act within marriage must be open to procreation. Sex acts must be of the type, and only of the type, that allow for conception (penile-vaginal penetration). They are also acts of self-giving, one spouse to the other. However, the self-giving quality of sexuality is denied if methods are in place that are intended to prevent conception. In other words, it is only when each sex act between spouses is open to children that sexuality is morally good. This is because the finality of the act is preserved. The function of sex is biological; its end is the production of children. In other words, procreation is the teleological significance of sex (4–5).

It is through this reasoning as well as its understanding of sex/gender that the church produces a theology of sex/gender complementarity, a very important concept in the church's theology of womanhood. While not described in detail in this document, a description of what is meant by complementarity and how it develops from these mentions into a full-fledged theological concept seems necessary. Here, *complementarity* means that given the biological makeup of males and females and the natural way in which it is only through heterosexual sex that can children be conceived, men/males and women/females are by their very nature marital partners for each other. In addition, biology separates social roles. We can see this in paragraph 5 of the document, which refers to *Gaudium et spes,* paragraphs 29 and 60. Women, because they give birth, are best suited for raising and educating children, while men are fit to work in the public sphere. A man cannot be in the home because of worldly obligations, and women who work outside the home frustrate their responsibilities and possibly endanger the home and children. These roles complement rather than compete against each other. In this way all humans share in equal dignity at the same time that males and females have different and complementary social roles to play.

Returning to the document, section 11 discusses virgins and their role in life. Celibate men and women give up their sexuality to God and channel their sexual energy into caring for others. *Persona humana* says virginity "is an eminent way of giving oneself more easily to God alone with an undivided heart" (11). With consecrated virginity, humans have an "undivided" focus on God and neighbor; this allows them to serve the world more wholly and to be able to give more of themselves to the world in charity.

The document also discusses various types of immoral sexuality in addition to contraception: masturbation, homosexuality, sex outside marriage (pre-marital, adultery, remarriage), and polygamy. First of all, any sex act that denies the finality or teleological purpose of sex (to produce children) is disordered and against God's plan (4, 8, and 9). This includes masturbation, which by design does not create the union of two people that every sex act should do. Homosexual activity, which could be seen as a union of two people,[4] cannot produce children (9). In addition, most sex outside of marriage also uses some form of contraception and is therefore immoral. Let us look at each one of these categories in more depth.

Masturbation is morally suspect because it does not connect a woman and man together in love. *Persona humana,* section 9, says,

> All deliberate exercise of sexuality must be reserved to this regular relationship [meaning marriage]. Even if it cannot be proved that Scripture condemns this sin by name, the tradition of the church has rightly understood it to be condemned in the New Testament when the latter speaks of "impurity," "unchasteness" and other vices contrary to chastity and continence.

In other words, masturbation, since it does not satisfy the requirements for sex to be open to procreation, is immoral.

Persona humana recognizes that homosexuality afflicts many humans around the world (8). However, these individuals should live chaste (in their case meaning celibate) lives and be respected by all members of the Christian community as they struggle to deal with their condition. The document shows that the issue is not settled for the church; it posits that homosexuality may have a few sources of origin and for these reasons homosexual individuals should be treated pastorally with compassion. First, homosexuality might be a biologically based pathology, or, second, it could come from poor education and poor examples. While homosexuality might seem natural to many homosexual individuals, homosexual sex acts are a "serious depravity" (8). Whatever excuses society makes for homosexual behavior can never justify the act because the act denies the divinely instituted complementarity of men and women. This is in addition to its inability to produce the teleological significance of sex: procreation. According to the document, homosexual sex acts are "intrinsically disordered and can in no case be approved of" (8).

As mentioned above, the church acknowledges that homosexual people struggle with their sexual desires on a daily basis and that society some-

---

[4] These are my words and not part of the document.

times even justifies homosexual acts and lifestyles as positive or normal (10). Nevertheless, in the realm of sexual ethics any sexual act outside of marriage or within marriage that prevents conception is a mortal sin. It disconnects the individual from God in a very serious way, even if that is not one's intention in the act. All people (even those in marriages) should live as virtuous and charitable lives as possible, and one of the ways this is accomplished is by not committing certain sexual sins.

INTER INSIGNIORES

In addition to sexual ethics and the place of women in society, the church also takes a firm stance on the priesthood, especially as it relates to women and the feminist language of equal rights. *Inter insigniores*, or *On the Question of Admission of Women to the Ministerial Priesthood,* promulgated on October 15, 1976, by the SCDF, explains and defends the church's tradition of a male-only priesthood. The church gives many reasons why the priesthood is reserved for men while taking into consideration women's entrance into the public realm and gender-based discrimination. The SCDF, throughout this document, also discusses the participation of women in larger society, in the history of the church, during Jesus' ministry, and in the life of the early Christian community.

The document begins by acknowledging the changing role of women in public life, the need to end oppression and discrimination against women in the world, and the history of important women in the life of the church. The document addresses the new roles of women in society matter-of-factly as part of the world's current social landscape. Yet, despite these changes, women continue to face various forms of cultural and institutionalized discrimination. Church leaders understand this to be contrary to God's plan for the world and ask for humanity to end this injustice. In the introduction to the document the church presents itself as a model of women's participation, given its long history of religious women who have enriched the faith and the church with their many gifts, writings, charity work, and strong faith.

The SCDF also realizes that it must expand the roles of women within the church. It considers Vatican II the first step in opening the doors to allow women to participate more fully in the life of the church. Women now participate on many levels of the church and in everyday parish life as well.

At this point in the document the church examines the changes in women's roles in Protestant denominations, including entry into "the pastoral office." The church acknowledges that this is a difficult issue, especially in terms of ecumenical dialogue. It is by citing this Protestant tradition, according to the church, that the church has been asked by its theologians if women can be ordained within the Roman Catholic Church as well. (This issue has been addressed by many Roman Catholic feminist theologians, although the introduction to the document is not clear whether these are the theologians it is referencing here or not.)

The church responds to the question of women's ordination by acknowledging the poor treatment of women in patristic and earlier church documents but wholeheartedly believes that women were not discriminated against by Jesus. This is crucial because it was Jesus who established the priestly office. Therefore, the church cannot change Jesus' established way and cannot admit women to the priesthood. In addition to this, there are other reasons why women would not be effective (one could even say convincing as) priests.

Let us examine the argument laid out in this document and the document's many reasons for a male-only priesthood, first with a brief summary and then a more in-depth explanation. One of the main arguments the document lays out is the church's lack of power to change the historical institution of the priesthood because God has not granted the church permission to do so. Church leaders also do not have the power to grant ordination to women because God chose to be incarnate as a male and commissioned only male apostles at the Last Supper even though he also had female disciples. In addition, women's bodies are not male and therefore do not establish the link to the priest "*en persona Christi*" (5), which is necessary for faith. Another reason given to exclude women from the priesthood is that a male-only priesthood is one of many eschatological mysteries. Finally, a male-only priesthood is in keeping with the tradition of the church; church teaching has never strayed on this point.

Let us explore these ideas in more depth. First, one important reason for a male-only priesthood is the historical fact of Jesus' maleness. God's choice to become male and Jesus' choice of an all-male apostolate were free of societal pressures. In this vein, *Inter insigniores* says:

> "Sacramental signs," says St. Thomas, "represent what they signify by natural resemblance." The same natural resemblance is required for persons as for things: when Christ's role in the Eucharist is to be expressed sacramentally, there would not be this 'natural resemblance' which must exist between Christ and his minister if the role of Christ were not taken by a man: in such a case it would be difficult to see in the minister the image of Christ. For Christ himself was and remains a man. (5)

This maleness of Jesus also points to another reason only men can be priests. Jesus was male, and the faithful need the direct connection between the maleness of Jesus and Jesus' representative on earth—the priest. In other words, if a woman were a priest, the femaleness of the priest and the maleness of Jesus would not match. The body of a woman cannot represent the body of a man (5).

Jesus also commissioned a male-only priesthood even though he had plenty of women disciples. As the document and the Gospels attest, Jesus treated women with respect and healed them often. Women were also the first to testify to Jesus' resurrection, even though Jewish custom of the day did not value women's testimony. Despite his closeness to many women, Jesus did not commission women to go out to the nations as he did the twelve apostles. Given the gospel's witness to the inclusive manner in which Jesus treated the women of his time, Jesus' decision to establish a male-only priesthood is especially easy to understand as truthfully free of societal pressure, according to *Inter insigniores*. In addition, while the Gospels record stories of women who accompany the apostles and are often portrayed as gaining converts and instructing men about Jesus, the document declares that the early church never considered women's ordination (4).

Because of the sacramental nature of the priesthood and the priest's role in dispensing the sacraments, especially consecrating the bread and wine into the body and blood of Jesus Christ, women cannot fulfill the priestly office. These sacraments form the foundation of Christianity, according to the document, and to go against its foundation would jeopardize salvation as well. They are also the basis of the structure of the church as commissioned by Jesus (5).

For the reasons mentioned above, the priesthood is a position about which human rights language is completely inapplicable. The priesthood is a mystery of salvation established by Jesus. In addition, the church tests men's vocations to the priesthood to ensure their authenticity and their call by God; not just any man can become a priest. It is not a right for men either. So, while women may feel called to the priesthood, the SCDF stresses the need to recognize this not as a truly vocational calling but rather as a misinterpretation of their real vocation to children and the family. According to *Inter insigniores*, confirming a male-only priesthood does not denigrate women as human beings or as mothers. Rather, it supports the complementary nature of men and women and their different but significant roles. In fact, a male-only priesthood is in keeping with God's plan and the mystery of salvation (6).

THE ROLE OF WOMEN IN THE PLAN OF SALVATION

According to this document, then, women have a different role to play in the mystery of salvation, one that does not allow them to be priests. What is that role? Some mention of this different role for women is described in the next document of the 1970s, although this role is not fully fleshed out until the next decade. The next document is referred to in English as "The Role of Women in the Plan of Salvation."[5] The Italian version of "The Role of Women in the Plan of Salvation" (of which there is no English translation currently available) does not have the same title. It seems to be more commonly known as Pope Paul VI's address to the people during the *Angelus Domini* on Sunday, January 30, 1977. The *Angelus Domini* is a prayer about and to Mary repeated three times daily, usually at 6 a.m., noon, and 6 p.m., with set words and intentions. When performed at the Vatican with the pope in attendance, it appears to be quite common for the pope to address the congregation at some point during the prayer.

On January 30, 1977, Pope Paul VI addressed women as a group and explained what the church understands women's role in salvation to be. One of the first things the message confirms is the male-only priesthood. It acknowledges feminists' challenge to this rule as one that continues inequality between the sexes. However, the pope responds by saying that because men and women have different functions, men and women also have different roles to play in society. In addition, Jesus established the priesthood as he did. Sexual difference does not mean that sex/gender has less dignity or deserves less respect. Women have the same ability to be virtuous, to show love, and to be holy as men do, as illustrated in the Letter to the Galatians, which states there is no difference between Greek and Jew, slave or free, or man or woman (3:28). Women should cultivate those virtues and talents given to them by God as part of God's divine plan.

On its own, this document does a poor job explaining what these virtues and talents are and how women should do their part for the salvation of the world. Nonetheless, some of these ideas have already been explained in the other documents of this decade and suggest what might be meant here. At the same time, the document summarizes well the theology produced within this decade.

Women (and men) are called to be virtuous. A woman should not procure an abortion, no matter what the circumstances, because by doing so she commits murder. She also sins against God and denies a human being their right to life. Procuring abortions can also lead to disrespect for life, which is extremely dangerous for humanity now and future generations. The church believes that feminist arguments for abortion as a human right deny the fact that life begins at conception. The human potential of an embryo is very significant because it means that in order to create a human being

---

[5] *Ordinatio sacerdotalis* calls it this.

out of some small collection of cells, a human being has been present from the first moment those cells began to multiply. Ridding the womb of those cells destroys a human life, and there are church and divine consequences for such actions.

Likewise, women must consider sexual ethics. The use of contraception is morally reprehensible because it interrupts the finality of the sex act between married people. Therefore, the spouses are not fully giving themselves to each other. Likewise, masturbation, homosexuality, and any sexual act outside of heterosexual vaginal penetration open to procreation is gravely sinful. Some of these acts deny the union of two people, while others do not allow conception to take place. It is for these reasons that they are sinful and disordered.

Related to sexual ethics is sexual differentiation. Men and women have different biological capacities and functions. It is from these biological differences that one can point to different roles for men and women in social, religious, and civic institutions, to name just a few. Whatever the differences may be, men and women should be accorded equal respect and dignity. Where this is lacking for women, laws, customs, and societies must change to accord all people equal respect and dignity. Women's rights must also be protected and secured. This is extremely important in those countries that do a particularly poor job of affording women the respect and dignity they deserve as human beings and creations of God.

At the same time, this biological difference also supports the complementarity of men and women. It is only through vaginal-penile penetration that the human species can procreate. Because each sex/gender is better or more suited for a specific task, it makes sense for the two to come together. In addition, women, because they bear children for nine months, birth them, and produce their first sustenance (breast milk), should be the primary caregivers of children.

Women should not become priests because that role does not align with the mystery of salvation or the way in which Jesus established the church. Rather, they have other important work to do that more suits their feminine psychological makeup. Women should work for world peace and just social, economic, and political relations among people. They should make society friendlier as they fulfill their roles as educators and participants in other areas of social and civic life. Women should also help the world by showing it their feminine psychological capacity for tenderness, understanding, perseverance, generosity, humility, and sensibility. In this way women will gain the respect, dignity, and place in this world that they seek for themselves and in which the church supports them; they will make the world a better place.

Rather than feel that the church continues to support women's inequality, women should see in the church the many ways it inspires respect, dignity, and protection of women around the world. The church acknowledges the discriminatory outlook of some of the early church fathers toward women in their writings. For the church, this acknowledgment is important so that it can be sure not to continue in discriminatory footsteps. The church acknowledges its long history of important female religious figures, including theologians and church doctors. The document also points to the fact that while Jesus did not choose women to be priests, Jesus' life and ministry show an unbiased and respectful attitude toward the women in his life. In fact, women were the first to witness to Jesus' resurrection. Finally, the church supports those parts of the feminist movements across the globe that fight to end discrimination based on sex/gender and secure women's civic and social rights. The church believes that women need to be protected from harm and granted the dignity and respect they deserve as human beings. It approves of feminist movements that support these goals. At the same time, it is leery of feminist movements that misunderstand gender equality and human rights language.

The theology of womanhood developed in the 1970s offers a firm defense of the priesthood as a male-only institution. It acknowledges the goodness of feminisms that fight for the end of sex/gender discrimination and for people and societal institutions to inspire equal respect and dignity of all human persons. The documents also show much theological concern over sexual ethics and the burgeoning sexual revolution and its promotion of looser sexual mores across the globe. In this regard the church defends all humans' right to life and disagrees with feminist gains in regard to abortion rights. It views women who procure abortions as murderers and sinners, and allocates punishment for those sins. Finally, it introduces the concept of gender complementarity, a highly significant theological concept for many reasons, even though the documents offer little explanation of what is meant by the term. This will be the subject of more comment in the following chapters.

In summary, the decade ended quite differently than it began. Women's roles as workers, wives, and mothers seem to be downplayed to focus on other more pressing issues such as the social and civic role of women, the priesthood, and sexual ethics. However, this trend does not last long. In the 1980s a renewed focus on women as mothers and wives is seen in the documents and once again becomes part of official Roman Catholic theological concern. After the texts "Declaration on Procured Abortion," *Persona Humana,* and *Inter insigniores,* we will turn to the 1980s.

DECLARATION ON PROCURED ABORTION

18 NOVEMBER 1974

1. The problem of procured abortion and of its possible legal liberalization has become more or less everywhere the subject of impassioned discussions. These debates would be less grave were it not a question of human life, a primordial value, which must be protected and promoted. Everyone understands this, although many look for reasons, even against all evidence, to promote the use of abortion. One cannot but be astonished to see a simultaneous increase of unqualified protests against the death penalty and every form of war and the vindication of the liberalization of abortion, either in its entirety or in ever broader indications. The Church is too conscious of the fact that it belongs to her vocation to defend man against everything that could disintegrate or lessen his dignity to remain silent on such a topic. Because the Son of God became man, there is no man who is not His brother in humanity and who is not called to become a Christian in order to receive salvation from Him.

2. In many countries the public authorities which resist the liberalization of abortion laws are the object of powerful pressures aimed at leading them to this goal. This, it is said, would violate no one's conscience, for each individual would be left free to follow his own opinion, while being prevented from imposing it on others. Ethical pluralism is claimed to be a normal consequence of ideological pluralism. There is, however, a great difference between the one and the other, for action affects the interests of others more quickly than does mere opinion. Moreover, one can never claim freedom of opinion as a pretext for attacking the rights of others, most especially the right to life.

3. Numerous Christian lay people, especially doctors, but also parents' associations, statesmen, or leading figures in posts of responsibility have vigorously reacted against this propaganda campaign. Above all, many episcopal conferences and many bishops acting in their own name have judged it opportune to recall very strongly the traditional doctrine of the Church. With a striking convergence these documents admirably emphasize an attitude of respect for life which is at the same time human and Christian. Nevertheless, it has happened that several

56

of these documents here or there have encountered reservation or even opposition.

4. Charged with the promotion and the defense of faith and morals in the universal Church, the SCDF proposes to recall this teaching in its essential aspects to all the faithful. Thus in showing the unity of the Church, it will confirm by the authority proper to the Holy See what the bishops have opportunely undertaken. It hopes that all the faithful, including those who might have been unsettled by the controversies and new opinions, will understand that it is not a question of opposing one opinion to another, but of transmitting to the faithful a constant teaching of the supreme Magisterium, which teaches moral norms in the light of faith. It is therefore clear that this declaration necessarily entails a grave obligation for Christian consciences. May God deign to enlighten also all men who strive with their whole heart to "act in truth" (*Jn*. 3:21).

5. "Death was not God's doing, he takes no pleasure in the extinction of the living" (*Wis*. 1:13). Certainly God has created beings who have only one lifetime and physical death cannot be absent from the world of those with a bodily existence. But what is immediately willed is life, and in the visible universe everything has been made for man, who is the image of God and the world's crowning glory (cf. *Gen*. 1:26–28). On the human level, "it was the devil's envy that brought death into the world" (*Wis*. 2:24). Introduced by sin, death remains bound up with it: death is the sign and fruit of sin. But there is no final triumph for death. Confirming faith in the Resurrection, the Lord proclaims in the Gospel: "God is God, not of the dead, but of the living" (*Mt*. 22:32). And death like sin will be definitively defeated by resurrection in Christ (cf. 1 *Cor*. 15:20–27). Thus we understand that human life, even on this earth, is precious. Infused by the Creator, life is again taken back by Him (cf. *Gen*. 2:7; *Wis*. 15:11). It remains under His protection: man's blood cries out to Him (cf. *Gen*. 4:10) and He will demand an account of it, "for in the image of God man was made" (*Gen*. 9:5–6). The commandment of God is formal: "You shall not kill" (*Ex*. 20:13). Life is at the same time a gift and a responsibility. It is received as a "talent" (cf. *Mt*. 25:14–30); it must be put to proper use. In order that life may bring forth fruit, many tasks are offered to man in this world and he must not shirk them. More important still, the Christian knows that eternal life depends on what, with the grace of God, he does with his life on earth.

6. The tradition of the Church has always held that human life must be protected and favored from the beginning, just as at the various stages of its development. Opposing the morals of the Greco-Roman world, the Church of the first centuries insisted on the difference that exists on this point between those morals and Christian morals. In the Didache it is clearly said: "You shall not kill by abortion the fruit of the womb and you shall not murder the infant already born." Athenagoras emphasizes that Christians consider as murderers those women who

take medicines to procure an abortion; he condemns the killers of children, including those still living in their mother's womb, "where they are already the object of the care of divine Providence." Tertullian did not always perhaps use the same language; he nevertheless clearly affirms the essential principle: "To prevent birth is anticipated murder; it makes little difference whether one destroys a life already born or does away with it in its nascent stage. The one who will be a man is already one."

7. In the course of history, the Fathers of the Church, her Pastors and her Doctors have taught the same doctrine—the various opinions on the infusion of the spiritual soul did not introduce any doubt about the illicitness of abortion. It is true that in the Middle Ages, when the opinion was generally held that the spiritual soul was not present until after the first few weeks, a distinction was made in the evaluation of the sin and the gravity of penal sanctions. Excellent authors allowed for this first period more lenient case solutions which they rejected for following periods. But it was never denied at that time that procured abortion, even during the first days, was objectively grave fault. This condemnation was in fact unanimous. Among the many documents it is sufficient to recall certain ones. The first Council of Mainz in 847 reconsidered the penalties against abortion which had been established by preceding Councils. It decided that the most rigorous penance would be imposed "on women who procure the elimination of the fruit conceived in their womb." The Decree of Gratian reported the following words of Pope Stephen V: "That person is a murderer who causes to perish by abortion what has been conceived." St. Thomas, the Common Doctor of the Church, teaches that abortion is a grave sin against the natural law." At the time of the Renaissance Pope Sixtus V condemned abortion with the greatest severity. A century later, Innocent XI rejected the propositions of certain lax canonists who sought to excuse an abortion procured before the moment accepted by some as the moment of the spiritual animation of the new being. In our days the recent Roman Pontiffs have proclaimed the same doctrine with the greatest clarity. Pius XI explicitly answered the most serious objections. Pius XII clearly excluded all direct abortion, that is, abortion which is either an end or a means. John XXIII recalled the teaching of the Fathers on the sacred character of life "which from its beginning demands the action of God the Creator." Most recently, the Second Vatican Council, presided over by Paul VI, has most severely condemned abortion: "Life must be safeguarded with extreme care from conception; abortion and infanticide are abominable crimes." The same Paul VI, speaking on this subject on many occasions, has not been afraid to declare that this teaching of the Church "has not changed and is unchangeable."

8. Respect for human life is not just a Christian obligation. Human reason is sufficient to impose it on the basis of the analysis of what a

human person is and should be. Constituted by a rational nature, man is a personal subject capable of reflecting on himself and of determining his acts and hence his own destiny: he is free. He is consequently master of himself; or rather, because this takes place in the course of time, he has the means of becoming so: this is his task. Created immediately by God, man's soul is spiritual and therefore immortal. Hence man is open to God, he finds his fulfillment only in Him. But man lives in the community of his equals; he is nourished by interpersonal communication with men in the indispensable social setting. In the face of society and other men, each human person possesses himself, he possesses life and different goods, he has these as a right. It is this that strict justice demands from all in his regard.

9. Nevertheless, temporal life lived in this world is not identified with the person. The person possesses as his own a level of life that is more profound and that cannot end. Bodily life is a fundamental good, here below it is the condition for all other goods. But there are higher values for which it could be legitimate or even necessary to be willing to expose oneself to the risk of losing bodily life. In a society of persons the common good is for each individual an end which he must serve and to which he must subordinate his particular interest. But it is not his last end and, from this point of view, it is society which is at the service of the person, because the person will not fulfill his destiny except in God. The person can be definitively subordinated only to God. Man can never be treated simply as a means to be disposed of in order to obtain a higher end.

10. In regard to the mutual rights and duties of the person and of society, it belongs to moral teaching to enlighten consciences; it belongs to the law to specify and organize external behavior. There is precisely a certain number of rights which society is not in a position to grant since these rights precede society; but society has the function to preserve and to enforce them. These are the greater part of those which are today called "human rights" and which our age boasts of having formulated.

11. The first right of the human person is his life. He has other goods and some are more precious, but this one is fundamental—the condition of all the others. Hence it must be protected above all others. It does not belong to society, nor does it belong to public authority in any form to recognize this right for some and not for others: all discrimination is evil, whether it be founded on race, sex, color or religion. It is not recognition by another that constitutes this right. This right is antecedent to its recognition; it demands recognition and it is strictly unjust to refuse it.

12. Any discrimination based on the various stages of life is no more justified than any other discrimination. The right to life remains complete in an old person, even one greatly weakened; it is not lost by one who is incurably sick. The right to life is no less to be respected in the small

infant just born than in the mature person. In reality, respect for human life is called for from the time that the process of generation begins. From the time that the ovum is fertilized, a life is begun which is neither that of the father nor of the mother, it is rather the life of a new human being with his own growth. It would never be made human if it were not human already.

13. To this perpetual evidence—perfectly independent of the discussions on the moment of animation—modern genetic science brings valuable confirmation. It has demonstrated that, from the first instant, there is established the program of what this living being will be: a man, this individual man with his characteristic aspects already well determined. Right from fertilization is begun the adventure of a human life, and each of its capacities requires time—a rather lengthy time—to find its place and to be in a position to act. The least that can be said is that present science, in its most evolved state, does not give any substantial support to those who defend abortion. Moreover, it is not up to biological sciences to make a definitive judgment on questions which are properly philosophical and moral such as the moment when a human person is constituted or the legitimacy of abortion. From a moral point of view this is certain: even if a doubt existed concerning whether the fruit of conception is already a human person, it is objectively a grave sin to dare to risk murder. "The one who will be a man is already one."

14. Divine law and natural reason, therefore, exclude all right to the direct killing of an innocent man. However, if the reasons given to justify an abortion were always manifestly evil and valueless the problem would not be so dramatic. The gravity of the problem comes from the fact that in certain cases, perhaps in quite a considerable number of cases, by denying abortion one endangers important values to which it is normal to attach great value, and which may sometimes even seem to have priority. We do not deny these very great difficulties. It may be a serious question of health, sometimes of life or death, for the mother; it may be the burden represented by an additional child, especially if there are good reasons to fear that the child will be abnormal or retarded; it may be the importance attributed in different classes of society to considerations of honor or dishonor, of loss of social standing, and so forth. We proclaim only that none of these reasons can ever objectively confer the right to dispose of another's life, even when that life is only beginning. With regard to the future unhappiness of the child, no one, not even the father or mother, can act as its substitute—even if it is still in the embryonic stage—to choose in the child's name, life or death. The child itself, when grown up, will never have the right to choose suicide; no more may his parents choose death for the child while it is not of an age to decide for itself. Life is too fundamental a value to be weighed against even very serious disadvantages.

15. The movement for the emancipation of women, insofar as it seeks essentially to free them from all unjust discrimination, is on perfectly sound ground. In the different forms of cultural background there is a great deal to be done in this regard. But one cannot change nature. Nor can one exempt women, any more than men, from what nature demands of them. Furthermore, all publicly recognized freedom is always limited by the certain rights of others.

16. The same must be said of the claim to sexual freedom. If by this expression one is to understand the mastery progressively acquired by reason and by authentic love over instinctive impulse, without diminishing pleasure but keeping it in its proper place—and in this sphere this is the only authentic freedom—then there is nothing to object to. But this kind of freedom will always be careful not to violate justice. If, on the contrary, one is to understand that men and women are "free" to seek sexual pleasure to the point of satiety, without taking into account any law or the essential orientation of sexual life to its fruits of fertility, then this idea has nothing Christian in it. It is even unworthy of man. In any case it does not confer any right to dispose of human life—even if embryonic—or to suppress it on the pretext that it is burdensome.

17. Scientific progress is opening to technology—and will open still more—the possibility of delicate interventions, the consequences of which can be very serious, for good as well as for evil. These are achievements of the human spirit which in themselves are admirable. But technology can never be independent of the criterion of morality, since technology exists for man and must respect his finality. Just as there is no right to use nuclear energy for every possible purpose, so there is no right to manipulate human life in every possible direction. Technology must be at the service of man, so as better to ensure the functioning of his normal abilities, to prevent or to cure his illnesses, and to contribute to his better human development. It is true that the evolution of technology makes early abortion more and more easy, but the moral evaluation is in no way modified because of this.

18. We know what seriousness the problem of birth control can assume for some families and for some countries. That is why the last Council and subsequently the encyclical "*Humanae vitae*" of July 25, 1968, spoke of "responsible parenthood." What we wish to say again with emphasis, as was pointed out in the conciliar constitution "*Gaudium et spes*," in the encyclical "*Populorum progressio*" and in other papal documents, is that never, under any pretext, may abortion be resorted to, either by a family or by the political authority, as a legitimate means of regulating births. The damage to moral values is always a greater evil for the common good than any disadvantage in the economic or demographic order.

19. The moral discussion is being accompanied more or less everywhere by serious juridical debates. There is no country where legislation

does not forbid and punish murder. Furthermore, many countries had specifically applied this condemnation and these penalties to the particular case of procured abortion. In these days a vast body of opinion petitions the liberalization of this latter prohibition. There already exists a fairly general tendency which seeks to limit, as far as possible, all restrictive legislation, especially when it seems to touch upon private life. The argument of pluralism is also used. Although many citizens, in particular the Catholic faithful, condemn abortion, many others hold that it is licit, at least as a lesser evil. Why force them to follow an opinion which is not theirs, especially in a country where they are in the majority? In addition it is apparent that, where they still exist, the laws condemning abortion appear difficult to apply. The crime has become too common for it to be punished every time, and the public authorities often find that it is wiser to close their eyes to it. But the preservation of a law which is not applied is always to the detriment of authority and of all the other laws. It must be added that clandestine abortion puts women, who resign themselves to it and have recourse to it, in the most serious dangers for future pregnancies and also in many cases for their lives. Even if the legislator continues to regard abortion as an evil, may he not propose to restrict its damage?

20. These arguments and others in addition that are heard from varying quarters are not conclusive. It is true that civil law cannot expect to cover the whole field of morality or to punish all faults. No one expects it to do so. It must often tolerate what is in fact a lesser evil, in order to avoid a greater one. One must, however, be attentive to what a change in legislation can represent. Many will take as authorization what is perhaps only the abstention from punishment. Even more, in the present case, this very renunciation seems at the very least to admit that the legislator no longer considers abortion a crime against human life, since murder is still always severely punished. It is true that it is not the task of the law to choose between points of view or to impose one rather than another. But the life of the child takes precedence over all opinions. One cannot invoke freedom of thought to destroy this life.

21. The role of law is not to record what is done, but to help in promoting improvement. It is at all times the task of the State to preserve each person's rights and to protect the weakest. In order to do so the State will have to right many wrongs. The law is not obliged to sanction everything, but it cannot act contrary to a law which is deeper and more majestic than any human law: the natural law engraved in men's hearts by the Creator as a norm which reason clarifies and strives to formulate properly, and which one must always struggle to understand better, but which it is always wrong to contradict. Human law can abstain from punishment, but it cannot declare to be right what would be opposed to the natural law, for this opposition suffices to give the assurance that a law is not a law at all.

22. It must in any case be clearly understood that whatever may be laid down by civil law in this matter, man can never obey a law which is in itself immoral, and such is the case of a law which would admit in principle the liceity of abortion. Nor can he take part in a propaganda campaign in favor of such a law, or vote for it. Moreover, he may not collaborate in its application. It is, for instance, inadmissible that doctors or nurses should find themselves obliged to cooperate closely in abortions and have to choose between the law of God and their professional situation.

23. On the contrary, it is the task of law to pursue a reform of society and of conditions of life in all milieux, starting with the most deprived, so that always and everywhere it may be possible to give every child coming into this world a welcome worthy of a person. Help for families and for unmarried mothers, assured grants for children, a statute for illegitimate children and reasonable arrangements for adoption—a whole positive policy must be put into force so that there will always be a concrete, honorable and possible alternative to abortion.

24. Following one's conscience in obedience to the law of God is not always the easy way. One must not fail to recognize the weight of the sacrifices and the burdens which it can impose. Heroism is sometimes called for in order to remain faithful to the requirements of the divine law. Therefore, we must emphasize that the path of true progress of the human person passes through this constant fidelity to a conscience maintained in uprightness and truth; and we must exhort all those who are able to do so to lighten the burdens still crushing so many men and women, families and children, who are placed in situations to which, in human terms, there is no solution.

25. A Christian's outlook cannot be limited to the horizon of life in this world. He knows that during the present life another one is being prepared, one of such importance that it is in its light that judgments must be made. From this viewpoint there is no absolute misfortune here below, not even the terrible sorrow of bringing up a handicapped child. This is the contradiction proclaimed by the Lord: "Happy those who mourn: they shall be comforted" (*Mt.* 5:5). To measure happiness by the absence of sorrow and misery in this world is to turn one's back on the Gospel.

26. But this does not mean that one can remain indifferent to these sorrows and miseries. Every man and woman with feeling, and certainly every Christian, must be ready to do what he can to remedy them. This is the law of charity, of which the first preoccupation must always be the establishment of justice. One can never approve of abortion; but it is above all necessary to combat its causes. This includes political action, which will be in particular the task of the law. But it is necessary at the same time to influence morality and to do everything possible to help families, mothers and children. Considerable progress in the service

of life has been accomplished by medicine. One can hope that such progress will continue, in accordance with the vocation of doctors, which is not to suppress life but to care for it and favor it as much as possible. It is equally desirable that, in suitable institutions, or, in their absence, in the outpouring of Christian generosity and charity every form of assistance should be developed.

27. There will be no effective action on the level of morality unless at the same time an effort is made on the level of ideas. A point of view—or even more, perhaps a way of thinking—which considers fertility as an evil cannot be allowed to spread without contradiction. It is true that not all forms of culture are equally in favor of large families. Such families come up against much greater difficulties in an industrial and urban civilization. Thus in recent times the Church has insisted on the idea of responsible parenthood, the exercise of true human and Christian prudence.

Such prudence would not be authentic if it did not include generosity. It must preserve awareness of the grandeur of the task of cooperating with the Creator in the transmission of life, which gives new members to society and new children to the Church. Christ's Church has the fundamental solicitude of protecting and favoring life. She certainly thinks before all else of the life which Christ came to bring: "I have come so that they may have life and have it to the full" (*Jn.* 10:10). But life at all its levels comes from God, and bodily life is for man the indispensable beginning. In this life on earth sin has introduced, multiplied and made harder to bear suffering and death. But in taking their burden upon Himself, Jesus Christ has transformed them: for whoever believes in Him, suffering and death itself become instruments of resurrection. Hence Saint Paul can say: "I think that what we suffer in this life can never be compared to the glory, as yet unrevealed, which is waiting for us" (*Rom.* 8:18). And, if we make this comparison we shall add with him: "Yes, the troubles which are soon over, though they weigh little, train us for the carrying of a weight of eternal glory which is out of all proportion to them" (2 *Cor.* 4:17).

The Supreme Pontiff Pope Paul VI, in an audience granted to the undersigned Secretary of the Sacred Congregation for the Doctrine of the Faith on June 28, 1974, has ratified this Declaration on Procured Abortion and has confirmed it and ordered it to be promulgated.

Given in Rome, at the Sacred Congregation for the Doctrine of the Faith, on November 18, the Commemoration of the Dedication of the Basilicas of Saints Peter and Paul, in the year 1974.

PERSONA HUMANA

DECLARATION ON CERTAIN QUESTIONS
CONCERNING SEXUAL ETHICS

29 DECEMBER 1975

I

According to contemporary scientific research, the human person is so profoundly affected by sexuality that it must be considered as one of the factors which give to each individual's life the principal traits that distinguish it. In fact it is from sex that the human person receives the characteristics which, on the biological, psychological and spiritual levels, make that person a man or a woman, and thereby largely condition his or her progress towards maturity and insertion into society. Hence sexual matters, as is obvious to everyone, today constitute a theme frequently and openly dealt with in books, reviews, magazines and other means of social communication.

In the present period, the corruption of morals has increased, and one of the most serious indications of this corruption is the unbridled exaltation of sex. Moreover, through the means of social communication and through public entertainment this corruption has reached the point of invading the field of education and of infecting the general mentality.

In this context certain educators, teachers and moralists have been able to contribute to a better understanding and integration into life of the values proper to each of the sexes; on the other hand there are those who have put forward concepts and modes of behavior which are contrary to the true moral exigencies of the human person. Some members of the latter group have even gone so far as to favor a licentious hedonism.

As a result, in the course of a few years, teachings, moral criteria and modes of living hitherto faithfully preserved have been very much unsettled, even among Christians. There are many people today who, being confronted with widespread opinions opposed to the teaching which they received from the Church, have come to wonder what must still hold as true.

II

The Church cannot remain indifferent to this confusion of minds and relaxation of morals. It is a question, in fact, of a matter which is of the utmost importance both for the personal lives of Christians and for the social life of our time.

The Bishops are daily led to note the growing difficulties experienced by the faithful in obtaining knowledge of wholesome moral teaching, especially in sexual matters, and of the growing difficulties experienced by pastors in expounding this teaching effectively. The Bishops know that by their pastoral charge they are called upon to meet the needs of their faithful in this very serious matter, and important documents dealing with it have already been published by some of them or by episcopal conferences. Nevertheless, since the erroneous opinions and resulting deviations are continuing to spread everywhere, the Sacred Congregation for the Doctrine of the Faith, by virtue of its function in the universal Church and by a mandate of the Supreme Pontiff, has judged it necessary to publish the present Declaration.

III

The people of our time are more and more convinced that the human person's dignity and vocation demand that they should discover, by the light of their own intelligence, the values innate in their nature, that they should ceaselessly develop these values and realize them in their lives, in order to achieve an ever greater development.

In moral matters man cannot make value judgments according to his personal whim: "In the depths of his conscience, man detects a law which he does not impose on himself, but which holds him to obedience. . . . For man has in his heart a law written by God. To obey it is the very dignity of man; according to it he will be judged."

Moreover, through His revelation God has made known to us Christians His plan of salvation, and He has held up to us Christ, the Savior and Sanctifier, in His teaching and example, as the supreme and immutable Law of life: "I am the light of the world; anyone who follows Me will not be walking in the dark, he will have the light of life."

Therefore there can be no true promotion of man's dignity unless the essential order of his nature is respected. Of course, in the history of civilization many of the concrete conditions and needs of human life have changed and will continue to change. But all evolution of morals and every type of life must be kept within the limits imposed by the immutable principles based upon every human person's constitutive elements and essential relations—elements and relations which transcend historical contingency.

These fundamental principles, which can be grasped by reason, are contained in "the Divine Law—eternal, objective and universal—whereby God orders, directs and governs the entire universe and all the ways of the human community, by a plan conceived in wisdom and love. Man has been made by God to participate in this law, with the result that, under the gentle disposition of Divine Providence, he can come to perceive ever increasingly the unchanging truth." This Divine Law is accessible to our minds.

IV

Hence, those many people are in error who today assert that one can find neither in human nature nor in the revealed law any absolute and immutable norm to serve for particular actions other than the one which expresses itself in the general law of charity and respect for human dignity. As a proof of their assertion they put forward the view that so-called norms of the natural law or precepts of Sacred Scripture are to be regarded only as given expressions of a form of particular culture at a certain moment of history.

But in fact, Divine Revelation and, in its own proper order, philosophical wisdom, emphasize the authentic exigencies of human nature. They thereby necessarily manifest the existence of immutable laws inscribed in the constitutive elements of human nature and which are revealed to be identical in all beings endowed with reason.

Furthermore, Christ instituted His Church as "the pillar and bulwark of truth." With the Holy Spirit's assistance, she ceaselessly preserves and transmits without error the truths of the moral order, and she authentically interprets not only the revealed positive law but "also . . . those principles of the moral order which have their origin in human nature itself" and which concern man's full development and sanctification. Now in fact the Church throughout her history has always considered a certain number of precepts of the natural law as having an absolute and immutable value, and in their transgression she has seen a contradiction of the teaching and spirit of the Gospel.

V

Since sexual ethics concern fundamental values of human and Christian life, this general teaching equally applies to sexual ethics. In this domain there exist principles and norms which the Church has always unhesitatingly transmitted as part of her teaching, however much the opinions and morals of the world may have been opposed to them. These principles and norms in no way owe their origin to a certain type of culture, but rather to knowledge of the Divine Law and of human nature. They therefore cannot be considered as having become out of date or doubtful under the pretext that a new cultural situation has arisen.

It is these principles which inspired the exhortations and directives given by the Second Vatican Council for an education and an organization of social life taking account of the equal dignity of man and woman while respecting their difference.

Speaking of "the sexual nature of man and the human faculty of pro-creation," the Council noted that they "wonderfully exceed the disposi-tions of lower forms of life." It then took particular care to expound the principles and criteria which concern human sexuality in marriage, and which are based upon the finality of the specific function of sexuality.

In this regard the Council declares that the moral goodness of the acts proper to conjugal life, acts which are ordered according to true human dignity, "does not depend solely on sincere intentions or on an evaluation of motives. It must be determined by objective standards. These, based on the nature of the human person and his acts, preserve the full sense of mutual self-giving and human procreation in the context of true love."

These final words briefly sum up the Council's teaching—more fully expounded in an earlier part of the same Constitution—on the finality of the sexual act and on the principal criterion of its morality: it is respect for its finality that ensures the moral goodness of this act.

This same principle, which the Church holds from Divine Revela-tion and from her authentic interpretation of the natural law, is also the basis of her traditional doctrine, which states that the use of the sexual function has its true meaning and moral rectitude only in true marriage.

VI

It is not the purpose of the present Declaration to deal with all the abuses of the sexual faculty, nor with all the elements involved in the practice of chastity. Its object is rather to repeat the Church's doctrine on certain particular points, in view of the urgent need to oppose serious errors and widespread aberrant modes of behavior.

VII

Today there are many who vindicate the right to sexual union before marriage, at least in those cases where a firm intention to marry and an affection which is already in some way conjugal in the psychology of the subjects require this completion, which they judge to be connatural. This is especially the case when the celebration of the marriage is impeded by circumstances or when this intimate relationship seems necessary in order for love to be preserved.

This opinion is contrary to Christian doctrine, which states that every genital act must be within the framework of marriage. However firm the intention of those who practice such premature sexual relations may be, the fact remains that these relations cannot ensure, in sincerity and fidelity, the interpersonal relationship between a man and a woman, nor especially can they protect this relationship from whims and caprices. Now it is a stable union that Jesus willed, and He restored its original requirement, beginning with the sexual difference. "Have you not read that the Creator from the beginning made them male and female and that He said: This is why a man must leave father and mother, and cling to his wife, and the two become one body? They are no longer two, therefore, but one body. So then, what God has united, man must not divide." St. Paul will be even more explicit when he shows that if unmarried people or widows cannot live chastely they have no other alternative than the stable union of marriage: " . . . it is better to marry than to be aflame with passion." Through marriage, in fact, the love of married people is taken up into that love which Christ irrevocably has for the Church, while dissolute sexual union defiles the temple of the Holy Spirit which the Christian has become. Sexual union therefore is only legitimate if a definitive community of life has been established between the man and the woman.

This is what the Church has always understood and taught, and she finds a profound agreement with her doctrine in men's reflection and in the lessons of history.

Experience teaches us that love must find its safeguard in the stability of marriage, if sexual intercourse is truly to respond to the requirements of its own finality and to those of human dignity. These requirements call for a conjugal contract sanctioned and guaranteed by society—a contract which establishes a state of life of capital importance both for the exclusive union of the man and the woman and for the good of their family and of the human community. Most often, in fact, premarital relations exclude the possibility of children. What is represented to be conjugal love is not able, as it absolutely should be, to develop into paternal and maternal love. Or, if it does happen to do so, this will be to the detriment of the children, who will be deprived of the stable environment in which they ought to develop in order to find in it the way and the means of their insertion into society as a whole.

The consent given by people who wish to be united in marriage must therefore be manifested externally and in a manner which makes it valid in the eyes of society. As far as the faithful are concerned, their consent to the setting up of a community of conjugal life must be expressed according to the laws of the Church. It is a consent which makes their marriage a Sacrament of Christ.

VIII

At the present time there are those who, basing themselves on observations in the psychological order, have begun to judge indulgently, and even to excuse completely, homosexual relations between certain people. This they do in opposition to the constant teaching of the Magisterium and to the moral sense of the Christian people.

A distinction is drawn, and it seems with some reason, between homosexuals whose tendency comes from a false education, from a lack of normal sexual development, from habit, from bad example, or from other similar causes, and is transitory or at least not incurable; and homosexuals who are definitively such because of some kind of innate instinct or a pathological constitution judged to be incurable.

In regard to this second category of subjects, some people conclude that their tendency is so natural that it justifies in their case homosexual relations within a sincere communion of life and love analogous to marriage, in so far as such homosexuals feel incapable of enduring a solitary life.

In the pastoral field, these homosexuals must certainly be treated with understanding and sustained in the hope of overcoming their personal difficulties and their inability to fit into society. Their culpability will be judged with prudence. But no pastoral method can be employed which would give moral justification to these acts on the grounds that they would be consonant with the condition of such people. For according to the objective moral order, homosexual relations are acts which lack an essential and indispensable finality. In Sacred Scripture they are condemned as a serious depravity and even presented as the sad consequence of rejecting God. This judgment of Scripture does not of course permit us to conclude that all those who suffer from this anomaly are personally responsible for it, but it does attest to the fact that homosexual acts are intrinsically disordered and can in no case be approved of.

IX

The traditional Catholic doctrine that masturbation constitutes a grave moral disorder is often called into doubt or expressly denied today. It is said that psychology and sociology show that it is a normal phenomenon of sexual development, especially among the young. It is stated that there is real and serious fault only in the measure that the subject deliberately indulges in solitary pleasure closed in on self ("ipsation"), because in this case the act would indeed be radically opposed to the loving communion between persons of different sex which some hold is what is principally sought in the use of the sexual faculty.

This opinion is contradictory to the teaching and pastoral practice of the Catholic Church. Whatever the force of certain arguments of a biological and philosophical nature, which have sometimes been used by theologians, in fact both the Magisterium of the Church—in the course of a constant tradition—and the moral sense of the faithful have declared without hesitation that masturbation is an intrinsically and seriously disordered act. The main reason is that, whatever the motive for acting this way, the deliberate use of the sexual faculty outside normal conjugal relations essentially contradicts the finality of the faculty. For it lacks the sexual relationship called for by the moral order, namely the relationship which realizes "the full sense of mutual self-giving and human procreation in the context of true love." All deliberate exercise of sexuality must be reserved to this regular relationship. Even if it cannot be proved that Scripture condemns this sin by name, the tradition of the Church has rightly understood it to be condemned in the New Testament when the latter speaks of "impurity," "unchasteness" and other vices contrary to chastity and continence.

Sociological surveys are able to show the frequency of this disorder according to the places, populations or circumstances studied. In this way facts are discovered, but facts do not constitute a criterion for judging the moral value of human acts. The frequency of the phenomenon in question is certainly to be linked with man's innate weakness following original sin; but it is also to be linked with the loss of a sense of God, with the corruption of morals engendered by the commercialization of vice, with the unrestrained licentiousness of so many public entertainments and publications, as well as with the neglect of modesty, which is the guardian of chastity.

On the subject of masturbation modern psychology provides much valid and useful information for formulating a more equitable judgment on moral responsibility and for orienting pastoral action. Psychology helps one to see how the immaturity of adolescence (which can sometimes persist after that age), psychological imbalance or habit can influence behavior, diminishing the deliberate character of the act and bringing about a situation whereby subjectively there may not always be serious fault. But in general, the absence of serious responsibility must not be presumed; this would be to misunderstand people's moral capacity.

In the pastoral ministry, in order to form an adequate judgment in concrete cases, the habitual behavior of people will be considered in its totality, not only with regard to the individual's practice of charity and of justice but also with regard to the individual's care in observing the particular precepts of chastity. In particular, one will have to examine whether the individual is using the necessary means, both natural and supernatural, which Christian asceticism from its long experience recommends for overcoming the passions and progressing in virtue.

X

The observance of the moral law in the field of sexuality and the practice of chastity have been considerably endangered, especially among less fervent Christians, by the current tendency to minimize as far as possible, when not denying outright, the reality of grave sin, at least in people's actual lives.

There are those who go as far as to affirm that mortal sin, which causes separation from God, only exists in the formal refusal directly opposed to God's call, or in that selfishness which completely and deliberately closes itself to the love of neighbor. They say that it is only then that there comes into play the fundamental option, that is to say the decision which totally commits the person and which is necessary if mortal sin is to exist; by this option the person, from the depths of the personality, takes up or ratifies a fundamental attitude towards God or people. On the contrary, so-called "peripheral" actions (which, it is said, usually do not involve decisive choice), do not go so far as to change the fundamental option, the less so since they often come, as is observed, from habit. Thus such actions can weaken the fundamental option, but not to such a degree as to change it completely. Now according to these authors, a change of the fundamental option towards God less easily comes about in the field of sexual activity, where a person generally does not transgress the moral order in a fully deliberate and responsible manner but rather under the influence of passion, weakness, immaturity, sometimes even through the illusion of thus showing love for someone else. To these causes there is often added the pressure of the social environment.

In reality, it is precisely the fundamental option which in the last resort defines a person's moral disposition. But it can be completely changed by particular acts, especially when, as often happens, these have been prepared for by previous more superficial acts. Whatever the case, it is wrong to say that particular acts are not enough to constitute mortal sin.

According to the Church's teaching, mortal sin, which is opposed to God, does not consist only in formal and direct resistance to the commandment of charity. It is equally to be found in this opposition to authentic love which is included in every deliberate transgression, in serious matter, of each of the moral laws.

Christ Himself has indicated the double commandment of love as the basis of the moral life. But on this commandment depends "the whole Law, and the Prophets also." It therefore includes the other particular precepts. In fact, to the young man who asked, ". . . what good deed must I do to possess eternal life?" Jesus replied: ". . . if you wish to enter into life, keep the commandments. . . . You must not kill. You must not commit adultery. You must not steal. You must not bring false witness. Honor your father and mother, and: you must love your neighbor as yourself."

A person therefore sins mortally not only when his action comes from direct contempt for love of God and neighbor, but also when he consciously and freely, for whatever reason, chooses something which is seriously disordered. For in this choice, as has been said above, there is already included contempt for the Divine commandment: the person turns himself away from God and loses charity. Now according to Christian tradition and the Church's teaching, and as right reason also recognizes, the moral order of sexuality involves such high values of human life that every direct violation of this order is objectively serious.

It is true that in sins of the sexual order, in view of their kind and their causes, it more easily happens that free consent is not fully given; this is a fact which calls for caution in all judgment as to the subject's responsibility. In this matter it is particularly opportune to recall the following words of Scripture: "Man looks at appearances but God looks at the heart." However, although prudence is recommended in judging the subjective seriousness of a particular sinful act, it in no way follows that one can hold the view that in the sexual field mortal sins are not committed.

Pastors of souls must therefore exercise patience and goodness; but they are not allowed to render God's commandments null, nor to reduce unreasonably people's responsibility. "To diminish in no way the saving teaching of Christ constitutes an eminent form of charity for souls. But this must ever be accompanied by patience and goodness, such as the Lord Himself gave example of in dealing with people. Having come not to condemn but to save, He was indeed intransigent with evil, but merciful towards individuals."

XI

As has been said above, the purpose of this Declaration is to draw the attention of the faithful in present-day circumstances to certain errors and modes of behavior which they must guard against. The virtue of chastity, however, is in no way confined solely to avoiding the faults already listed. It is aimed at attaining higher and more positive goals. It is a virtue which concerns the whole personality, as regards both interior and outward behavior.

Individuals should be endowed with this virtue according to their state in life: for some it will mean virginity or celibacy consecrated to God, which is an eminent way of giving oneself more easily to God alone with an undivided heart. For others it will take the form determined by the moral law, according to whether they are married or single. But whatever the state of life, chastity is not simply an external state; it must make a person's heart pure in accordance with Christ's words: "You have learned how it was said: You must not commit adultery. But I say this to you: if a man looks at a woman lustfully, he has already committed adultery with her in his heart."

Chastity is included in that continence which St. Paul numbers among the gifts of the Holy Spirit, while he condemns sensuality as a vice particularly unworthy of the Christian and one which precludes entry into the Kingdom of Heaven. "What God wants is for all to be holy. He wants you to keep away from fornication, and each one of you knows how to use the body that belongs to him in a way that is holy and honorable, not giving way to selfish lust like the pagans who do not know God. He wants nobody at all ever to sin by taking advantage of a brother in these matters. . . . We have been called by God to be holy, not to be immoral. In other words, anyone who objects is not objecting to a human authority, but to God, Who gives you His Holy Spirit." "Among you there must not be even a mention of fornication or impurity in any of its forms, or promiscuity: this would hardly become the saints! For you can be quite certain that nobody who actually indulges in fornication or impurity or promiscuity—which is worshipping a false god—can inherit anything of the Kingdom of God. Do not let anyone deceive you with empty arguments: it is for this loose living that God's anger comes down on those who rebel against Him. Make sure that you are not included with them. You were darkness once, but now you are light in the Lord; be like children of light, for the effects of the light are seen in complete goodness and right living and truth."

In addition, the Apostle points out the specifically Christian motive for practising chastity when he condemns the sin of fornication not only in the measure that this action is injurious to one's neighbor or to the social order but because the fornicator offends against Christ Who has redeemed him with His blood and of Whom he is a member, and against the Holy Spirit of Whom he is the temple. "You know, surely, that your bodies are members making up the body of Christ. . . . All the other sins are committed outside the body; but to fornicate is to sin against your own body. Your body, you know, is the temple of the Holy Spirit, Who is in you since you received Him from God. You are not your own property; you have been bought and paid for. That is why you should use your body for the glory of God."

The more the faithful appreciate the value of chastity and its necessary role in their lives as men and women, the better they will understand, by a kind of spiritual instinct, its moral requirements and counsels. In the same way they will know better how to accept and carry out, in a spirit of docility to the Church's teaching, what an upright conscience dictates in concrete cases.

XII

The Apostle St. Paul describes in vivid terms the painful interior conflict of the person enslaved to sin: the conflict between "the law of his mind" and the "law of sin which dwells in his members" and which holds him captive. But man can achieve liberation from his "body doomed to death" through the grace of Jesus Christ. This grace is enjoyed by those who have been justified by it and whom "the law of the spirit of life in Christ Jesus has set free from the law of sin and death." It is for this reason that the Apostle adjures them: "That is why you must not let sin reign in your mortal bodies or command your obedience to bodily passions."

This liberation, which fits one to serve God in newness of life, does not however suppress the concupiscence deriving from original sin, nor the promptings to evil in this world, which is "in the power of the evil one." This is why the Apostle exhorts the faithful to overcome temptations by the power of God and to "stand against the wiles of the Devil" by faith, watchful prayer and an austerity of life that brings the body into subjection to the Spirit.

Living the Christian life by following in the footsteps of Christ requires that everyone should "deny himself and take up his cross daily," sustained by the hope of reward, for "if we have died with Him, we shall also reign with Him." In accordance with these pressing exhortations, the faithful of the present time, and indeed today more than ever, must use the means which have always been recommended by the Church for living a chaste life. These means are: discipline of the senses and the mind, watchfulness and prudence in avoiding occasions of sin, the observance of modesty, moderation in recreation, wholesome pursuits, assiduous prayer and frequent reception of the Sacraments of Penance and the Eucharist. Young people especially should earnestly foster devotion to the Immaculate Mother of God, and take as examples the lives of saints and other faithful people, especially young ones, who excelled in the practice of chastity.

It is important in particular that everyone should have a high esteem for the virtue of chastity, its beauty and its power of attraction. This virtue increases the human person's dignity and enables him to love truly, disinterestedly, unselfishly and with respect for others.

XIII

It is up to the Bishops to instruct the faithful in the moral teaching concerning sexual morality, however great may be the difficulties in carrying out this work in the face of ideas and practices generally prevailing today. This traditional doctrine must be studied more deeply. It must be handed on in a way capable of properly enlightening the consciences of those confronted with new situations and it must be enriched with a discernment of all the elements that can truthfully and usefully be brought forward about the meaning and value of human sexuality. But the principles and norms of moral living reaffirmed in this Declaration must be faithfully held and taught. It will especially be necessary to bring the faithful to understand that the Church holds these principles not as old and inviolable superstitions, nor out of some Manichaean prejudice, as is often alleged, but rather because she knows with certainty that they are in complete harmony with the Divine order of creation and with the spirit of Christ, and therefore also with human dignity.

It is likewise the Bishops' mission to see that a sound doctrine enlightened by faith and directed by the Magisterium of the Church is taught in faculties of theology and in seminaries. Bishops must also ensure that confessors enlighten people's consciences and that catechetical instruction is given in perfect fidelity to Catholic doctrine.

It rests with the Bishops, the priests and their collaborators to alert the faithful against the erroneous opinions often expressed in books, reviews and public meetings.

Parents, in the first place, and also teachers of the young must endeavor to lead their children and their pupils, by way of a complete education, to the psychological, emotional and moral maturity befitting their age. They will therefore prudently give them information suited to their age; and they will assiduously form their wills in accordance with

Christian morals, not only by advice but above all by the example of their own lives, relying on God's help, which they will obtain in prayer. They will likewise protect the young from the many dangers of which they are quite unaware.

Artists, writers and all those who use the means of social communication should exercise their profession in accordance with their Christian faith and with a clear awareness of the enormous influence which they can have. They should remember that "the primacy of the objective moral order must be regarded as absolute by all," and that it is wrong for them to give priority above it to any so-called aesthetic purpose, or to material advantage or to success. Whether it be a question of artistic or literary works, public entertainment or providing information, each individual in his or her own domain must show tact, discretion, moderation and a true sense of values. In this way, far from adding to the growing permissiveness of behavior, each individual will contribute towards controlling it and even towards making the moral climate of society more wholesome.

All lay people, for their part, by virtue of their rights and duties in the work of the apostolate, should endeavor to act in the same way.

Finally, it is necessary to remind everyone of the words of the Second Vatican Council: "This Holy Synod likewise affirms that children and young people have a right to be encouraged to weigh moral values with an upright conscience, and to embrace them by personal choice, to know and love more adequately. Hence, it earnestly entreats all who exercise government over people or preside over the work of education to see that youth is never deprived of this sacred right."

At the audience granted on November 7, 1975, to the undersigned Prefect of the Sacred Congregation for the Doctrine of the Faith, the Sovereign Pontiff by Divine Providence Pope Paul VI approved this Declaration "On certain questions concerning sexual ethics," confirmed it and ordered its publication.

Given in Rome, at the Sacred Congregation for the Doctrine of the Faith, on December 29th, 1975.

INTER INSIGNIORES

DECLARATION ON THE QUESTION OF ADMISSION OF WOMEN TO THE MINISTERIAL PRIESTHOOD

15 OCTOBER 1976

Introduction: The Role of Women in Modern Society and the Church

Among the characteristics that mark our present age, Pope John XXIII indicated, in his Encyclical *Pacem in Terris* of 11 April 1963, "the part that women are now taking in public life. . . . This is a development that is perhaps of swifter growth among Christian nations, but it is also happening extensively, if more slowly, among nations that are heirs to different traditions and imbued with a different culture." Along the same lines, the Second Vatican Council, enumerating in its Pastoral Constitution *Gaudium et Spes* the forms of discrimination touching upon the basic rights of the person which must be overcome and eliminated as being contrary to God's plan, gives first place to discrimination based upon sex. The resulting equality will secure the building up of a world that is not leveled out and uniform but harmonious and unified, if men and women contribute to it their own resources and dynamism, as Pope Paul VI recently stated.

In the life of the Church herself, as history shows us, women have played a decisive role and accomplished tasks of outstanding value. One has only to think of the foundresses of the great religious families, such as Saint Clare and Saint Teresa of Avila. The latter, moreover, and Saint Catherine of Siena, have left writings so rich in spiritual doctrine that Pope Paul VI has included them among the Doctors of the Church. Nor could one forget the great number of women who have consecrated themselves to the Lord for the exercise of charity or for the missions, and the Christian wives who have had a profound influence on their families, particularly for the passing on of the faith to their children.

But our age gives rise to increased demands: "Since in our time women have an ever more active share in the whole life of society, it

77

is very important that they participate more widely also in the various sectors of the Church's apostolate." This charge of the Second Vatican Council has already set in motion the whole process of change now taking place: these various experiences of course need to come to maturity. But as Pope Paul VI also remarked, a very large number of Christian communities are already benefiting from the apostolic commitment of women. Some of these women are called to take part in councils set up for pastoral reflection, at the diocesan or parish level; and the Apostolic See has brought women into some of its working bodies.

For some years now various Christian communities stemming from the sixteenth-century Reformation or of later origin have been admitting women to the pastoral office on a par with men. This initiative has led to petitions and writings by members of these communities and similar groups, directed towards making this admission a general thing; it has also led to contrary reactions. This therefore constitutes an ecumenical problem, and the Catholic Church must make her thinking known on it, all the more because in various sectors of opinion the question has been asked whether she too could not modify her discipline and admit women to priestly ordination. A number of Catholic theologians have even posed this question publicly, evoking studies not only in the sphere of exegesis, patrology and Church history but also in the field of the history of institutions and customs, of sociology and of psychology. The various arguments capable of clarifying this important problem have been submitted to a critical examination. As we are dealing with a debate which classical theology scarcely touched upon, the current argumentation runs the risk of neglecting essential elements.

For these reasons, in execution of a mandate received from the Holy Father and echoing the declaration which he himself made in his letter of 30 November 1975, the Sacred Congregation for the Doctrine of the Faith judges it necessary to recall that the Church, in fidelity to the example of the Lord, does not consider herself authorized to admit women to priestly ordination. The Sacred Congregation deems it opportune at the present juncture to explain this position of the Church. It is a position which will perhaps cause pain but whose positive value will become apparent in the long run, since it can be of help in deepening understanding of the respective roles of men and of women.

1. The Church's Constant Tradition

The Catholic Church has never felt that priestly or episcopal ordination can be validly conferred on women. A few heretical sects in the first centuries, especially Gnostic ones, entrusted the exercise of the priestly ministry to women: This innovation was immediately noted and condemned by the Fathers, who considered it as unacceptable in the Church. It is true that in the writings of the Fathers, one will find the undeniable influence of prejudices unfavourable to woman, but never-theless, it should be noted that these prejudices had hardly any influ-ences on their pastoral activity, and still less on their spiritual direction. But over and above these considerations inspired by the spirit of the times, one finds expressed—especially in the canonical documents of the Antiochan and Egyptian traditions—this essential reason, namely, that by calling only men to the priestly Order and ministry in its true sense, the Church intends to remain faithful to the type of ordained ministry willed by the Lord Jesus Christ and carefully maintained by the Apostles.

The same conviction animates medieval theology, even if the Scholastic doctors, in their desire to clarify by reason the data of faith, often present arguments on this point that modern thought would have difficulty in admitting, or would even rightly reject. Since that period and up till our own time, it can be said that the question has not been raised again for the practice has enjoyed peaceful and universal acceptance.

The Church's tradition in the matter has thus been so firm in the course of the centuries that the Magisterium has not felt the need to intervene in order to formulate a principle which was not attacked, or to defend a law which was not challenged. But each time that this tradition had the occasion to manifest itself, it witnessed to the Church's desire to conform to the model left her by the Lord.

The same tradition has been faithfully safeguarded by the Churches of the East. Their unanimity on this point is all the more remarkable since in many other questions their discipline admits of a great diversity. At present time these same Churches refuse to associate themselves with requests directed towards securing the accession of women to priestly ordination.

2. The Attitude of Christ

Jesus Christ did not call any women to become part of the Twelve. If he acted in this way, it was not in order to conform to the customs of his time, for his attitude towards women was quite different from that of his milieu, and he deliberately and courageously broke with it.

For example, to the great astonishment of his own disciples Jesus converses publicly with the Samaritan woman (Jn 4:27); he takes no notice of the state of legal impurity of the woman who had suffered from hemorrhages (Mt 9:20); he allows a sinful woman to approach him in the house of Simon the Pharisee (Lk 7:37); and by pardoning the woman taken in adultery, he means to show that one must not be more severe towards the fault of a woman than towards that of a man (Jn 8:11). He does not hesitate to depart from the Mosaic Law in order to affirm the equality of the rights and duties of men and women with regard to the marriage bond (Mk 10:2; Mt 19:3).

In his itinerant ministry Jesus was accompanied not only by the Twelve but also by a group of women (Lk 8:2). Contrary to the Jewish mentality, which did not accord great value to the testimony of women, as Jewish law attests, it was nevertheless women who were the first to have the privilege of seeing the risen Lord, and it was they who were charged by Jesus to take the first paschal message to the Apostles themselves (Mt 28:7; Lk 24:9; Jn 20:11), in order to prepare the latter to become the official witnesses to the Resurrection.

It is true that these facts do not make the matter immediately obvious. This is no surprise, for the questions that the Word of God brings before us go beyond the obvious. In order to reach the ultimate meaning of the mission of Jesus and the ultimate meaning of Scripture, a purely historical exegesis of the texts cannot suffice. But it must be recognised that we have here a number of convergent indications that make all the more remarkable that Jesus did not entrust the apostolic charge to women. Even his Mother, who was so closely associated with the mystery of her Son, and whose incomparable role is emphasized by the Gospels of Luke and John, was not invested with the apostolic ministry. This fact was to lead the Fathers to present her as an example of Christ's will in this domain; as Pope Innocent III repeated later, at the beginning of the thirteenth century, "Although the Blessed Virgin Mary surpassed in dignity and in excellence all the Apostles, nevertheless it was not to her but to them that the Lord entrusted the keys of the Kingdom of Heaven."

3.   The Practice of the Apostles

The apostolic community remained faithful to the attitude of Jesus towards women. Although Mary occupied a privileged place in the little circle of those gathered in the Upper Room after the Lord's Ascension (Acts 1:14), it was not she who was called to enter the College of the Twelve at the time of the election that resulted in the choice of Mathias: those who were put forward were two disciples whom the Gospels do not even mention.

On the day of Pentecost, the Holy Spirit filled them all, men and women (Acts 2:1, 1:14), yet the proclamation of the fulfillment of the prophecies in Jesus was made only by "Peter and the Eleven" (Acts 2:14).

When they and Paul went beyond the confines of the Jewish world, the preaching of the Gospel and the Christian life in the Greco-Roman civilisation impelled them to break with Mosaic practices, sometimes regretfully. They could therefore have envisaged conferring ordination on women, if they had not been convinced of their duty of fidelity to the Lord on this point. In fact the Greeks did not share the ideas of the Jews: although their philosophers taught the inferiority of women, historians nevertheless emphasize the existence of a certain movement for the advancement of women during the Imperial period. In fact we know from the book of Acts and from the letter of Saint Paul, that certain women worked with the Apostle for the Gospel (Rom 16:3–12; Phil 4:3). Saint Paul lists their names with gratitude in the final salutations of the Letters. Some of them often exercised an important influence on conversions: Priscilla, Lydia and others; especially Priscilla, who took it on herself to complete the instruction of Apollos (Acts 18:26); Phoebe, in the service of the Church of Cenchreae (Rom 16:1). All these facts manifest within the Apostolic Church a considerable evolution vis-à-vis the customs of Judaism. Nevertheless at no time was there a question of conferring ordination on these women.

In the Pauline letters, exegetes of authority have noted a difference between two formulas used by the Apostle: he writes indiscriminately "My fellow workers" (Rom 16:3; Phil 4:2–3) when referring to men and women helping him in his apostolate in one way or another; but he reserves the title of "God's fellow workers" (1 Cor 3–9; 1 Thess 3:2) to Apollos, Timothy and himself, thus designated because they are directly set apart for the apostolic ministry and the preaching of the Word of God. In spite of the so important role played by women on the day of the Resurrection, their collaboration was not extended by Saint Paul to the official and public proclamation of the message, since this proclamation belongs exclusively to the apostolic mission.

4. Permanent Value of the Attitude of Jesus and the Apostles

Could the Church today depart from this attitude of Jesus and the Apostles, which has been considered as normative by the whole of tradition up to our own day? Various arguments have been put forward in favour of a positive reply to this question, and these must now be examined.

It has been claimed in particular that the attitude of Jesus and the Apostles is explained by the influence of their milieu and their times. It is said that, if Jesus did not entrust to women and not even to his Mother a ministry assimilating them to the Twelve, this was because historical circumstances did not permit him to do so. No one however has ever proved—and it is clearly impossible to prove—that this attitude is inspired only by social and cultural reasons. As we have seen, and examination of the Gospels shows on the contrary that Jesus broke with the prejudices of his time, by widely contravening the discriminations practiced with regard to women. One therefore cannot maintain that, by not calling women to enter the group of the Apostles, Jesus was simply letting himself be guided by reasons of expediency. For all the more reason, social and cultural conditioning did not hold back the Apostles working in the Greek milieu, where the same forms of discrimination did not exist.

Another objection is based upon the transitory character that one claims to see today in some of the prescriptions of Saint Paul concerning women, and upon the difficulties that some aspects of his teaching raise in this regard. But it must be noted that these ordinances, probably inspired by the customs of the period, concern scarcely more than disciplinary practices of minor importance, such as the obligation imposed upon women to wear a veil on their head (1 Cor 11:2–16); such requirements no longer have a normative value. However, the Apostle's forbidding of women to speak in the assemblies (1 Cor 14:34–35; 1 Ti 2:12) is of a different nature, and exegetes define its meaning in this way: Paul in no way opposes the right, which he elsewhere recognises as possessed by women, to prophesy in the assembly (1 Cor 11:15); the prohibition solely concerns the official function of teaching in the Christian assembly. For Saint Paul this prescription is bound up with the divine plan of creation (1 Cor 11:7; Gen 2:18–24): it would be difficult to see in it the expression of a cultural fact. Nor should it be forgotten that we owe to Saint Paul one of the most vigorous texts in the New Testament on the fundamental equality of men and women, as children of God in Christ (Gal 3:28). Therefore there is no reason for accusing him of prejudices against women, when we note the trust that he shows towards them and the collaboration that he asks of them in his apostolate.

But over and above these objections taken from the history of apostolic times, those who support the legitimacy of change in the matter turn to the Church's practice in her sacramental discipline. It has been noted, in our day especially, to what extent the Church is conscious of possessing a certain power over the sacraments, even though they were instituted by Christ. She has used this power down the centuries in order to determine their signs and the conditions of their administration: recent decisions of Popes Pius XII and Paul IV are proof of this. However, it must be emphasized that this power, which is a real one, has definite limits. As Pope Pius XII recalled: "The Church has no power over the substance of the sacraments, that is to say, over what Christ the Lord, as the sources of Revelation bear witness, determined should be maintained in the sacramental sign." This was already the teaching of the council of Trent, which declared: "In the Church there has always existed this power, that in the administration of the sacraments, provided that their substance remains unaltered, she can lay down or modify what she considers more fitting either for the benefit of those who receive them or for respect towards those same sacraments, according to varying circumstances, times or places."

Moreover, it must not be forgotten that the sacramental signs are not conventional ones. Not only is it true that, in many respects, they are natural signs because they respond to the deep symbolism of actions and things, but they are more than this: they are principally meant to link the person of every period to the supreme Event of the history of salvation, in order to enable that person to understand, through all the Bible's wealth of pedagogy and symbolism, what grace they signify and produce. For example, the sacrament of the Eucharist is not only a fraternal meal, but at the same time a memorial which makes present and actual Christ's sacrifice and his offering by the Church. Again the priestly ministry is not just a pastoral service; it ensures the continuity of the functions entrusted by Christ to the Apostles and the continuity of the powers related to those functions. Adaptations to civilizations and times therefore cannot abolish on essential points the sacramental reference to constitutive events of Christianity and to Christ himself.

In the final analysis it is the Church through the voice of the Magisterium, that, in these various domains, decides what can change and what must remain immutable. When she judges she cannot accept certain changes, it is because she knows she is bound by Christ's manner of acting. Her attitude, despite appearances, is therefore not one of archaism but of fidelity: it can be truly understood only in this light. The Church makes pronouncements in virtue of the Lord's promise and the presence of the Holy Spirit, in order to proclaim better the mystery of Christ and to safeguard and manifest the whole of its rich content.

The practice of the Church therefore has a normative character: in the fact of conferring priestly ordination only on men, it is a question of unbroken tradition throughout the history of the Church, universal in the East and in the West, and alert to repress abuses immediately. This norm, based on Christ's example, has been and is still observed because it is considered to conform to God's plan for his Church.

5. The Ministerial Priesthood in the Light of the Mystery of Christ

Having recalled the Church's norm and the basis thereof, it seems useful and opportune to illustrate this norm by showing the profound fittingness that theological reflection discovers between the proper nature of the sacrament of Order, with its specific reference to the mystery of Christ, and the fact that only men have been called to receive priestly ordination. It is not a question here of bringing forward a demonstrative argument, but of clarifying this teaching by the analogy of faith.

The Church's constant teaching, repeated and clarified by the Second Vatican Council and again recalled by the 1971 Synod of Bishops and by the Sacred Congregation for the Doctrine of the Faith in its Declaration of 24th. June 1973, declares that the bishop or the priest in the exercise of his ministry, does not act in his own name, *in persona propria*: he represents Christ, who acts through him: "the priest truly acts in the place of Christ", as Saint Cyprian already wrote in the third century. It is this ability to represent Christ that Saint Paul considered as characteristic of his apostolic function (2 Cor 5:20; Gal 4:14). The supreme expression of this representation is found in the altogether special form it assumes in the celebration of the Eucharist, which is the source and centre of the Church's unity, the sacrificial meal in which the People of God are associated in the sacrifice of Christ: the priest, who alone has the power to perform it, then acts not only through the effective power conferred on him by Christ, but *in persona Christi*, taking the role of Christ, to the point of being his very image, when he pronounces the words of consecration.

The Christian priesthood is therefore of a sacramental nature: the priest is a sign, the supernatural effectiveness of which comes from the ordination received, but a sign that must be perceptible and which the faithful must be able to recognise with ease. The whole sacramental economy is in fact based upon natural signs, on symbols imprinted on the human psychology: "Sacramental signs," says Saint Thomas, "represent what they signify by natural resemblance." The same natural resemblance is required for persons as for things: when Christ's role in the Eucharist is to be expressed sacramentally, there would not be this "natural resemblance" which must exist between Christ and his minister if the role of Christ were not taken by a man: in such a case it would be difficult to see in the minister the image of Christ. For Christ himself was and remains a man.

Christ is of course the firstborn of all humanity, of women as well as men: the unity which he re-established after sin is such that there are no more distinctions between Jew and Greek, slave and free, male and female, but all are one in Christ Jesus (Gal 3:28). Nevertheless, the incarnation of the Word took place according to the male sex: this is indeed a question of fact, and this fact, while not implying an alleged natural superiority of man over woman, cannot be disassociated from the economy of salvation: it is indeed in harmony with the entirety of God's plan as God himself has revealed it, and of which the mystery of the Covenant is the nucleus.

For the salvation offered by God to men and women, the union with him to which they are called—in short, the Covenant—took on, from the Old Testament Prophets onwards, the privileged form of a nuptial mystery: for God the Chosen People is seen as his ardently loved spouse. Both Jewish and Christian tradition has discovered the depth of this intimacy of love by reading and rereading the Song of Songs; the divine Bridegroom will remain faithful even when the Bride betrays his love, when Israel is unfaithful to God (Hos 1–3; Jer 2). When the "fullness of time" (Gal 4:4) comes, the Word, the Son of God, takes on flesh in order to establish and seal the new and eternal Covenant in his blood, which will be shed for many so that sins may be forgiven. His death will gather together again the scattered children of God; from his pierced side will be born the Church, as Eve was born from Adam's side. At that time there is fully and eternally accomplished the nuptial mystery proclaimed and hymned in the Old Testament: Christ is the Bridegroom; the Church his Bride, whom he loves because he has gained her by his blood and made her glorious, holy and without blemish, and henceforth he is inseparable from her. This nuptial theme, which is developed from the Letters of Saint Paul onwards (2 Cor 11:2; Eph 5:22–23) to the writings of Saint John (especially in Jn 3:29; Rev 19:7, 9), is present also in the Synoptic Gospels: the Bridegroom's friends must not fast as long as he is with them (Mk 2:19); the Kingdom of Heaven is like a king who gave a feast for his son's wedding (Mt 22:1–14). It is through this Scriptural language, all interwoven with symbols, and which expresses and affects man and women in their profound identity, that there is revealed to us the mystery of God and Christ, a mystery which of itself is unfathomable.

That is why we can never ignore the fact that Christ is a man. And therefore, unless one is to disregard the importance of this symbolism for the economy of Revelation, it must be admitted that, in actions which demand the character of ordination and in which Christ himself, the author of the Covenant, the Bridegroom, the Head of the Church, is represented, exercising his ministry of salvation—which is in the highest degree the case of the Eucharist—his role (this is the original sense of the word *persona*) must be taken by a man. This does not stem from any personal superiority of the latter in the order of values, but only from a difference of fact on the level of functions and service.

Could one say that, since Christ is now in the heavenly condition, from now on it is a matter of indifference whether he be represented by a man or by a woman, since "at the resurrection men and women do not marry" (Mt 22:30)? But this text does not mean that the distinction between man and women, insofar as it determines the identity proper to the person, is suppressed in the glorified state; what holds for us also holds for Christ. It is indeed evident that in human beings the difference of sex exercises an important influence, much deeper than, for example, ethnic differences: the latter do not affect the human person as intimately as the difference of sex, which is directly ordained both for the communion of persons and for the generation of human beings. In Biblical Revelation this difference is the effect of God's will from the beginning: "male and female he created them" (Gen 1:27).

However, it will perhaps be further objected that the priest, especially when he presides at the liturgical and sacramental functions, equally represents the Church: he acts in her name with "the intention of doing what she does". In this sense, the theologians of the Middle Ages said that the minister also acts *in persona Ecclesiae*, that is to say, in the name of the whole Church and in order to represent her. And in fact, leaving aside the question of the participation of the faithful in a liturgical action, it is indeed in the name of the whole Church that the action is celebrated by the priest: he prays in the name of all, and in the Mass he offers the sacrifice of the whole Church. In the new Passover, the Church, under visible signs, immolates Christ through the ministry of the priest.

And so, it is asserted, since the priest also represents the Church, would it not be possible to think that this representation could be carried out by a woman, according to the symbolism already explained? It is true that the priest represents the Church, which is the Body of Christ. But if he does so, it is precisely because he first represents Christ himself, who is the Head and the Shepherd of the Church. The Second Vatican Council used this phrase to make more precise and complete the expression *in persona Christi*. It is in this quality that the priest presides over the Christian assembly and celebrates the Eucharistic sacrifice "in which the whole Church offers and is herself wholly offered."

If one does justice to these reflections, one will better understand how well-founded is the basis of the Church's practice; and will conclude that the controversies raised in our days over the ordination of women are for all Christians a pressing invitation to meditate on the mystery of the Church, to study in greater detail the meaning of the episcopate and the priesthood, and to rediscover the real and pre-eminent place of the priest in the community of the baptized, of which he indeed forms part but from which he is distinguished because, in the actions that call for the character of ordination, for the community he is—with all the effectiveness proper to the sacraments—the image and symbol of Christ himself who calls, forgives, and accomplishes the sacrifice of the Covenant.

6. The Ministerial Priesthood Illustrated by The Mystery of the Church

It is opportune to recall that problems of sacramental theology, especially when they concern the ministerial priesthood, as is the case here, cannot be solved except in the light of Revelation. The human sciences, however valuable their contribution in their own domain, cannot suffice here, for they cannot grasp the realities of faith: the properly supernatural content of these realities is beyond their competence.

Thus one must note the extent to which the Church is a society different from other societies, original in her nature and in her structures. The pastoral charge in the Church is normally linked to the sacrament of Order; it is not a simple government, comparable to the modes of authority found in the States. It is not granted by people's spontaneous choice: even when it involves designation through election, it is the laying on of hands and the prayer of the successors of the Apostles which guarantee God's choice; and it is the Holy Spirit, given by ordination, who grants participation in the ruling power of the Supreme Pastor, Christ (Acts 20:28). It is a charge of service and love: "If you love me, feed my sheep" (Jn 21:15–17).

For this reason one cannot see how it is possible to propose the admission of women to the priesthood in virtue of the equality of rights of the human person, an equality which holds good also for Christians. To this end, use is sometimes made of the text quoted above, from the Letter to the Galatians (3:28), which says that in Christ there is no longer any distinction between men and women. But this passage does not concern ministries: it only affirms the universal calling to divine filiation, which is the same for all. Moreover, and above all, to consider the ministerial priesthood as a human right would be to misjudge its nature completely: baptism does not confer any personal title to public ministry within the Church. The priesthood is not conferred for the honour or advantage of the recipient, but for the service of God and the Church; it is the object of a specific and totally gratuitous vocation: "You did not choose me, no, I chose you; and I commissioned you . . ." (Jn 15:16; Heb 5:4).

It is sometimes said and written in books and periodicals that some women feel that they have a vocation to the priesthood. Such an attraction however noble and understandable, still does not suffice for a genuine vocation. In fact a vocation cannot be reduced to a mere personal attraction, which can remain purely subjective. Since the priesthood is a particular ministry of which the Church has received the charge and the control, authentication by the Church is indispensable here and is a constitutive part of the vocation: Christ chose "those he wanted" (Mk 3:13). On the other hand, there is a universal vocation of all the baptized to the exercise of the royal priesthood by offering their lives to God and by giving witness for his praise.

Women who express a desire for the ministerial priesthood are doubtless motivated by the desire to serve Christ and the Church. And it is not surprising that, at a time when they are becoming more aware of the discriminations to which they have been subjected, they should desire the ministerial priesthood itself. But it must not be forgotten that the priesthood does not form part of the rights of the individual, but stems from the economy of the mystery of Christ and the Church. The priestly office cannot become the goal of social advancement: no merely human progress of society or of the individual can of itself give access to it: it is of another order.

It therefore remains for us to meditate more deeply on the nature of the real equality of the baptized which is one of the great affirmations of Christianity; equality is in no way identity, for the Church is a differentiated body, in which each individual has his or her role. The roles are distinct, and must not be confused; they do not favour the superiority of some vis-à-vis the others, nor do they provide an excuse for jealousy; the only better gift, which can and must be desired, is love (1 Cor

12–13). The greatest in the Kingdom of Heaven are not the ministers but the saints.

The Church desires that Christian women should become more fully aware of the greatness of their mission; today their role is of capital importance, both for the renewal and humanization of society and for the rediscovery of believers of the true face of the Church.

His Holiness Pope Paul VI, during the audience granted to the undersigned Prefect of the Sacred Congregation on 15 October 1976, approved this Declaration, confirmed it and ordered its publication.

Given in Rome, at the Sacred Congregation for the Doctrine of the Faith, on 15 October 1976, the feast of Saint Theresa of Avila.

Chapter 3

THE 1980s

If one could or even had to choose a decade in which the theology of womanhood expressed by the Roman Catholic Church was richly developed, it would be the 1980s. This decade contains two of the most significant documents to come out of official Vatican teachings regarding women and their changing role, status, and place in contemporary society: *Familiaris consortio*, or *On the Role of the Christian Family in the Modern World*, published by Pope John Paul II on November 22, 1981; and *Mulieris dignitatem*, or *On the Dignity and Vocation of Women on the Occasion of the Marian Year*, released by Pope John Paul II on August 15, 1988. Selections from these two documents are included at the end of this chapter.

Examining these two documents provides ample fruit for understanding the theology of womanhood as it develops in the 1980s. However, there are two other important documents that must also be summarized because they provide additional insight into women's roles in the family, in society, and in the church. They are "Educational Guidance in Human Love," published by the Sacred Congregation on Christian Education's (SCCE) on November 1, 1983; and *Donum vitae*, or *Instruction on Respect for Human Life in Its Origin and on the Dignity of Procreation: Replies to Certain Questions of the Day*, released by the SCDF on February 22, 1987.

FAMILIARIS CONSORTIO

As already mentioned, Pope John Paul II promulgated the Apostolic Exhortation *Familiaris consortio* on November 22, 1981. The document begins with the church proposing that the document be used by members of the Roman Catholic Church as a source of help regarding the institution of marriage and family life. This document responds to various contemporary challenges to marriage and family life experienced by Catholic clergy and laity by offering the church's perspective on how best to live within a marriage and to be part of a family. The document specifically says that it wishes to help young people understand the dignity of married life as well as its fulfilling nature (1).

Next, the church offers its definition of the family, which is very significant in the context of the rest of the document. The church affirms what previous church synods have decided: "The Christian family, in fact, is the first community called to announce the Gospel to the human person during growth and to bring him or her, through a progressive education and catechesis, to full human and Christian maturity" (2). In other words, the family is the first place where children encounter the saving message of Jesus and learn to understand the loving nature of God and the community of the Catholic Church. The idea that humans grow within families and through this growth and development become fully developed members of the Christian community places a large responsibility on the family, specifically the mother, whose primary responsibility includes birthing, caring for, and educating children, especially in their earliest years.

In addition to this definition of marriage, the church argues that the gospel message is intimately connected to the success of marriage and the fulfillment of family life. Marriage, as an institution created by God, was also in need of Jesus' redemption. The institution is to be remade in a way that accords its life and mission with the beginning intentions for human life as instilled within creation by the Creator and before the Fall. One of the duties of the church in times that threaten to obliterate and/or distort marriage as an institution is to remind all of the Catholic faithful what God intended marriage and family life to be (3). In fact, the church makes a very clear statement of the significance of all of this when it says, "*The future of humanity passes by way of the family*" (86).

The problems faced in marriage today are varied, according to the document. First, the mass media reports ways in which to improve marriage or solve marital problems that ignore the true dignity and respect for the human person; in this way they threaten the institution of marriage itself. This is especially true when mixed messages from the media undermine human freedom and dignity (4 and 7). The church also insists that the world has other misconceptions concerning marriage that hurt the institution as God designed it to be.

> Signs are not lacking of a disturbing degradation of some fundamental values: a mistaken theoretical and practical concept of the independence of the spouses in relation to each other; serious misconceptions regarding the relationship of authority between parents and children; the concrete difficulties that the family itself experiences in the transmission of values; the growing number of divorces; the scourge

of abortion; the ever more frequent recourse to sterilization; the appearance of a truly contraceptive mentality. (6)

The modern world also suffers from great confusion over what marriage means, what its purpose is, and what the significance of sexuality is (7). For example, polygamy offends the uniting, bonding, and self-giving characteristic of sex between wife and husband (19). The root of many of these misperceptions, according to the church, is the modern world's concept of human freedom. Freedom is not an autonomous existence with a range of choices and a lack of responsibility and accountability to other human beings. This notion threatens to seriously hurt and possibly destroy the family. More will be said about freedom shortly.

There are other factors that add to this threat to the family, especially in poorer countries and for those who live in the Third World. *Familiaris consortio* acknowledges that poverty, disease, and even the stress concerned with an unpredictable future further complicate and enlarge threats to family life. Many people living in poverty do not know when they will next eat, let alone when they will find a job or be secure enough to support a family. Adding the possibility of another mouth to feed, care for, and protect to already-existing families can increase tenfold the threat to the family and all that the family means, according to the church in *Familiaris consortio*. Likewise, population explosion in many countries leads to lack of land space and food (30). Developed countries are not immune to these problems, especially in light of the modern-day consumerist mindset prevalent in many well-to-do countries and among the wealthier of the poorer countries (6).

The Roman Catholic Church, through Pope John Paul II in this document, also recognizes positive contributions by society to family life, especially as they relate to the position of women in the family and in the world. The church declares "a more lively awareness of personal freedom and greater attention to the quality of interpersonal relationships in marriage, to promoting the dignity of women, to responsible procreation, to the education of children" (6) as good aspects that the modern age has introduced into the institution of marriage and into larger society in general. Modern society has also developed and expanded the role and need for the family in the modern world, and the church understands this to be a good development as well. Society, according to the document, does well when it encourages families to take a more active part in building and shaping society, in concern for the poor, and in working for justice and for more reciprocal intergenerational and interpersonal relationships within families. Society also recognizes that families must develop a more clear and careful understanding of their role as Christian families within the world.

Let us return to the concept of freedom and expand on it. One of the main tasks the church takes upon itself within this document is to understand the modern concept of freedom gone amuck and replace it with the kind of human freedom that comes through a thorough understanding of the gospel message (6). According to *Familiaris consortio*, true freedom is tempered by Christian charity, commitments, responsibilities, and duties to God and other members of the human family. In other words, true freedom is not individualistic but comes within the context of families and human relationships and responsibilities.

Modern society and modern families by extension struggle with how to be free and remain thoroughly committed to the Christian message. The church describes this struggle using the understanding of these conflicts that Saint Augustine so insightfully recounted. According to the document, Saint Augustine was known to say that "history is a struggle between freedoms that are in mutual conflict . . . a conflict between two loves: the love of God to the point of disregarding self, and the love of self to the point of disregarding God" (6). One of the many things the church wants to teach the world through this document is how to balance these two conflicting loves and how to understand modern society in a way that makes life better and more secure for families.

One of the first ways it does this is by defining the four main responsibilities of families: "(1) forming a community of persons; (2) serving life; (3) participating in the development of society; and (4) sharing in the life and mission of the Church" (17). Marriage begins as a commitment between two people to live together, to form a community, and to work toward the betterment of the world. The family should be a place in which love is fostered between two people first and then expanded to children of the union and from there to the world as a whole. Two baptized individuals should marry within the church, and this marriage should be witnessed to and supported by the couple's local Christian community and the larger global Christian community. One very significant aspect of this marriage commitment is that it can never be dissolved by any human institution (and it is only rarely annulled by the church).

Respecting life means that marriage is the only proper place for sexuality and that all sexual acts within marriage should be open to the possibility of children (11–13, 28–29). Yet, the Roman Catholic Church realizes that this is not happening and draws attention to this "anti-life mentality" (30). The divine design of marriage requires that it be open to children since it is through the family first that children first come to know about Jesus, God, and the Christian faith. The family is the first Christian community for children (39). In this way, besides being a place of community, support, love, and growth for the spouses within the marriage, marriage's main purpose as created and understood by God and the church is the conception, birth, raising, education, and support of children that result from the love between husband and wife. The church considers children to be God's "gift of a new responsibility" (14); by using contraception or by procuring abortions married couples disrupt God's plan, debase human sexuality, and fail to fully give of themselves in the sex act (32). Some couples through no fault of their own may not be able to have children; when this occurs their marriage is no less valid in God's eyes. Likewise, people who choose not to marry and to remain celibate and dedicate their virginity to God also validate marriage as an institution according to the church because humans can serve God equally through married life or consecrated virginity (16).

Families are also called to better society. One of the ways the family does this is through the practice of hospitality, according to *Familiaris consortio*. Some good examples of hospitality are sharing with others, feeding them, clothing them, and welcoming them into the home. In other words, follow Jesus' example and show God's love to the world. Another way the family can better society is through political participation. The church believes the family should be active in political life so that it can defend the family from laws and directives that might undermine the institution or threaten its foundation (44). Likewise, families should better society by working with public and Christian associations that promote good values, "the development of the human person, the medical, juridical and social protection of mothers and young children, the just advancement of women and the struggle against all that is detrimental to their dignity. . . . [The family should also support] other associations [that] work for the building of a more just and human world" (72).

The family is also called to be an active participant in the church. This is done by participating in one's local parish, attending mass together regularly, and receiving the sacraments. Children should receive religious education at home and when necessary at church as well. Family members should pray regularly as a family and individually.

It is important to look at women in relationship to the family. In sections 22 through 24, the church addresses women as wives within marriage, as members of society, and as victims of oppression, disrespect, and mistreatment. Based on marriage's first duty to be a community of persons, women have certain roles and responsibilities within the family. Likewise, a community assumes mutual respect, dignity, love, encouragement, and support. Women within marriage must be afforded the same respect and dignity as men are. Women are also equally responsible within the institution to be wives who give of themselves fully to their husbands and to their children. Men are expected to do the same (22).

The dignity of women is stressed as well. The document emphasizes that the Bible continuously testifies to the dignity of women. Jesus treated women well. Likewise, women were the first to report his resurrection. Women missionaries are reported in the Acts of the Apostles (54). Mary is a good example of God's manifestation of the true dignity of women because God chose Mary to be the mother of Jesus (22).

In addition to biblical evidence, human rationality also leads to the conclusion that women should be accorded equal dignity with men, according to *Familiaris consortio*. In fact, in light of Jesus' actions and human reason, women's dignity is a significant part of the history of salvation.

Moving on from a strong statement about the respect and dignity women should be accorded, the document acknowledges that women are often the first to lose that dignity and the first to suffer within society. Many women face strong oppression and violence because some people view women as objects, things, and possessions rather than as human beings. Human slavery, pornography, prostitution, and discrimination in educational opportunities and pay rates illustrate some of the ways women continue to be victims of violence and oppression in the world today. Women are often also victims of violence and discrimination because of their status in society. Widows, unwed mothers, and divorced women are often treated as less than human and not afforded the respect they deserve as human beings. The church adamantly denies all forms of discrimination and supports all change and work toward ending them (24).

One of the viewpoints that the church believes does harm to women is the bias that women should only be in the home. This is wrong. To think that women should only be in the home goes against women's equal dignity with men as well as their equal responsibility within the family to the spouse and the children. Women should be able to participate in public life and have public roles, according to *Familiar consortio* (23).

However, the church warns that women will never reach their full potential if they are not valued also as wives and mothers. Women's public participation and domestic responsibilities should be equally valued. In fact, public and private life for women should be a seamless combination of the two. Only then will women really have the opportunity to thrive, and only then will society be truly just and "human" (23). Within the church's commitment to a renewed understanding of a "theology of work," women's work in the home should be "recognized and respected by all for its irreplaceable value" (23).

One of women's roles as mothers includes the duty to be the primary educators of their children, especially in the Christian faith. In *Familiaris consortio* Pope John Paul II draws on the words of Pope Paul VI, who asked women if they are teaching their children the proper prayers and preparing them for the sacraments (60). One can see a difference between the roles of men and women here. Men were asked by the pope if they joined their families in prayer, at least occasionally, and if they brought peace into their homes.

While women should be allowed to pursue jobs and careers within the public sector, society should not be structured in such a way that women must work outside of the home. Women who work in the public world should not be valued more than women whose only work is in the house. Likewise, women who work outside the home should not put aside their femininity. Devaluing femininity and domestic work is destructive to family life and human dignity, according to *Familiaris consortio* (23).

EDUCATIONAL GUIDANCE IN HUMAN LOVE: OUTLINES FOR SEX EDUCATION

On November 1, 1983, the SCCE published "Educational Guidance in Human Love: Outlines for Sex Education." Given the role of women within marriage and the requirement that each sex act be open to procreation, what the church has to say about sex education merits consideration. If a woman chooses to enter married life, much of her life should center around the children. Women have also been accorded a primary role in their children's education, especially as it relates to the faith. Thus, this document is important in the Roman Catholic Church's theology of womanhood.

This document begins by affirming the Christian anthropology laid out concerning humanity in *Persona humana* and *Familiaris consortio*. First, sex is for procreation. Next, even at birth human beings are sexed and gendered beings through and through. Their sex/gender is biological, psychological, and also spiritual. Based on this essentially gendered nature of being human, women and men complement each other. In addition, a person's gender affects his or her role in society (4–5).

Related to humans as sexed/gendered beings, all human bodies, based on their sex, are divinely designed to serve a function. First, the body reveals to humanity its mortal and bodily nature. It is through the body that humans express themselves. Bodies are also reminders of God because they are gifts from God, who created them. The sexual function of the body is love and mutual self-giving, which leads to another function: procreation. This biological function of the body distinguishes men and women, as do other bodily characteristics. This bodily difference does not and *should* not mean lesser dignity or respect for one sex. Rather, difference, and the complementarity such difference brings, should be embraced and celebrated as part of

God's divine design. Echoing *Gaudium et spes,* the document emphasizes that both male and female beings are created in the likeness and image of God and therefore are equal in dignity and respect (4–25).

According to the document, it has recently been brought to the attention of the church that the whole person has become separated from the sex act because of the church's concern only with genital acts. Sexual relations between husbands and wives are meant to show love, mutual self-giving, respect, and intimacy. While they are also genital in nature, and each sex act should be open to procreation, sex is more than just genital stimulation or pleasure. The document declares that there is a distinct difference between genital sex and true love (one expression of true love is sexual intercourse):

> True love is the capacity to open oneself to one's neighbour in gener-
> osity, and in devotion of the other for the other's good; it knows how
> to respect the personality and the freedom of the other, it is self-giv-
> ing, not possessive. The sex instinct, on the other hand, if abandoned
> to itself, is reduced to the merely genital, and tends to take possession
> of the other, immediately seeking personal gratification (94).

In other words, sex is one true expression of love, and it is through communion with one's spouse that love grows. This overabundance of love as well as mutual love for each other naturally translates into greater love for one's neighbor.

There is another vocation besides married life in which human beings can love the world by serving it and also grow in love for the world. That other possibility is consecrated virginity. The SCCE considers celibacy a life that better serves God and one's neighbor than married life: "Free of the duties of conjugal love, the virgin heart can feel, therefore, more disposed to the gratuitous love of one's brothers and sisters. In consequence, virginity for the sake of the kingdom of heaven better expresses the gift of Christ to the Father on behalf of us and prefigures with greater precision the reality of eternal life, all substantiated in charity" (31). While the SCCE considers consecrated virginity better for showing love—because it is free from familial responsibility—it is safe to say that both married individuals and consecrated virgins express God's love for the world. More important, both states are necessary for the world. Just as with sex/gender difference, difference does not mean each state is accorded different degrees of respect and/ or dignity. Each state of life is occupied by a human person, and humanity already grants all people equal respect and dignity as God's creations.

With these two vocations in mind, Christian sex education should include an introduction to these two states of life as choices for each human being

(56). In fact, all Christians, no matter what their vocation in life, are called to be instruments of God's love in the world. The document stresses that these two roles both offer fulfilling ways for Christians to show the world love. At some point individuals should choose the path they believe they are called by God to take.

Following this exploration of vocation, the document discusses sexuality more specifically. There are many problems in current societal views of sexuality, it states. One of the problems many people face that threatens to derail God's plan and the ability for humans to show love in the ways God intended is contraception. This has been discussed many times already within this book as it relates to married life, the mutual self-giving of spouses, and God's divine design of the human person. The document does not add anything to this teaching.

There is another problem that many people also face that threatens human development. In fact, it also seems to threaten humans' capacity to show love to God and neighbor as well. This problem is homosexuality. As already mentioned in the Introduction, one of the discussions raised by feminism and also the sexual revolution is the question of greater sexual freedom. For many, greater sexual freedom also means choice of one's sexual partner's sex/gender. Second-wave feminism also saw a movement within its ranks of lesbian separatism and lesbianism as a political identity. As it does with many societal changes and societal discussions, the document spends a number of paragraphs discussing homosexuality and its understanding of the human in relationship to homosexual disorders, identities, and sexual acts.

Homosexuality, according to this document, is an impediment of one's ability to reach human sexual maturity. Homosexual individuals show "social mal-adaption" (101). Homosexuality is a condition that has many causes. It may come from bad influences, be biological, or manifest some sort of physiological imbalance. Nonetheless, all sex acts outside of married life are severely disordered. Still, homosexual sex acts are no graver than disordered heterosexual ones, such as heterosexual sex within marriage that uses contraception.

Yet, the homosexual individual has more of a problem than just learning self-control and the joys that come from celibacy. The homosexual individual is developmentally delayed in some ways. The church also seems to suggest that the homosexual individual does not know love of God or neighbor. Therefore, whatever the cause of the disorder, sex educators, family members, and others must help the individual develop into sexual maturity and should "promote [within the individual] an authentic moral force towards conversion to the love of God and neighbour" (103). Once converted to this love, the individual will reach sexual maturity and be able to choose his or her vocation: consecrated celibacy or married life.[1]

DONUM VITAE

Donum vitae, or *Instruction on Respect for Human Life in Its Origin and on the Dignity of Procreation: Replies to Certain Questions of the Day*, was promulgated on February 22, 1987, by the SCDF. As may seem obvious from the English title, it discusses modern questions about procreation, yet unlike the other documents examined thus far, this document focuses on specific medical and technological developments relating to conception as well as scientific research done on embryos and fetuses.

An important note about the relationship between science and religion seems relevant at this junction. For much of church history, church leadership was at best skeptical about the good science can offer to humanity and at worst outright suspicious of its purpose, benefits, and explanations, seeing them as seeking to undermine religious truth. Much of this suspiciousness halted at Vatican II, even though the church is still hesitant about the moral value and ethical quality of many scientific discoveries and developments. *Gaudium et spes* discusses science and the way in which it should always work for the benefit of humanity (15, 32–36). It should help humanity fulfill its religious and spiritual goals as well as provide new insights into how to tackle world problems such as environmental destruction, disease, hunger, poverty, and the like. This same fundamental idea that science should work to the benefit of humanity is also mentioned in section 2 of *Donum vitae*. As *Gaudium et spes* makes clear, and as this document repeats by referencing *Gaudium et spes*, "science without conscience can only lead to man's

---

[1] It should be noted that this is the document's understanding of homosexuality; the church's understanding of it as a sexual orientation has not yet developed. The LGBT movement within the United States attracted public attention in 1969 with the Stonewall Riots and the rising up of transgendered women to free themselves of police harassment and brutality. Homosexual individuals had lobbied for rights and acceptance in the United States and elsewhere for decades before this. In 1973 the American Psychological Association removed homosexuality as a mental disorder from its diagnostic manual. The church's understanding of homosexuality will also evolve as time moves on, as we will see. One of the societal changes that sparked renewed interest in the church's understanding of sexuality and new theologies of sexuality apart from feminism was the clergy sexual-abuse scandal that took place mainly in Europe and the United States in the early 2000s. This book cannot cover all of this material as it beyond its scope and has been extensively covered in other works. It will cover some of the changing understandings of sexuality and homosexuality as they relate to the theology of womanhood. One significant scientific discussion that affects church theology and doctrine in this regard is the idea of sexual orientation as biologically determined.

ruin" (*Donum vitae*, Introduction, 2). The church's concern for the moral and ethical quality that science must contain explains why the church feels the need to comment on these scientific developments.

The church acknowledges help from the scientific community to understand many of these scientific developments. With a basic and hopefully good grasp on the information, the church published this document to comment on it from a moral, ethical, and overall religious perspective. The document begins with a definition of human life: humans are creations of God and therefore have not only the right to life but also deserve dignity and basic human and civil rights.

In light of this moral value of the person, the document continues by laying out what it considers to be the basis of its moral criteria regarding new scientific developments, especially as they affect and shape human life at its very beginning. "The criteria are the respect, defence and promotion of man, his 'primary and fundamental right' to life, his dignity as a person who is endowed with a spiritual soul and with moral responsibility and who is called to beatific communion with God" (Introduction, 1). In addition, the church judges these scientific developments concerning human life from a place of a deep concern for humanity, one that comes from Jesus' love and one that hopes to explain God's laws and commandments concerning human life so that people may know what they need to be good, moral persons (Introduction).

The church moves on to define the moment of creation of the human being first by denying scientific terminology. It declares that all developmental stages within the womb—embryo, zygote, fetus, or the like—have the same ethical basis and fundamental human value (Foreword). This moment of creation concerns the soul, which the church argues is immediately created by God at conception (Introduction, 5). The divinely designed place for such creation of human life is the marital union between husband and wife. Their love and self-giving expressed in sexual union is the only rightful and natural place in which to co-create with God a new human life. Likewise, the document reaffirms what it has already defined at Vatican II in *Gaudium et spes* (51), in the 1974 document "Declaration on Procured Abortion," and in the 1983 "Charter of the Rights of the Family"[2]: Life begins at conception and must be respected from that point forward (*Donum vitae*, I, 1).

The document then addresses specific questions concerning prenatal testing, medical intervention *in utero*, medical research on human embryos, various types of *in vitro* fertilization, surrogate motherhood, artificial insemination, and the right to have children. The church argues that any method or intervention that does not respect human life, especially living

---

[2] This document can be found on the Vatican website, www.vatican.va.

human beings, is contrary to God's law and church precept. For example, artificial insemination is immoral because it takes place outside the marital union. Women and couples should not have prenatal testing done if their intent is to abort an unhealthy or deformed baby. Medical procedures within the womb are permissible as long as they respect the life of the baby and work toward its betterment. Surrogate motherhood, much like artificial insemination and *in vitro* fertilization (IVF) procedures, takes place outside of the marital union and therefore is immoral (I–II). The church believes that no couple has a right to have children, no matter how much they may want them (II, 8). Rather, children are a gift from God and must be respected and treated as such.

Why has this document been included in a book on the theology of womanhood? As laid out before, a large part of a woman's role and responsibility within marriage revolves around family life, and the church believes that family life includes children. Women are also the physical bearers of children, and therefore any discussion of children concerns women as well. Likewise, these issues illustrate the influences of both science and feminism on the church and the church's need to comment, define, and often redefine its stance on various issues of the day. In all of these ways this document contributes to the church's theology of womanhood, specifically its understanding of woman's dignity, rights, and place in this world.

MULIERIS DIGNITATEM

The final document of this decade is also probably the most significant document ever published on women and their place in society and the church. In *Mulieris dignitatem,* or *On the Dignity and Vocation of Women on the Occasion of the Marian Year,* Pope John Paul II lays out a thorough theology of womanhood, drawing on previous documents and developing some new ideas based on societal change. This document was "the first in the history of the church"[3] specifically to address what it means according to the official teachings of the church to be human, to be a female, and the nature of women's divine vocation. It describes femininity and advocates that women, in order to be fulfilled, should be mothers.

The Marian Year of 1988 was proclaimed by Pope John Paul II in *Redemptoris mater.* He explains that the purpose of this Marian Year is to increase the clergy's and laity's devotion to Mary and Mary's role in the mystery of the church (48). The pope's immense devotion to Mary was evident in all of his papal writings and theological discussions. It makes

---

[3] Joan Chittister, O.S.B., "Coming Soon: 'An Effective and Intelligent Campaign,'" *The National Catholic Reporter*, October 14, 2003; nationalcatholicreporter.org website.

sense that this concentration on Mary and her role in the life of the Christian community would spark a theological document on the place of women in society. In fact, *Redemptoris mater* says:

> This Marian dimension of Christian life takes on special importance in relation to women and their status. In fact, femininity has a unique relationship with the Mother of the Redeemer. . . . It can thus be said that women, by looking to Mary, find in her the secret of living their femininity with dignity and of achieving their own true advancement. In the light of Mary, the church sees in the face of women the reflection of a beauty which mirrors the loftiest sentiments of which the human heart is capable: the self-offering totality of love; the strength that is capable of bearing the greatest sorrows; limitless fidelity and tireless devotion to work; the ability to combine penetrating intuition with words of support and encouragement. (46)

The document *Mulieris dignitatem* further explains the connections among Mary, femininity, and women. The importance of Mary for the church and as an example of women and their roles is quite obvious in the document. The mother of God offers all mothers, whether actual physical mothers or spiritual mothers, the perfect example of motherhood and femininity.

The document also cites many documents that have recognized this changing place, status, and role of women in contemporary society. A few examples are

- Pope Paul VI's "Address to Women," which we examined in Chapter 1;
- Vatican II's *Gaudium et spes* and *Apostolicam actuositatem*, which we examined in Chapter 1; and
- Pope John XXIII's *Pacem in terris*, also examined in Chapter 1.

At the same time the document acknowledges three key concepts about women. First, women are undervalued; second, their true gifts to the world are not completely acknowledged; and third, and most important, they have not been allowed to develop their true potential, which they would then use to help make the world a better place.

With these three ideas in mind the document understands itself as a meditation in light of the Marian Year. It reflects on a number of key understandings of womanhood and woman's potential. One of the first ideas it addresses is what Mary as mother of God means in relationship to the dignity and vocation of women in the world. Pope John Paul II, through the

document, also describes what it means to be a woman, describes femininity, and lays out what he think God intended women's vocation and mission
in the world to be. Finally, the document acknowledges that the world will
not be as just, fair, and equal as it should be and that the church's Christian
mission will not be fully realized without women using their God-given
gifts and talents to help make the world a better place (I, 2).

Mulieris dignitatem begins with an explanation of Mary and her relationship to creation, redemption, and the greater plan of God and God's
creation. The church—through Pope John Paul II, who called Mary *co-
redemptrix* with Jesus during an address in Guayaquil, Ecuador—considers
Mary to be part of salvation history. The birth, life, and death of Jesus took
place within her, through her, and with her significant influence. It cannot
be denied that God was birthed by a woman, and she therefore holds a key
place within humanity's salvation and God's divine plan (II, 3).

Mary's role as mother of God shows humanity women's dignity as well.
First, Mary chooses to become the mother of God and therefore exercises
what the church calls her free will, "her personal and feminine 'I'" (II, 4).
Mary's free choice to be the mother of God is the basis that "*determines the
essential horizon of reflection on the dignity and the vocation of women*"
(II, 5). Mary's care for Jesus in his youth as well as her commitment to his
ministry and her journey with him to the cross show the world the nature
of free will, choice, dedication, faith, and true love. In other words, it is
through Mary that we can better understand human dignity, potential, and
the concept of free will. More important, it is through Mary that we can
understand how women should conduct themselves by following her example of caring, loving, dedication, and mothering (IV, 11).

Next, the document addresses women as created in the image and likeness of God and therefore deserving of equal respect and dignity as human
beings. It starts by discussing the two different Genesis stories about humanity's creation: the one in which men and women are created at the same
time (Gn 1:1—2:3) and the one in which man is created first and woman
is created from man's rib (Gn 2:4–24). The document insists that while the
idea that woman comes from a man's rib is more like other mythical stories present in the era in which this story was written, both stories support
the same conclusion: men and women are human beings who have equal
rational capacity, equal dignity, and should merit equal respect, given that
both were created in the image and likeness of God (III, 6).

The document then addresses marriage and gender complementarity.
God created marriage as a divine institution. The creation stories show how
men and women were, from the very moment of creation, made for each
other. They help each other, work together, and correctly combine the masculine and feminine aspects of themselves into one flesh, as God intended

humanity to be (III, 7). Men and women were made male and female, and in this way both masculinity and femininity have much to offer the world and both should be honored, cherished, and cultivated. Nonetheless, there is a difference between men and women, and it is important to acknowledge this and respect its boundaries (IV, 10).

Pope John Paul II acknowledges that the situation of women in the world is not one of equality in dignity, respect, and treatment. Another aspect of human existence that is described in the Genesis retelling of the Fall is an account of the unequal status of women in society and the recognition that this is not how God intended the relationship between the sexes to be. Humanity needs to correct this. The Hebrew scriptures say the inequality of the sexes will be resolved in the "fullness of time" (IV, 10). From a Christian perspective, the document believes that the fullness of time has come. Mary, as the new Eve, participates in the incarnation in a way that should create a new situation on earth, one that should right this inequality. Jesus' life, ministry, and death on the cross put an end to the pull and influence of original sin over humanity (IV, 11). In other words, the salvific power of Jesus' life and death should restore humanity to its fullness, to its original creation, and end the inequality that exists between the sexes. It is up to humans to help make this new creation, the saved world, come to fulfillment.

Is it important to remember that the point of the document is also to define women's role in this new earthly creation. For instance, Mary's role in salvation is distinctly as a woman, and it is her femininity that the document wishes to emphasize. The document says, "*this is the discovery of all the richness and personal resources of femininity* [her ability to say yes to God], all the eternal originality of the 'woman,' just as God wanted her to be, a person for her own sake, who discovers herself 'by means of a sincere gift of self'" (IV, 11). In other words, a woman played a key role in salvation. That role included the gift of herself, which was distinct from the role played by her son and the men who surrounded her. It is women's gift of self that will help bring about a new creation at the same time that it fulfills women's divinely appointed vocation. This gift of self is not only good for the world and the future of humanity, but it is also good for each individual woman because it helps her reach her true potential by being who God intended her to be.

Let us look at these ideas in more detail. Women, as we have already seen, are sexed and gendered down to their souls. Femininity is not just something women do; it is something women are. All women should be feminine in their comportment and demeanor. Being feminine means taking on God's divine design for women. One thing women excel at is a respect for life (V, 14). This respect for life translates into a host of other characteristics and qualities that make women who God intended them to be. Being a woman means being feminine. It means accepting new life in the womb (V, 14), responding well to others, being a good listener, being sensitive, offering others the gift of herself, being a mother, being attentive to others, teaching men how to be good fathers, being able to resist suffering better than men because of her sensitive nature, and being entrusted with the care of humans in a way that differs significantly from the role men are given by God (V, 13). Women, according to Pope John Paul II, operate out of the "order of love." This means that a woman's primary role and responsibility is to love others, to show others that love, and to teach others (men) what love means. It is as if love is part of the nature of femininity and God's intention for women as well. Women operate from the place of love and should have love as their number one concern and priority.

According to *Mulieris dignitatem*, a woman's femininity and its order of love can be fulfilled in two different ways: physical motherhood or spiritual motherhood. In physical motherhood "it is the woman who 'pays' directly for this shared generation which literally absorbs the energies of her body and soul . . . but men owe a special debt to the woman" (VI, 18) because of this. It is therefore a shame that some women find themselves in positions where men try to convince them to have abortions. The document says women never forget about the life that once occupied their wombs (V, 14).

Spiritual motherhood is characteristic of women who have never had children because of their love and care for human beings in the world (VI, 21). Many of these women are nuns, yet some are not. Nonetheless, spiritual mothers dedicate their lives to helping others. They work in jails, with the poor, cook for soup kitchens, tutor children, advocate justice, and care for the sick. Educating children and instilling and cultivating the Roman Catholic faith are other important parts of spiritual motherhood. Women's lives should revolve around helping others because this is what God created them to do. Most of the time, caring for others is best accomplished at home.

These two roles are also defended through an examination of the Gospels. First, the church argues, as we have seen many times before, that Jesus treated women with the dignity and respect they deserved even when it was contrary to societal norms of the time. In fact, the document points out that Jesus affirmed the personhood and dignity of women when he told men to love their wives. The affirmation of women given by Jesus during his ministry now means that women can develop into full human beings the way in which God meant (VII, 24). The document also addresses the femininity of Martha and her faith-filled and loving response to Jesus as an example of specifically feminine response to God (V, 15). However, a woman's role precludes membership in the priesthood because at the Last Supper Jesus commissioned only men to act on his behalf in the eucharistic meal, a choice free of societal pressures (VII, 26).

The church acknowledges that discrimination against women still exists in this world. It believes that Jesus' mission was to help right this effect of the Fall. It also maintains that women's femininity, their literal self-gift to the world, should be valued more. The document ends by saying that men and women are responsible for the future of the world. Women, in the Spirit of Christ, can "discover the entire meaning of their femininity and thus be disposed to making a 'sincere gift of self' to others, thereby finding themselves" (IX, 31). More important, by being gifts of self, women participate in the world in a way that instructs the world to be centered on love as well. There are many aspects of the world and its current arrangement that urgently need women's gifts of love and sensitivity to make the world a better place. This is their genius.[4]

Likewise, the world must further women's growth and development. A woman's gift of self means little if no one respects her and affords her the dignity she deserves as a member of the human race. Mary is the model woman who shows all humanity what true self-giving love means, a model the whole church needs to acknowledge and become more attuned to, but one also that women, specifically, should try to emulate. Using Mary as a basis to show the world the respect women deserve and the ways in which their gifts can make the world a better place, the church, throughout the document, explains how women should be treated by the world and also how they should interact with the world.

Women, as feminine beings who, by being in tune with their feminine nature, offer the world the gift of themselves, not only make the world a better place, but also fulfill their God-given destinies. Of all of the descriptions of women we have encountered up to this point, the 1980s explain most succinctly the church's theology of womanhood. The church recognizes that the position, status, and role of women are changing in the world and also that there are ways in which women are not respected and treated as they deserve to be as human beings and God's creations. Many women are the first to suffer oppression, disease, poverty, and destitution. In many countries they lack essential rights and freedoms of personhood. The church urges humanity to work toward improving women's situation by explaining who women are, what their true potential can be, and what they have to offer the world.

Women operate out of the order of love. This means that women prioritize love in their lives by loving, caring for, and supporting others. Women offer the world the gifts of themselves to make the world a better place.

---

[4] For more on this concept, see Pope John Paul II, *The Genius of Women* (Washington DC: U.S. Catholic Conference, 1997).

Women respect life and teach others how to do so as well. Women are good listeners and are sensitive to the needs of others, which helps to make them more attuned to the suffering of others and better able to cope with suffering as well. Women are mothers who care for children in their infancy. Women also mother by caring for the sick, hungry, needy, and imprisoned. Women are the first educators of infants and the ones who teach children about the Christian faith. Women are wives who offer the gift of themselves in sexual union with their husbands. Women also work alongside their husbands as partners. Women are full members of the human race; they deserve dignity and respect equal to that of men, given that they too are creations of God. Yet, women are also different from men and find fulfillment not by becoming like men but by cultivating their feminine nature and talents. Women are members of families who help make the world a better place by working to protect the family and cultivating within the family a space of communion and love. Women can work inside and outside of the home, even though their priorities focus on family life, the raising of young children, and the home. Women's bodies were created by God to bear life, which also helps define their God-given roles as mothers.

Yet, who women are and what women should be and how they should be treated varies significantly. For example, women's work in the home should be more valued. There are countries in which women do not have freedom and the opportunity to exercise their free will. There are many places where women are not treated with the respect and dignity they deserve. Women are often victims of severe poverty and face a daily struggle to survive. Women are often pressured into abortions by men who do not want to help care for the child. Women are discriminated against when they are viewed as only biological vessels for new life or as individuals whose only proper place is in the home.

The world needs to make sure women are properly cared for and treated with the respect and dignity equal to that which men are accorded. Women should be allowed to choose to work outside the home. The world needs to secure women's freedoms and rights as well. Until women are treated well, they cannot realize their full potential as human beings. The world suffers along with women and will continue to suffer until women gain the rights, freedoms, and proper treatment they deserve.

At the same time, women must also work to make the world a better place through the use of their feminine qualities. Women should teach men how to be better fathers, better listeners, better people, and in that way help the world become a more just, equitable, and fair place. Women need to show the world how to love. Women need to introduce their children to the Catholic faith and be good mothers whose children are good Christians. Women need always to respect life, marriage, and sexuality.

It seems women need to help change the world as much as the world needs to change to help women. God created women a certain way, and it is through the cultivation of their very nature that they can find fulfillment as human beings. Jesus defined women's roles in the church he established by not treating women as the rest of his society did and therefore not showing bias in his choice of a male-only priesthood.

In the 1980s the Roman Catholic Church provided its most complete understanding of women and a theology of womanhood. In many ways men and women have different roles to play in society, in the church, and in family life. Those roles have been ordained by God since the very beginning of creation. While the next decade adds some detail, the 1980s marked a turning point in how the church understands womanhood; in no other decade is womanhood defined as well as it is in the following documents.

FAMILIARIS CONSORTIO

APOSTOLIC EXHORTATION
OF POPE JOHN PAUL II TO THE EPISCOPATE
TO THE CLERGY AND TO THE FAITHFUL
OF THE WHOLE CATHOLIC CHURCH
ON THE ROLE
OF THE CHRISTIAN FAMILY
IN THE MODERN WORLD

22 NOVEMBER 1981

INTRODUCTION

The Church at the Service of the Family

1. The family in the modern world, as much as and perhaps more than any other institution, has been beset by the many profound and rapid changes that have affected society and culture. Many families are living this situation in fidelity to those values that constitute the foundation of the institution of the family. Others have become uncertain and bewildered over their role or even doubtful and almost unaware of the ultimate meaning and truth of conjugal and family life. Finally, there are others who are hindered by various situations of injustice in the realization of their fundamental rights.

Knowing that marriage and the family constitute one of the most precious of human values, the Church wishes to speak and offer her help to those who are already aware of the value of marriage and the family and seek to live it faithfully, to those who are uncertain and anxious and searching for the truth, and to those who are unjustly impeded from living freely their family lives. Supporting the first, illuminating the second and assisting the others, the Church offers her services to every person who wonders about the destiny of marriage and the family.

In a particular way the Church addresses the young, who are beginning their journey towards marriage and family life, for the purpose of presenting them with new horizons, helping them to discover the beauty and grandeur of the vocation to love and the service of life.

The Synod of 1980 in Continuity with Preceding Synods

2. A sign of this profound interest of the Church in the family was the last Synod of Bishops, held in Rome from September 26 to October 25, 1980. This was a natural continuation of the two preceding Synods: the Christian family, in fact, is the first community called to announce the Gospel to the human person during growth and to bring him or her, through a progressive education and catechesis, to full human and Christian maturity.

Furthermore, the recent Synod is logically connected in some way as well with that on the ministeriIal priesthood and on justice in the modern world. In fact, as an educating community, the family must help man to discern his own vocation and to accept responsibility in the search for greater justice, educating him from the beginning in interpersonal relationships, rich in justice and in love.

At the close of their assembly, the Synod Fathers presented me with a long list of proposals in which they had gathered the fruits of their reflections, which had matured over intense days of work, and they asked me unanimously to be a spokesman before humanity of the Church's lively care for the family and to give suitable indications for renewed pastoral effort in this fundamental sector of the life of man and of the Church.

As I fulfill that mission with this Exhortation, thus actuating in a particular matter the apostolic ministry with which I am entrusted, I wish to thank all the members of the Synod for the very valuable contribution of teaching and experience that they made especially through the *Propositiones*, the text of which I am entrusting to the Pontifical Council for the Family with instructions to study it so as to bring out every aspect of its rich content.

The Precious Value of Marriage and of the Family

3. Illuminated by the faith that gives her an understanding of all the truth concerning the great value of marriage and the family and their deepest meaning, the Church once again feels the pressing need to proclaim the Gospel, that is the "good news," to all people without exception, in particular to all those who are called to marriage and are preparing for it, to all married couples and parents in the world.

The Church is deeply convinced that only by the acceptance of the Gospel are the hopes that man legitimately places in marriage and in the family capable of being fulfilled.

Willed by God in the very act of creation, marriage and the family are interiorly ordained to fulfillment in Christ and have need of His graces in order to be healed from the wounds of sin and restored to their "beginning," that is, to full understanding and the full realization of God's plan.

At a moment of history in which the family is the object of numerous forces that seek to destroy it or in some way to deform it, and aware that the well-being of society and her own good are intimately tied to the good of the family, the Church perceives in a more urgent and compelling way her mission of proclaiming to all people the plan of God for marriage and the family, ensuring their full vitality and human and Christian development, and thus contributing to the renewal of society and of the People of God.

PART ONE

BRIGHT SPOTS AND SHADOWS FOR THE FAMILY TODAY

The Need to Understand the Situation

4. Since God's plan for marriage and the family touches men and women in the concreteness of their daily existence in specific social and cultural situations, the Church ought to apply herself to understanding the situations within which marriage and the family are lived today, in order to fulfill her task of serving.

This understanding is, therefore, an inescapable requirement of the work of evangelization. It is, in fact, to the families of our times that the Church must bring the unchangeable and ever new Gospel of Jesus Christ, just as it is the families involved in the present conditions of the world that are called to accept and to live the plan of God that pertains to them. Moreover, the call and demands of the Spirit resound in the very events of history, and so the Church can also be guided to a more profound understanding of the inexhaustible mystery of marriage and the family by the circumstances, the questions and the anxieties and hopes of the young people, married couples and parents of today.

To this ought to be added a further reflection of particular importance at the present time. Not infrequently ideas and solutions which are very appealing but which obscure in varying degrees the truth and the dignity of the human person, are offered to the men and women of today, in their sincere and deep search for a response to the important daily problems that affect their married and family life. These views are often supported by the powerful and pervasive organization of the means of social communication, which subtly endanger freedom and the capacity for objective judgment.

Many are already aware of this danger to the human person and are working for the truth. The Church, with her evangelical discernment, joins with them, offering her own service to the truth, to freedom and to the dignity of every man and every woman.

The Situation of the Family in the World Today

6. The situation in which the family finds itself presents positive and negative aspects: the first are a sign of the salvation of Christ operating in the world; the second, a sign of the refusal that man gives to the love of God.

On the one hand, in fact, there is a more lively awareness of personal freedom and greater attention to the quality of interpersonal relationships in marriage, to promoting the dignity of women, to responsible procreation, to the education of children. There is also an awareness of the need for the development of interfamily relationships, for reciprocal spiritual and material assistance, the rediscovery of the ecclesial mission proper to the family and its responsibility for the building of a more just society. On the other hand, however, signs are not lacking of a disturbing degradation of some fundamental values: a mistaken theoretical and practical concept of the independence of the spouses in relation to each other; serious misconceptions regarding the relationship of authority between parents and children; the concrete difficulties that the family itself experiences in the transmission of values; the growing number of divorces; the scourge of abortion; the ever more frequent recourse to sterilization; the appearance of a truly contraceptive mentality.

At the root of these negative phenomena there frequently lies a corruption of the idea and the experience of freedom, conceived not as a capacity for realizing the truth of God's plan for marriage and the family, but as an autonomous power of self-affirmation, often against others, for one's own selfish well-being.

Worthy of our attention also is the fact that, in the countries of the so-called Third World, families often lack both the means necessary for survival, such as food, work, housing and medicine, and the most elementary freedoms. In the richer countries, on the contrary, excessive prosperity and the consumer mentality, paradoxically joined to a certain anguish and uncertainty about the future, deprive married couples of the generosity and courage needed for raising up new human life: thus life is often perceived not as a blessing, but as a danger from which to defend oneself.

The historical situation in which the family lives therefore appears as an interplay of light and darkness.

This shows that history is not simply a fixed progression towards what is better, but rather an event of freedom, and even a struggle between freedoms that are in mutual conflict, that is, according to the well-known expression of St. Augustine, a conflict between two loves: the love of

God to the point of disregarding self, and the love of self to the point of disregarding God.

It follows that only an education for love rooted in faith can lead to the capacity of interpreting "the signs of the times," which are the historical expression of this twofold love. . . .

PART TWO

THE PLAN OF GOD FOR MARRIAGE AND THE FAMILY

Man, the Image of the God Who Is Love

11. God created man in His own image and likeness: calling him to existence through love, He called him at the same time for love.

God is love and in Himself He lives a mystery of personal loving communion. Creating the human race in His own image and continually keeping it in being, God inscribed in the humanity of man and woman the vocation, and thus the capacity and responsibility, of love and communion. Love is therefore the fundamental and innate vocation of every human being.

As an incarnate spirit, that is a soul which expresses itself in a body and a body informed by an immortal spirit, man is called to love in his unified totality. Love includes the human body, and the body is made a sharer in spiritual love.

Christian revelation recognizes two specific ways of realizing the vocation of the human person in its entirety, to love: marriage and virginity or celibacy. Either one is, in its own proper form, an actuation of the most profound truth of man, of his being "created in the image of God."

Consequently, sexuality, by means of which man and woman give themselves to one another through the acts which are proper and exclusive to spouses, is by no means something purely biological, but concerns the innermost being of the human person as such. It is realized in a truly human way only if it is an integral part of the love by which a man and a woman commit themselves totally to one another until death. The total physical self-giving would be a lie if it were not the sign and fruit of a total personal self-giving, in which the whole person, including the temporal dimension, is present: if the person were to withhold something or reserve the possibility of deciding otherwise in the future, by this very fact he or she would not be giving totally.

This totality which is required by conjugal love also corresponds to the demands of responsible fertility. This fertility is directed to the generation of a human being, and so by its nature it surpasses the purely biological order and involves a whole series of personal values. For the harmonious growth of these values a persevering and unified contribution by both parents is necessary.

The only "place" in which this self-giving in its whole truth is made possible is marriage, the covenant of conjugal love freely and consciously chosen, whereby man and woman accept the intimate community of life and love willed by God Himself which only in this light manifests its true meaning. The institution of marriage is not an undue interference by society or authority, nor the extrinsic imposition of a form. Rather it is an interior requirement of the covenant of conjugal love which is publicly affirmed as unique and exclusive, in order to live in complete fidelity to the plan of God, the Creator. A person's freedom, far from being restricted by this fidelity, is secured against every form of subjectivism or relativism and is made a sharer in creative Wisdom.

Marriage and Communion between God and People

12. The communion of love between God and people, a fundamental part of the Revelation and faith experience of Israel, finds a meaningful expression in the marriage covenant which is established between a man and a woman.

For this reason the central word of Revelation, "God loves His people," is likewise proclaimed through the living and concrete word whereby a man and a woman express their conjugal love. Their bond of love becomes the image and the symbol of the covenant which unites God and His people. And the same sin which can harm the conjugal covenant becomes an image of the infidelity of the people to their God: idolatry is prostitution, infidelity is adultery, disobedience to the law is abandonment of the spousal love of the Lord. But the infidelity of Israel does not destroy the eternal fidelity of the Lord, and therefore the ever faithful love of God is put forward as the model of the faithful love which should exist between spouses.

Jesus Christ, Bridegroom of the Church, and the Sacrament of Matrimony

13. The communion between God and His people finds its definitive fulfillment in Jesus Christ, the Bridegroom who loves and gives Himself as the Savior of humanity, uniting it to Himself as His body.

He reveals the original truth of marriage, the truth of the "beginning," and, freeing man from his hardness of heart, He makes man capable of realizing this truth in its entirety.

This revelation reaches its definitive fullness in the gift of love which the Word of God makes to humanity in assuming a human nature, and in the sacrifice which Jesus Christ makes of Himself on the Cross for His bride, the Church. In this sacrifice there is entirely revealed that plan which God has imprinted on the humanity of man and woman since their creation; the marriage of baptized persons thus becomes a real symbol of that new and eternal covenant sanctioned in the blood of Christ. The Spirit which the Lord pours forth gives a new heart, and renders man and woman capable of loving one another as Christ has loved us. Conjugal love reaches that fullness to which it is interiorly ordained, conjugal charity, which is the proper and specific way in which the spouses participate in and are called to live the very charity of Christ who gave Himself on the Cross.

In a deservedly famous page, Tertullian has well expressed the greatness of this conjugal life in Christ and its beauty: "How can I ever express the happiness of the marriage that is joined together by the Church strengthened by an offering, sealed by a blessing, announced by angels and ratified by the Father? . . . How wonderful the bond between two believers with a single hope, a single desire, a single observance, a single service! They are both brethren and both fellow-servants; there is no separation between them in spirit or flesh; in fact they are truly two in one flesh and where the flesh is one, one is the spirit."

Receiving and meditating faithfully on the word of God, the Church has solemnly taught and continues to teach that the marriage of the baptized is one of the seven sacraments of the New Covenant.

Indeed, by means of baptism, man and woman are definitively placed within the new and eternal covenant, in the spousal covenant of Christ with the Church. And it is because of this indestructible insertion that the intimate community of conjugal life and love, founded by the Creator, is elevated and assumed into the spousal charity of Christ, sustained and enriched by His redeeming power.

By virtue of the sacramentality of their marriage, spouses are bound to one another in the most profoundly indissoluble manner. Their belonging to each other is the real representation, by means of the sacramental sign, of the very relationship of Christ with the Church.

Spouses are therefore the permanent reminder to the Church of what happened on the Cross; they are for one another and for the children witnesses to the salvation in which the sacrament makes them sharers. Of this salvation event marriage, like every sacrament, is a memorial, actuation and prophecy: "As a memorial, the sacrament gives them the grace and duty of commemorating the great works of God and of bearing witness to them before their children. As actuation, it gives them the grace and duty of putting into practice in the present, towards each other and their children, the demands of a love which forgives and redeems. As prophecy, it gives them the grace and duty of living and bearing witness to the hope of the future encounter with Christ."

Like each of the seven sacraments, so also marriage is a real symbol of the event of salvation, but in its own way. "The spouses participate in it as spouses, together, as a couple, so that the first and immediate effect of marriage *(res et sacramentum)* is not supernatural grace itself, but the Christian conjugal bond, a typically Christian communion of two persons because it represents the mystery of Christ's incarnation and the mystery of His covenant. The content of participation in Christ's life is also specific: conjugal love involves a totality, in which all the elements of the person enter – appeal of the body and instinct, power of feeling and affectivity, aspiration of the spirit and of will. It aims at a deeply personal unity, the unity that, beyond union in one flesh, leads to forming one heart and soul; it demands indissolubility and faithfulness in definitive mutual giving; and it is open to fertility (cf. *Humanae vitae*, 9). In a word it is a question of the normal characteristics of all natural conjugal love, but with a new significance which not only purifies and strengthens them, but raises them to the extent of making them the expression of specifically Christian values."

Children, the Precious Gift of Marriage

14. According to the plan of God, marriage is the foundation of the wider community of the family, since the very institution of marriage and conjugal love are ordained to the procreation and education of children, in whom they find their crowning.

In its most profound reality, love is essentially a gift; and conjugal love, while leading the spouses to the reciprocal "knowledge" which makes them "one flesh," does not end with the couple, because it makes them capable of the greatest possible gift, the gift by which they become cooperators with God for giving life to a new human person. Thus the couple, while giving themselves to one another, give not just themselves but also the reality of children, who are a living reflection of their love, a permanent sign of conjugal unity and a living and inseparable synthesis of their being a father and a mother.

When they become parents, spouses receive from God the gift of a new responsibility. Their parental love is called to become for the children the visible sign of the very love of God, "from whom every family in heaven and on earth is named."

It must not be forgotten however that, even when procreation is not possible, conjugal life does not for this reason lose its value. Physical sterility in fact can be for spouses the occasion for other important services to the life of the human person, for example, adoption, various forms of educational work, and assistance to other families and to poor or handicapped children.

The Family, a Communion of Persons

15. In matrimony and in the family a complex of interpersonal relationships is set up – married life, fatherhood and motherhood, filiation

and fraternity – through which each human person is introduced into the "human family" and into the "family of God," which is the Church.

Christian marriage and the Christian family build up the Church: for in the family the human person is not only brought into being and progressively introduced by means of education into the human community, but by means of the rebirth of baptism and education in the faith the child is also introduced into God's family, which is the Church.

The human family, disunited by sin, is reconstituted in its unity by the redemptive power of the death and Resurrection of Christ. Christian marriage, by participating in the salvific efficacy of this event, constitutes the natural setting in which the human person is introduced into the great family of the Church.

The commandment to grow and multiply, given to man and woman in the beginning, in this way reaches its whole truth and full realization.

The Church thus finds in the family, born from the sacrament, the cradle and the setting in which she can enter the human generations, and where these in their turn can enter the Church.

Marriage and Virginity or Celibacy

16. Virginity or celibacy for the sake of the Kingdom of God not only does not contradict the dignity of marriage but presupposes it and confirms it. Marriage and virginity or celibacy are two ways of expressing and living the one mystery of the covenant of God with His people. When marriage is not esteemed, neither can consecrated virginity or celibacy exist; when human sexuality is not regarded as a great value given by the Creator, the renunciation of it for the sake of the Kingdom of Heaven loses its meaning.

Rightly indeed does St. John Chrysostom say: "Whoever denigrates marriage also diminishes the glory of virginity. Whoever praises it makes virginity more admirable and resplendent. What appears good only in comparison with evil would not be particularly good. It is something better than what is admitted to be good that is the most excellent good."

In virginity or celibacy, the human being is awaiting, also in a bodily way, the eschatological marriage of Christ with the Church, giving himself or herself completely to the Church in the hope that Christ may give Himself to the Church in the full truth of eternal life. The celibate person thus anticipates in his or her flesh the new world of the future resurrection.

By virtue of this witness, virginity or celibacy keeps alive in the Church a consciousness of the mystery of marriage and defends it from any reduction and impoverishment.

Virginity or celibacy, by liberating the human heart in a unique way, "so as to make it burn with greater love for God and all humanity," bears witness that the Kingdom of God and His justice is that pearl of great price which is preferred to every other value no matter how great, and hence must be sought as the only definitive value. It is for this reason that the Church, throughout her history, has always defended the superiority of this charism to that of marriage, by reason of the wholly singular link which it has with the Kingdom of God.

In spite of having renounced physical fecundity, the celibate person becomes spiritually fruitful, the father and mother of many, cooperating in the realization of the family according to God's plan.

Christian couples therefore have the right to expect from celibate persons a good example and a witness of fidelity to their vocation until death. Just as fidelity at times becomes difficult for married people and requires sacrifice, mortification and self-denial, the same can happen to celibate persons, and their fidelity, even in the trials that may occur, should strengthen the fidelity of married couples.

These reflections on virginity or celibacy can enlighten and help those who, for reasons independent of their own will, have been unable to marry and have then accepted their situation in a spirit of service.

PART THREE

THE ROLE OF THE CHRISTIAN FAMILY

Family, Become What You Are

17. The family finds in the plan of God the Creator and Redeemer not only its identity, what it is, but also its mission, what it can and should do. The role that God calls the family to perform in history derives from what the family is; its role represents the dynamic and existential development of what it is. Each family finds within itself a summons that cannot be ignored, and that specifies both its dignity and its responsibility: family, become what you are.

Accordingly, the family must go back to the "beginning" of God's creative act, if it is to attain self-knowledge and self-realization in accordance with the inner truth not only of what it is but also of what it does in history. And since in God's plan it has been established as an "intimate community of life and love," the family has the mission to become more and more what it is, that is to say, a community of life and love, in an effort that will find fulfillment, as will everything created and redeemed, in the Kingdom of God. Looking at it in such a way as to reach its very roots, we must say that the essence and role of the family are in the final analysis specified by love. Hence the family has the mission to guard, reveal and communicate love, and this is a living reflection of and a real sharing in God's love for humanity and the love of Christ the Lord for the Church His bride.

Every particular task of the family is an expressive and concrete actuation of that fundamental mission. We must therefore go deeper into the unique riches of the family's mission and probe its contents, which are both manifold and unified.

Thus, with love as its point of departure and making constant reference to it, the recent Synod emphasized four general tasks for the family:

1) forming a community of persons;
2) serving life;
3) participating in the development of society;
4) sharing in the life and mission of the Church.

I – FORMING A COMMUNITY OF PERSONS

Love as the Principle and Power of Communion

18. The family, which is founded and given life by love, is a community of persons: of husband and wife, of parents and children, of relatives. Its first task is to live with fidelity the reality of communion in a constant effort to develop an authentic community of persons.

The inner principle of that task, its permanent power and its final goal is love: without love the family is not a community of persons and, in the same way, without love the family cannot live, grow and perfect itself as a community of persons. What I wrote in the Encyclical Redemptor hominis applies primarily and especially within the family as such: "Man cannot live without love. He remains a being that is incomprehensible for himself, his life is senseless, if love is not revealed to him, if he does not encounter love, if he does not experience it and make it his own, if he does not participate intimately in it."

The love between husband and wife and, in a derivatory and broader way, the love between members of the same family – between parents and children, brothers and sisters and relatives and members of the household – is given life and sustenance by an unceasing inner dynamism leading the family to ever deeper and more intense communion, which is the foundation and soul of the community of marriage and the family.

The Indivisible Unity of Conjugal Communion

19. The first communion is the one which is established and which develops between husband and wife: by virtue of the covenant of married life, the man and woman "are no longer two but one flesh" and they are called to grow continually in their communion through day-to-day fidelity to their marriage promise of total mutual self-giving.

This conjugal communion sinks its roots in the natural complementarity that exists between man and woman, and is nurtured through the personal willingness of the spouses to share their entire life-project, what they have and what they are: for this reason such communion is the fruit and the sign of a profoundly human need. But in the Lord Christ God takes up this human need, confirms it, purifies it and elevates it, leading it to perfection through the sacrament of matrimony: the Holy Spirit who is poured out in the sacramental celebration offers Christian couples the gift of a new communion of love that is the living and real image of that unique unity which makes of the Church the indivisible Mystical Body of the Lord Jesus.

The gift of the Spirit is a commandment of life for Christian spouses and at the same time a stimulating impulse so that every day they may progress towards an ever richer union with each other on all levels – of the body, of the character, of the heart, of the intelligence and will, of the soul – revealing in this way to the Church and to the world the new communion of love, given by the grace of Christ.

Such a communion is radically contradicted by polygamy: this, in fact, directly negates the plan of God which was revealed from the beginning, because it is contrary to the equal personal dignity of men and women who in matrimony give themselves with a love that is total and therefore unique and exclusive. As the Second Vatican Council writes: "Firmly established by the Lord, the unity of marriage will radiate from the equal personal dignity of husband and wife, a dignity acknowledged by mutual and total love."

An Indissoluble Communion

20. Conjugal communion is characterized not only by its unity but also by its indissolubility: "As a mutual gift of two persons, this intimate union, as well as the good of children, imposes total fidelity on the spouses and argues for an unbreakable oneness between them."

It is a fundamental duty of the Church to reaffirm strongly, as the Synod Fathers did, the doctrine of the indissolubility of marriage. To all those who, in our times, consider it too difficult, or indeed impossible, to be bound to one person for the whole of life, and to those caught up in a culture that rejects the indissolubility of marriage and openly mocks the commitment of spouses to fidelity, it is necessary to reconfirm the good news of the definitive nature of that conjugal love that has in Christ its foundation and strength.

Being rooted in the personal and total self-giving of the couple, and being required by the good of the children, the indissolubility of marriage finds its ultimate truth in the plan that God has manifested in His revelation: He wills and He communicates the indissolubility of marriage as a fruit, a sign and a requirement of the absolutely faithful love that God has for man and that the Lord Jesus has for the Church.

Christ renews the first plan that the Creator inscribed in the hearts of man and woman, and in the celebration of the sacrament of matrimony offers a "new heart": thus the couples are not only able to overcome "hardness of heart," but also and above all they are able to share the full and definitive love of Christ, the new and eternal Covenant made flesh. Just as the Lord Jesus is the "faithful witness," the "yes" of the promises of God and thus the supreme realization of the unconditional faithfulness with which God loves His people, so Christian couples are called to participate truly in the irrevocable indissolubility that binds Christ to the Church His bride, loved by Him to the end.

The gift of the sacrament is at the same time a vocation and commandment for the Christian spouses, that they may remain faithful to each other forever, beyond every trial and difficulty, in generous obedience to the holy will of the Lord: "What therefore God has joined together, let not man put asunder."

To bear witness to the inestimable value of the indissolubility and fidelity of marriage is one of the most precious and most urgent tasks of Christian couples in our time. So, with all my Brothers who participated in the Synod of Bishops, I praise and encourage those numerous couples who, though encountering no small difficulty, preserve and develop the value of indissolubility: thus, in a humble and courageous manner, they perform the role committed to them of being in the world a "sign" – a small and precious sign, sometimes also subjected to temptation, but always renewed – of the unfailing fidelity with which God and Jesus Christ love each and every human being. But it is also proper to recognize the value of the witness of those spouses who, even when abandoned by their partner, with the strength of faith and of Christian hope have not entered a new union: these spouses too give an authentic witness to fidelity, of which the world today has a great need. For this reason they must be encouraged and helped by the pastors and the faithful of the Church. . . .

The Rights and Role of Women

22. In that it is, and ought always to become, a communion and community of persons, the family finds in love the source and the constant impetus for welcoming, respecting and promoting each one of its members in his or her lofty dignity as a person, that is, as a living image of God. As the Synod Fathers rightly stated, the moral criterion for the authenticity of conjugal and family relationships consists in fostering the dignity and vocation of the individual persons, who achieve their fullness by sincere self-giving.

In this perspective the Synod devoted special attention to women, to their rights and role within the family and society. In the same perspective are also to be considered men as husbands and fathers, and likewise children and the elderly.

Above all it is important to underline the equal dignity and responsibility of women with men. This equality is realized in a unique manner in that reciprocal self-giving by each one to the other and by both to the children which is proper to marriage and the family. What human reason intuitively perceives and acknowledges is fully revealed by the word of God: the history of salvation, in fact, is a continuous and luminous testimony of the dignity of women.

In creating the human race "male and female," God gives man and woman an equal personal dignity, endowing them with the inalienable rights and responsibilities proper to the human person. God then manifests the dignity of women in the highest form possible, by assuming human flesh from the Virgin Mary, whom the Church honors as the Mother of God, calling her the new Eve and presenting her as the model of redeemed woman. The sensitive respect of Jesus towards the women that He called to His following and His friendship, His appearing on Easter morning to a woman before the other disciples, the mission entrusted to women to carry the good news of the Resurrection to the apostles – these are all signs that confirm the special esteem of the Lord Jesus for women. The Apostle Paul will say: "In Christ Jesus you are all children of God through faith.... There is neither Jew nor Greek, there is neither slave nor free, there is neither male nor female; for you are all one in Christ Jesus."

Women and Society

23. Without intending to deal with all the various aspects of the vast and complex theme of the relationships between women and society, and limiting these remarks to a few essential points, one cannot but observe that in the specific area of family life a widespread social and cultural tradition has considered women's role to be exclusively that of wife and mother, without adequate access to public functions which have generally been reserved for men.

There is no doubt that the equal dignity and responsibility of men and women fully justifies women's access to public functions. On the other hand the true advancement of women requires that clear recognition be given to the value of their maternal and family role, by comparison with all other public roles and all other professions. Furthermore, these roles and professions should be harmoniously combined, if we wish the evolution of society and culture to be truly and fully human.

This will come about more easily if, in accordance with the wishes expressed by the Synod, a renewed "theology of work" can shed light upon and study in depth the meaning of work in the Christian life and determine the fundamental bond between work and the family, and therefore the original and irreplaceable meaning of work in the home and in rearing children. Therefore the Church can and should help modern society by tirelessly insisting that the work of women in the home be recognized and respected by all in its irreplaceable value. This is of particular importance in education: for possible discrimination between the different types of work and professions is eliminated at its very root once it is clear that all people, in every area, are working with equal rights and equal responsibilities. The image of God in man and in woman will thus be seen with added luster.

While it must be recognized that women have the same right as men to perform various public functions, society must be structured in such a way that wives and mothers are not in practice compelled to work outside the home, and that their families can live and prosper in a dignified way even when they themselves devote their full time to their own family.

Furthermore, the mentality which honors women more for their work outside the home than for their work within the family must be overcome. This requires that men should truly esteem and love women with total respect for their personal dignity, and that society should create and develop conditions favoring work in the home.

With due respect to the different vocations of men and women, the Church must in her own life promote as far as possible their equality of rights and dignity: and this for the good of all, the family, the Church and society.

But clearly all of this does not mean for women a renunciation of their femininity or an imitation of the male role, but the fullness of true feminine humanity which should be expressed in their activity, whether in the family or outside of it, without disregarding the differences of customs and cultures in this sphere.

Offenses against Women's Dignity

24. Unfortunately the Christian message about the dignity of women is contradicted by that persistent mentality which considers the human being not as a person but as a thing, as an object of trade, at the service of selfish interest and mere pleasure: the first victims of this mentality are women.

This mentality produces very bitter fruits, such as contempt for men and for women, slavery, oppression of the weak, pornography, prostitution – especially in an organized form – and all those various forms of discrimination that exist in the fields of education, employment, wages, etc.

Besides, many forms of degrading discrimination still persist today in a great part of our society that affect and seriously harm particular categories of women, as for example childless wives, widows, separated or divorced women, and unmarried mothers.

The Synod Fathers deplored these and other forms of discrimination as strongly as possible. I therefore ask that vigorous and incisive pastoral action be taken by all to overcome them definitively so that the image of God that shines in all human beings without exception may be fully respected. . . .

Associations of Families for Families

72. Still within the Church, which is the subject responsible for the pastoral care of the family, mention should be made of the various groupings of members of the faithful in which the mystery of Christ's Church is in some measure manifested and lived. One should therefore recognize and make good use of – each one in relationship to its own characteristics, purposes, effectiveness and methods – the different ecclesial communities, the various groups and the numerous movements engaged in various ways, for different reasons and at different levels, in the pastoral care of the family.

For this reason the Synod expressly recognized the useful contribution made by such associations of spirituality, formation and apostolate. It will be their task to foster among the faithful a lively sense of solidarity, to favor a manner of living inspired by the Gospel and by the faith of the Church, to form consciences according to Christian values and not according to the standards of public opinion; to stimulate people to perform works of charity for one another and for others with a spirit of openness which will make Christian families into a true source of light and a wholesome leaven for other families.

It is similarly desirable that, with a lively sense of the common good, Christian families should become actively engaged, at every level, in other non-ecclesial associations as well. Some of these associations work for the preservation, transmission and protection of the wholesome ethical and cultural values of each people, the development of the human person, the medical, juridical and social protection of mothers and young children, the just advancement of women and the struggle against all that is detrimental to their dignity, the increase of mutual solidarity, knowledge of the problems connected with the responsible regulation of fertility in accordance with natural methods that are in conformity with human dignity and the teaching of the Church. Other associations work for the building of a more just and human world; for the promotion of just laws favoring the right social order with full respect for the dignity and every legitimate freedom of the individual and the family, on both the national and international level; for collaboration with the school and with the other institutions that complete the education of children, and so forth. . . .

CONCLUSION

86. At the end of this Apostolic Exhortation my thoughts turn with earnest solicitude:

to you, married couples, to you, fathers and mothers of families;

to you, young men and women, the future and the hope of the Church and the world, destined to be the dynamic central nucleus of the family in the approaching third millennium;

to you, venerable and dear Brothers in the Episcopate and in the priesthood, beloved sons and daughters in the religious life, souls consecrated to the Lord, who bear witness before married couples to the ultimate reality of the love of God;

to you, upright men and women, who for any reason whatever give thought to the fate of the family.

The future of humanity passes by way of the family.

It is therefore indispensable and urgent that every person of good will should endeavor to save and foster the values and requirements of the family.

I feel that I must ask for a particular effort in this field from the sons and daughters of the Church. Faith gives them full knowledge of God's wonderful plan: they therefore have an extra reason for caring for the reality that is the family in this time of trial and of grace.

They must show the family special love. This is an injunction that calls for concrete action.

Loving the family means being able to appreciate its values and capabilities, fostering them always. Loving the family means identifying the dangers and the evils that menace it, in order to overcome them. Loving the family means endeavoring to create for it an environment favorable for its development. The modern Christian family is often tempted to be discouraged and is distressed at the growth of its difficulties; it is an eminent form of love to give it back its reasons for confidence in itself, in the riches that it possesses by nature and grace, and in the mission that God has entrusted to it. "Yes indeed, the families of today must be called back to their original position. They must follow Christ."

Christians also have the mission of proclaiming with joy and conviction the Good News about the family, for the family absolutely needs to hear ever anew and to understand ever more deeply the authentic words that reveal its identity, its inner resources and the importance of its mission in the City of God and in that of man.

The Church knows the path by which the family can reach the heart of the deepest truth about itself. The Church has learned this path at the school of Christ and the school of history interpreted in the light of the Spirit. She does not impose it but she feels an urgent need to propose it to everyone without fear and indeed with great confidence and hope, although she knows that the Good News includes the subject of the Cross. But it is through the Cross that the family can attain the fullness of its being and the perfection of its love.

Finally, I wish to call on all Christians to collaborate cordially and courageously with all people of good will who are serving the family in accordance with their responsibilities. The individuals and groups, movements and associations in the Church which devote themselves to the family's welfare, acting in the Church's name and under her inspiration, often find themselves side by side with other individuals and institutions working for the same ideal. With faithfulness to the values of the Gospel and of the human person and with respect for lawful pluralism in initiatives this collaboration can favor a more rapid and integral advancement of the family.

And now, at the end of my pastoral message, which is intended to draw everyone's attention to the demanding yet fascinating roles of the Christian family, I wish to invoke the protection of the Holy Family of Nazareth.

Through God's mysterious design, it was in that family that the Son of God spent long years of a hidden life. It is therefore the prototype and example for all Christian families. It was unique in the world. Its life was passed in anonymity and silence in a little town in Palestine. It underwent trials of poverty, persecution and exile. It glorified God in an incomparably exalted and pure way. And it will not fail to help Christian families – indeed, all the families in the world – to be faithful to their day-to-day duties, to bear the cares and tribulations of life, to be open and generous to the needs of others, and to fulfill with joy the plan of God in their regard.

St. Joseph was "a just man," a tireless worker, the upright guardian of those entrusted to his care. May he always guard, protect and enlighten families.

May the Virgin Mary, who is the Mother of the Church, also be the Mother of "the Church of the home." Thanks to her motherly aid, may each Christian family really become a "little Church" in which the mystery of the Church of Christ is mirrored and given new life. May she, the Handmaid of the Lord, be an example of humble and generous acceptance of the will of God. May she, the Sorrowful Mother at the foot of the Cross, comfort the sufferings and dry the tears of those in distress because of the difficulties of their families.

May Christ the Lord, the Universal King, the King of Families, be present in every Christian home as He was at Cana, bestowing light, joy, serenity and strength. On the solemn day dedicated to His Kingship I beg of Him that every family may generously make its own contribution to the coming of His Kingdom in the world – "a kingdom of truth and life, a kingdom of holiness and grace, a kingdom of justice, love, and peace," 183 towards which history is journeying.

I entrust each family to Him, to Mary, and to Joseph. To their hands and their hearts I offer this Exhortation: may it be they who present it to you, venerable Brothers and beloved sons and daughters, and may it be they who open your hearts to the light that the Gospel sheds on every family.

I assure you all of my constant prayers and I cordially impart the apostolic blessing to each and every one of you, in the name of the Father, and of the Son, and of the Holy Spirit.

Given in Rome, at St. Peter's, on the twenty-second day of November, the Solemnity of our Lord Jesus Christ, Universal King, in the year 1981, the fourth of the Pontificate.

MULIERIS DIGNITATEM

APOSTOLIC LETTER OF THE SUPREME PONTIFF
JOHN PAUL II
ON THE
DIGNITY AND VOCATION
OF WOMEN
ON THE OCCASION
OF THE MARIAN YEAR

15 AUGUST 1988

Venerable Brothers and dear Sons and Daughters,
Health and the Apostolic Blessing.

I

INTRODUCTION

A sign of the times

1. THE DIGNITY AND THE VOCATION OF WOMEN – a subject of constant human and Christian reflection – have gained exceptional prominence in recent years. This can be seen, for example, *in the statements of the Church's Magisterium* present in various documents *of the Second Vatican Council,* which declares in its Closing Message: "The hour is coming, in fact has come, when the vocation of women is being acknowledged in its fullness, the hour in which women acquire in the world an influence, an effect and a power never hitherto achieved. That is why, at his moment when the human race is undergoing so deep a transformation, women imbued with a spirit of the Gospel can do so much to aid humanity in not falling." *This Message* sums up what had already been expressed in the Council's teaching, specifically in the Pastoral Constitution *Gaudium et Spes* and in the Decree on the Apostolate of the Laity *Apostolicam Actuositatem*.
Similar thinking had already been put forth in the period before the Council, as can be seen in a number of Pope *Pius XII's* Discourses and

in the Encyclical *Pacem in Terris* of Pope *John XXIII*. After the Second Vatican Council, my predecessor *Paul VI* showed the relevance of this "sign of the times," when he conferred the title "Doctor of the Church" upon Saint Teresa of Jesus and Saint Catherine of Siena, and likewise when, at the request of the 1971 Assembly of the Synod of Bishops, he set up *a special Commission* for the study of contemporary problems concerning the *"effective promotion of the dignity and the responsibility of women."* In one of his Discourses Paul VI said: "Within Christianity, more than in any other religion, and since its very beginning, women have had a special dignity, of which the New Testament shows us many important aspects . . . ; it is evident that women are meant to form part of the living and working structure of Christianity in so prominent a manner that perhaps not all their potentialities have yet been made clear."

The Fathers of the recent Assembly of the Synod of Bishops (October 1987), which was devoted to "The Vocation and Mission of the Laity in the Church and in the World Twenty Years after the Second Vatican Council," once more dealt with the dignity and vocation of women. One of their recommendations was for a further study of the anthropological and theological bases that are needed in order to solve the problems connected with the meaning and dignity of being a woman and being a man. It is a question of understanding the reason for and the consequences of the Creator's decision that the human being should always and only exist as a woman or a man. It is only by beginning from these bases, which make it possible to understand the greatness of the dignity and vocation of women, that one is able to speak of their active presence in the Church and in society.

This is what I intend to deal with in this document. The Post-Synodal Exhortation, which will be published later, will present proposals of a pastoral nature on the place of women in the Church and in society. On this subject the Fathers offered some important reflections, after they had taken into consideration the testimonies of the lay Auditors – both women and men – from the particular Churches throughout the world. . . .

III

THE IMAGE AND LIKENESS OF GOD

The Book of Genesis

6. Let us enter into the setting of the biblical "beginning." In it the revealed truth concerning man as "the image and likeness" of God constitutes the immutable *basis of all Christian anthropology*. "God created

man in his own image, in the image of God he created him; male and female he created them" (*Gen* 1:27). This concise passage contains the fundamental anthropological truths: man is the highpoint of the whole order of creation in the visible world; the human race, which takes its origin from the calling into existence of man and woman, crowns the whole work of creation; *both man and woman are human beings to an equal degree,* both are created *in God's image.* This image and likeness of God, which is essential for the human being, is passed on by the man and woman, as spouses and parents, to their descendants: "Be fruitful and multiply, and fill the earth and subdue it" (*Gen* 1:28). The Creator entrusts dominion over the earth to the human race, to all persons, to all men and women, who derive their dignity and vocation from the common "beginning."

In the Book of Genesis we find another description of the creation of man – man and woman (cf. 2:18–25) – to which we shall refer shortly. At this point, however, we can say that the biblical account puts forth the truth about the personal character of the human being. *Man is a person, man and woman equally so*, since both were created in the image and likeness of the personal God. What makes man like God is the fact that – unlike the whole world of other living creatures, including those endowed with senses *(animalia)* – man is also a rational being *(animal rationale)*. Thanks to this property, man and woman are able to "dominate" the other creatures of the visible world (cf. *Gen* 1:28).

The second description of the creation of man (cf. *Gen* 2:18–25) makes use of different language to express the truth about the creation of man, and especially of woman. In a sense the language is less precise, and, one might say, more descriptive and metaphorical, closer to the language of the myths known at the time. Nevertheless, we find no essential contradiction between the two texts. The text of *Gen* 2:18–25 helps us to understand better what we find in the concise passage of *Gen* 1:27–28. At the same time, if it is read together with the latter, it *helps us to understand even more profoundly* the fundamental *truth* which it contains *concerning man* created as man and woman in the image and likeness of God.

In the description found in *Gen* 2:18–25, the woman is created by God "from the rib" of the man and is placed at his side as another "I," as the companion of the man, who is alone in the surrounding world of living creatures and who finds in none of them a "helper" suitable for himself. Called into existence in this way, the woman is immediately recognized by the man as "flesh of his flesh and bone of his bones" (cf. *Gen* 2:23) and for this very reason she is called "woman." In biblical language this name indicates her essential identity with regard to man – *'is-'issah* – something which unfortunately modern languages in general are unable to express: "She shall be called woman ('issah) because she was taken out of man ('is)": *Gen* 2:23.

The biblical text provides sufficient bases for recognizing the essential equality of man and woman from the point of view of their humanity. From the very beginning, both are persons, unlike the other living beings in the world about them. *The woman is another "I" in a common humanity.* From the very beginning they appear as a "unity of the two," and this signifies that the original solitude is overcome, the solitude in which man does not find "a helper fit for him" *(Gen* 2:20). Is it only a question here of a "helper" in activity, in "subduing the earth" (cf. *Gen* 1:28)? Certainly it is a matter of a life's companion, with whom, as a wife, the man can unite himself, becoming with her "one flesh" and for this reason leaving "his father and his mother" (cf. *Gen* 2:24). Thus in the same context as the creation of man and woman, the biblical account speaks of God's *instituting marriage* as an indispensable condition for the transmission of life to new generations, the transmission of life to which marriage and conjugal love are by their nature ordered: "Be fruitful and multiply, and fill the earth and subdue it" *(Gen* 1:28).

Person – Communion – Gift

7. By reflecting on the whole account found in *Gen* 2:18–25, and by interpreting it in light of the truth about the image and likeness of God (cf. *Gen* 1:26–27), we can *understand* even *more fully what constitutes the personal character* of the human being, thanks to which both man and woman are like God. For every individual is made in the image of God, insofar as he or she is a rational and free creature capable of knowing God and loving him. Moreover, we read that man cannot exist "alone" (cf. *Gen* 2:18); he can exist only as a "unity of the two," and therefore *in relation to another human person.* It is a question here of a mutual relationship: man to woman and woman to man. Being a person in the image and likeness of God thus also involves existing in a relationship, in relation to the other "I." This is a prelude to the definitive self-revelation of the Triune God: a living unity in the communion of the Father, Son and Holy Spirit.

At the beginning of the Bible this is not yet stated directly. The whole Old Testament is mainly concerned with revealing the truth about the oneness and unity of God. Within this fundamental truth about God the New Testament will reveal the inscrutable mystery of God's inner life. *God*, who allows himself to be known by human beings through Christ, is the *unity of the Trinity*: unity in communion. In this way new light is also thrown on man's image and likeness to God, spoken of in the Book of Genesis. The fact that man "created as man and woman" is the image of God means not only that each of them individually is like God, as a rational and free being. It also means that man and woman, created as a "unity of the two" in their common humanity, are called to live in a communion of love, and in this way to mirror in the world the communion of love that is in God, through which the Three Persons love each other in the intimate mystery of the one divine life. The Father, Son and Holy Spirit, one God through the unity of the divinity, exist as persons through the inscrutable divine relationship. Only in this way can we understand the truth that God in himself is love (cf. 1 *Jn* 4:16).

The image and likeness of God in man, created as man and woman (in the analogy that can be presumed between Creator and creature), thus also expresses the "unity of the two" in a common humanity. This "unity of the two," which is a sign of interpersonal communion, *shows that the creation of man is* also marked by a certain likeness to the divine communion (*"communio"*). This likeness is a quality of the personal being of both man and woman, and is also a call and a task. The foundation of the whole *human "ethos" is* rooted in the image and likeness of God which the human being bears within himself from the beginning. Both the Old and New Testament will develop that "ethos," which reaches its apex in the *commandment of love*.

In the "unity of the two," man and woman are called from the beginning not only to exist "side by side" or "together," but they are also called *to exist mutually "one for the other."*

This also explains the meaning of the "help" spoken of in Genesis 2:18–25: "I will make him *a helper fit for him*." The biblical context enables us to understand this in the sense that the woman must "help" the man – and in his turn he must help her – first of all by the very fact of their "being human persons." In a certain sense this enables man and woman to discover their humanity ever anew and to confirm its whole meaning. We can easily understand that – on this fundamental level – it is a question of a *"help" on the part of both, and at the same time a mutual "help."* To be human means to be called to interpersonal communion. The text of Genesis 2:18–25 shows that marriage is the first and, in a sense, the fundamental dimension of this call. But it is not the only one. The whole of human history unfolds within the context of this call. In this history, on the basis of the principle of mutually being "for" the other, in interpersonal "communion," there develops in humanity itself, in accordance with God's will, the integration of what is *"masculine" and what is "feminine."* The biblical texts, from Genesis onwards, constantly enable us to discover the ground in which the truth about man is rooted, the solid and inviolable ground amid the many changes of human existence.

This truth also has to do with *the history of salvation*. In this regard a statement of the Second Vatican Council is especially significant. In the chapter on "The Community of Mankind" in the Pastoral Constitution *Gaudium et Spes*, we read: "The Lord Jesus, when he prayed to the Father 'that all may be one . . . as we are one' (*Jn* 17: 21–22), opened up vistas closed to human reason. For he implied *a certain likeness* between the union of the divine Persons and the union of God's children in truth and charity. This likeness reveals that man, who is the only creature on earth which God willed for its own sake, cannot fully find himself except through a sincere gift of self."

With these words, the Council text presents a summary of the whole truth about man and woman – a truth which is already outlined in the first chapters of the Book of Genesis, and which is the structural basis of biblical and Christian anthropology. *Man* – whether man or woman – is *the only being among the creatures* of the visible world *that God the Creator "has willed for its own sake"*; that creature is thus a person. Being a person means striving towards self-realization (the Council text speaks of self-discovery), which can only be achieved *"through a sincere gift of self."* The model for this interpretation of the person is God himself as Trinity, as a communion of Persons. To say that man is created in the image and likeness of God means that man is called to exist "for" others, to become a gift.

This applies to every human being, whether woman or man, who live it out in accordance with the special qualities proper to each. Within the framework of the present meditation on the dignity and vocation of women, this truth about being human constitutes the *indispensable point of departure*. Already in the Book of Genesis we can discern, in preliminary outline, the spousal character of the relationship between persons, which will serve as the basis for the subsequent development of the truth about motherhood, and about virginity, as two particular dimensions of the vocation of women in the light of divine Revelation. These two dimensions will find their loftiest expression at the "fullness of time" (cf. *Gal* 4:4) in the "woman" of Nazareth: the Virgin-Mother.

The anthropomorphism of biblical language

8. The presentation of man as "the image and likeness of God" at the very beginning of Sacred Scripture has *another significance too*. It is the key for understanding biblical Revelation as God's word about himself. Speaking about himself, whether through the prophets, or through the Son" (cf. *Heb* 1:1, 2) who became man, *God speaks in human language*, using human concepts and images. If this manner of expressing himself is characterized by a certain anthropomorphism, the reason is that man is "like" God: created in his image and likeness. But then, *God too is* in some measure "like man," and precisely because of this likeness, he can be humanly known. At the same time, the language of the Bible is sufficiently precise to indicate the limits of the "likeness," the limits of the "analogy." For biblical Revelation says that, while man's "likeness" to God is true, the *"non-likeness"* which separates the whole of creation from the Creator is *still more essentially true*. Although man is created in

God's likeness, God does not cease to be for him the one "who dwells in unapproachable light" (1 *Tim* 6:16): he is the "Different One," by essence the "totally Other."

This observation on the limits of the analogy – the limits of man's likeness to God in biblical language – must also be kept in mind when, in different passages of Sacred Scripture (especially in the Old Testament), we find *comparisons that attribute to God "masculine" or "feminine" qualities*. We find in these passages an indirect confirmation of the truth that both man and woman were created in the image and likeness of God. If there is a likeness between Creator and creatures, it is understandable that the Bible would refer to God using expressions that attribute to him both "masculine" and "feminine" qualities.

We may quote here some characteristic passages from the prophet *Isaiah*: "But Zion said, 'The Lord has forsaken me, my Lord has forgotten me.' *'Can a woman forget* her sucking child, that she should have no compassion on the son of her womb? Even these may forget, yet I will *not* forget you'" (49:14–15). And elsewhere: "As one whom his *mother* comforts, so will I comfort you; you shall be comforted in Jerusalem" (66:13). In the Psalms too God is compared to a caring mother: "Like a child quieted at its mother's breast; like a child that is quieted is my soul. O Israel, hope in the Lord" (*Ps* 131:2–3). In various passages the love of God who cares for his people is shown to be like that of a mother: thus, *like a mother God* "has carried" humanity, and in particular, his Chosen People, within his own womb; he has given birth to it in travail, has nourished and comforted it (cf. *Is* 42:14; 46:3–4). In many passages God's love is presented as the "masculine" love of the bridegroom and father (cf. *Hosea* 11:1–4; *Jer* 3:4–19), but also sometimes as the "feminine" love of a mother.

This characteristic of biblical language – its anthropomorphic way of speaking about God – *points* indirectly *to the mystery of the eternal "generating"* which belongs to the inner life of God. Nevertheless, in itself this "generating" has neither "masculine" nor "feminine" qualities. It is by nature totally divine. It is spiritual in the most perfect way, since "God is spirit" (*Jn* 4:24) and possesses no property typical of the body, neither "feminine" nor "masculine." Thus even *"fatherhood" in God is completely divine* and free of the "masculine" bodily characteristics proper to human fatherhood. In this sense the Old Testament spoke of God as a Father and turned to him as a Father. Jesus Christ – who called God "Abba Father" (*Mk* 14: 36), and who as the only-begotten and consubstantial Son placed this truth at the very centre of his Gospel, thus establishing the norm of Christian prayer – referred to fatherhood in this ultra-corporeal, superhuman and completely divine sense. He spoke as the Son, joined to the Father by the eternal mystery of divine generation, and he did so while being at the same time the truly human Son of his Virgin Mother.

Although it is not possible to attribute human qualities to the eternal generation of the Word of God, and although the divine fatherhood does not possess "masculine" characteristics in a physical sense, we must nevertheless seek in God the absolute *model* of all "*generation*" among human beings. This would seem to be the sense of the Letter to the Ephesians: "I bow my knees before the Father, from whom every family in heaven and on earth is named" (3:14–15). All "generating" among creatures finds its primary model in that generating which in God is completely divine, that is, spiritual. All "generating" in the created world is to be likened to this absolute and uncreated model. Thus every element of human generation which is proper to man, and every element which is proper to woman, namely human "*fatherhood*" and "*motherhood*," bears within itself a likeness to, or analogy with the divine "generating" and with that "fatherhood" which in God is "totally different," that is, completely spiritual and divine in essence; whereas in the human order, generation is proper to the "unity of the two": both are "parents," the man and the woman alike.

IV

EVE-MARY

The "beginning" and the sin

9. "Although he was made by God in a state of justice, from the very dawn of history man abused his liberty, at the urging of the Evil One. Man set himself against God and sought to find fulfillment apart from God." With these words the teaching of the last Council recalls the revealed doctrine about sin and in particular about that first sin, which is the "original" one. The biblical "beginning" – the creation of the world and of man in the world – *contains* in itself *the truth* about *this sin*, which can also be called the sin of man's "beginning" on the earth. Even though what is written in the Book of Genesis is expressed in the form of a symbolic narrative, as is the case in the description of the creation of man as male and female (cf. *Gen* 2:18–25), at the same time it reveals what should be called "the mystery of sin," and even more fully, "the mystery of evil" which exists in the world created by God.

It is not possible to read "the mystery of sin" without making reference to the whole truth about the "image and likeness" to God, which is the basis of biblical anthropology. This truth presents the creation of man as a special gift from the Creator, containing not only the foundation and source of the essential dignity of the human being – man and woman – in the created world, but also *the beginning of the call to both of them to share in the intimate life of God himself.* In the light of

Revelation, *creation likewise means the beginning of salvation history.* It is precisely in this beginning that sin is situated and manifests itself as opposition and negation.

It can be said, paradoxically, that the sin presented in the third chapter of Genesis confirms the truth about the image and likeness of God in man, since this truth means freedom, that is, man's use of free will by choosing good or his abuse of it by choosing evil, against the will of God. In its essence, however, sin is a negation of God as Creator in his relationship to man, and of what God wills for man, from the beginning and for ever. Creating man and woman in his own image and likeness, God wills for them the fullness of good, or supernatural happiness, which flows from sharing in his own life. *By committing sin man rejects this gift* and at the same time wills to become "as God, knowing good and evil" (*Gen* 3:5), that is to say, deciding what is good and what is evil independently of God, his Creator. The sin of the first parents has its own human "measure": an interior standard of its own in man's free will, and it also has within itself a certain "diabolic" characteristic, which is clearly shown in the Book of Genesis (3:15). Sin brings about a break in the original unity which man enjoyed in the state of original justice: union with God as the source of the unity within his own "I," in the mutual relationship between man and woman ("*communio personarum*") as well as in regard to the external world, to nature.

The biblical description of original sin in the third chapter of Genesis in a certain way "distinguishes the roles" which the woman and the man had in it. This is also referred to later in certain passages of the Bible, for example, Paul's Letter to Timothy: "For Adam was formed first, then Eve; and Adam was not deceived, but the woman was deceived and became a transgressor" (1 *Tim* 2:13–14). But there is no doubt that, independent of this "distinction of roles" in the biblical description, *that first sin is the sin of man,* created by God as male and female. It is also *the sin of the "first parents,"* to which is connected its hereditary character. In this sense we call it "original sin."

This sin, as already said, *cannot be properly understood without reference to the mystery of the creation* of the human being – man and woman – *in the image and likeness of God.* By means of this reference one can also understand the mystery of that "non-likeness" to God in which sin consists, and which manifests itself in the evil present in the history of the world. Similarly one can understand the mystery of that "non-likeness" to God, who "alone is good" (cf. *Mt* 19:17) and – the fullness of good. If sin's "non-likeness" to God, who is Holiness itself, presupposes "likeness" in the sphere of freedom and free will, it can then be said that for this very reason the *"non-likeness" contained in sin* is all the more tragic and sad. It must be admitted that God, as Creator and Father, is here wounded, "offended" – obviously offended – in the very heart of that gift which belongs to God's eternal plan for man.

At the same time, however, as the author of the evil of sin, *the human being – man and woman – is affected by it.* The third chapter of Genesis shows this with the words which clearly describe the new situation of man in the created world. It shows the perspective of "toil," by which man will earn his living (cf. *Gen* 3:17–19) and likewise the great "pain" with which the woman will give birth to her children (cf. *Gen* 3:16). And all this is marked by the necessity of death, which is the end of human life on earth. In this way man, as dust, will "return to the ground, for out of it he was taken": "you are dust, and to dust you shall return" (cf. *Gen* 3:19).

These words are confirmed generation after generation. They do not mean that *the image and the likeness of God in the human being,* whether woman or man, has been destroyed by sin; they mean rather that it has been "*obscured*" and in a sense "diminished." Sin in fact "diminishes" man, as the Second Vatican Council also recalls. If man is the image and likeness of God by his very nature as a person, then his greatness and his dignity are achieved in the covenant with God, in union with him, in striving towards that fundamental unity which belongs to the internal "logic" of the very mystery of creation. This unity corresponds to the profound truth concerning all intelligent creatures and in particular concerning man, who among all the creatures of the visible world was *elevated* from the beginning through the eternal choice of God in Jesus: "He chose us in (Christ) before the foundation of the world, . . . He destined us in love to be his sons through Jesus Christ, according to the purpose of his will" (*Eph* 1:4–6). The biblical teaching taken as a whole enables us to say that predestination concerns all human persons, men and women, each and every one without exception.

"He shall rule over you"

10. The biblical description in the Book of Genesis outlines the truth about the consequences of man's sin, as it is shown by *the disturbance* of that original *relationship between man and woman* which corresponds to their individual dignity as persons. A human being, whether male or female, is a person, and therefore, "the only creature on earth which God willed for its own sake"; and at the same time this unique and unrepeatable creature "cannot fully find himself except through a sincere gift of self." Here begins the relationship of "communion" in which the "unity of the two" and the personal dignity of both man and woman find expression. Therefore when we read in the biblical description the words addressed to the woman: "*Your desire shall be for your husband, and he shall rule over you*" (*Gen* 3:16), we discover a break and a constant threat precisely in regard to this "unity of the two" which corresponds to the dignity of the image and likeness of God in both of them. But this threat is more serious for the woman, since domination takes the

place of "being a sincere gift" and therefore living "for" the other: "he shall rule over you." This "domination" indicates the disturbance and *loss of the stability* of that *fundamental equality* which the man and the woman possess in the "unity of the two": and this is especially to the disadvantage of the woman, whereas only the equality resulting from their dignity as persons can give to their mutual relationship the character of an authentic *"communio personarum."* While the violation of this equality, which is both a gift and a right deriving from God the Creator, involves an element to the disadvantage of the woman, at the same time it also diminishes the true dignity of the man. Here we touch upon *an extremely sensitive point in the dimension of that "ethos"* which was originally inscribed by the Creator in the very creation of both of them in his own image and likeness.

This statement in Genesis 3:16 is of great significance. It implies a reference to the mutual relationship of man and woman *in marriage*. It refers to the desire born in the atmosphere of spousal love whereby the woman's "sincere gift of self" is responded to and matched by a corresponding "gift" on the part of the husband. Only on the basis of this principle can both of them, and in particular the woman, "discover themselves" as a true "unity of the two" according to the dignity of the person. The matrimonial union requires respect for and a perfecting of the true personal subjectivity of both of them. *The woman cannot become the "object" of "domination" and male "possession."* But the words of the biblical text directly concern original sin and its lasting consequences in man and woman. Burdened by hereditary sinfulness, they bear within themselves the constant *"inclination to sin,"* the tendency to go against the moral order which corresponds to the rational nature and dignity of man and woman as persons. This tendency is expressed in *a threefold concupiscence*, which Saint John defines as the lust of the eyes, the lust of the flesh and the pride of life (cf. 1 *Jn* 2:16). The words of the Book of Genesis quoted previously (3:16) show how this threefold concupiscence, the "inclination to sin," will burden the mutual relationship of man and woman.

These words of Genesis refer directly to marriage, but indirectly *they concern the different spheres of social life*: the situations in which the woman remains disadvantaged or discriminated against by the fact of being a woman. The revealed truth concerning the creation of the human being as male and female constitutes the principal argument against all the objectively injurious and unjust situations which contain and express the inheritance of the sin which all human beings bear within themselves. The books of Sacred Scripture confirm in various places *the actual existence of such situations* and at the same time proclaim the need for conversion, that is to say, for purification from evil and liberation from sin: from what offends neighbour, what "diminishes" man, not only the one who is offended but also the one who causes the offence. This is the unchangeable message of the Word revealed by God. In it is expressed the biblical "ethos" until the end of time.

In our times the question of "women's rights" has taken on new significance in the broad context of the rights of the human person. *The biblical and evangelical message* sheds light on this cause, which is the object of much attention today, *by safeguarding the truth about the "unity" of the "two,"* that is to say the truth about that dignity and vocation that result from the specific diversity and personal originality of man and woman. Consequently, even the rightful opposition of women to what is expressed in the biblical words "He shall rule over you" (*Gen* 3:16) must not under any condition lead to the "masculinization" of women. In the name of liberation from male "domination," women must not appropriate to themselves male characteristics contrary to their own feminine "originality." There is a well-founded fear that if they take this path, women will not "reach fulfilment," but instead will *deform and lose what constitutes their essential richness.* It is indeed an enormous richness. In the biblical description, the words of the first man at the sight of the woman who had been created are words of admiration and enchantment, words which fill the whole history of man on earth.

The personal resources of femininity are certainly no less than the resources of masculinity: they are merely different. Hence a woman, as well as a man, must understand her "fulfilment" as a person, her dignity and vocation, on the basis of these resources, according to the richness of the femininity which she received on the day of creation and which she inherits as an expression of the "image and likeness of God" that is specifically hers. *The inheritance of sin* suggested by the words of the Bible – "Your desire shall be for your husband, and he shall rule over you" – *can be conquered* only by following this path. The overcoming of this evil inheritance is, generation after generation, the task of every human being, whether woman or man. For whenever man is responsible for offending a woman's personal dignity and vocation, he acts contrary to his own personal dignity and his own vocation.

Proto-evangelium

11. The Book of Genesis attests to the fact that sin is the evil at man's "beginning" and that since then its consequences weigh upon the whole human race. At the same time it contains *the first foretelling of victory* over evil, *over sin*. This is proved by the words which we read in Genesis 3:15, usually called the "*Proto-evangelium*": "I will put enmity between you and the woman, and between your seed and her seed; he shall bruise your head, and you shall bruise his heel." It is significant that the foretelling of the Redeemer contained in these words refers to "the woman." She is assigned the first place in the

Proto-evangelium as the progenitrix of him who will be the Redeemer of man. And since the redemption is to be accomplished through a struggle against evil – through the "enmity" between the offspring of the woman and the offspring of him who, as "the father of lies" (*Jn* 8:44), *is* the first author of sin in human history – it is also *an enmity between him and the woman.*

These words give us a comprehensive view of the whole of Revelation, first as a preparation for the Gospel and later as the Gospel itself. From this vantage point the two female figures, *Eve* and *Mary,* are joined under the *name of woman.*

The words of the Proto-evangelium, re-read in the light of the New Testament, express well the mission of woman in the Redeemer's salvific struggle against the author of evil in human history.

The comparison Eve-Mary constantly recurs in the course of reflection on the deposit of faith received from divine Revelation. It is one of the themes frequently taken up by the Fathers, ecclesiastical writers and theologians. As a rule, from this comparison there emerges at first sight a difference, a contrast. *Eve*, as "the mother of all the living" (*Gen* 3:20), is *the witness to the biblical "beginning,"* which contains the truth about the creation of man made in the image and likeness of God and the truth about original sin. *Mary is the witness to the new "beginning"* and the "new creation" (cf. *2 Cor* 5:17), since she herself, as the first of the redeemed in salvation history, is "a new creation": she is "full of grace." It is difficult to grasp why the words of the Proto-evangelium place such strong emphasis on the "woman," if it is not admitted that *in her the new and definitive Covenant* of God with humanity *has its beginning,* the *Covenant* in the redeeming blood of Christ. The Covenant begins with a woman, the "woman" of the Annunciation at Nazareth. Herein lies the absolute originality of the Gospel: many times in the Old Testament, in order to intervene in the history of his people, God addressed himself to women, as in the case of the mothers of Samuel and Samson. However, to make his Covenant with humanity, he addressed himself only to men: *Noah, Abraham, and Moses.* At the beginning of the New Covenant, which is to be eternal and irrevocable, there is a woman: the Virgin of Nazareth. It is a *sign* that points to the fact that "in Jesus Christ" *"there is neither male nor female"* (*Gal* 3:28). In Christ the mutual opposition between man and woman – which is the inheritance of original sin – is essentially overcome. "For you are all *one* in Jesus Christ," Saint Paul will write (ibid.).

These words concern that original "unity of the two" which is linked with the creation of the human being as male and female, made in the image and likeness of God, and based on the model of that most perfect communion of Persons which is God himself. Saint Paul states that the mystery of man's redemption in Jesus Christ, the son of Mary, resumes and renews that which in the mystery of creation corresponded to the eternal design of God the Creator. Precisely for this reason, on the day of the creation of the human being as male and female "God saw everything that he had made, and behold, it was very good" (*Gen* 1:31). *The Redemption restores*, in a sense, at its very root, *the good* that was essentially "diminished" by sin and its heritage in human history.

The "woman" of the Proto-evangelium fits into the perspective of the Redemption. The comparison Eve-Mary can be understood also in the sense that *Mary assumes* in herself and embraces the *mystery of the "woman"* whose beginning is Eve, "the mother of all the living" (*Gen* 3:20). First of all she assumes and embraces it within the mystery of Christ, "the new and the last Adam" (cf. 1 *Cor* 15:45), who assumed in his own person the nature of the first Adam. The essence of the New Covenant consists in the fact that the Son of God, who is of one substance with the eternal Father, becomes man: he takes humanity into the unity of the divine Person of the Word. The one who accomplishes the Redemption is also a true man. The mystery of the world's Redemption presupposes that *God the Son assumed humanity* as *the inheritance of Adam*, becoming like him and like every man in all things, "yet without sinning" (*Heb* 4:15). In this way he "fully reveals man to himself and makes man's supreme calling clear," as the Second Vatican Council teaches. In a certain sense, he has helped man to discover "who he is" (cf. *Ps* 8:5).

In the tradition of faith and of Christian reflection throughout the ages, *the coupling Adam-Christ* is often linked with that of *Eve-Mary.* If Mary is described also as the "new Eve," what are the meanings of this analogy? Certainly there are many. Particularly noteworthy is the meaning which sees Mary as the full revelation of all that is included in the biblical word "woman": a revelation commensurate with the mystery of the Redemption. *Mary* means, in a sense, a going beyond the limit spoken of in the Book of Genesis (3:16) and a return to that "beginning" in which one finds the "woman" as she was intended to be in *creation,* and therefore in the eternal mind of God: in the bosom of the Most Holy Trinity. Mary is "the new beginning" of the *dignity and vocation of women,* of each and every woman.

A particular key for understanding this can be found in the words which the Evangelist puts on Mary's lips after the Annunciation, during her visit to Elizabeth: "He who is mighty has done great things for me" (*Lk* 1:49). These words certainly refer to the conception of her Son, who is the "Son of the Most High" (*Lk* 1:32), the "holy one" of God; but they can also signify *the discovery of her own feminine humanity. He "has done great things for me":* this is the *discovery of all the richness and personal resources of femininity*, all the eternal originality of the "woman," just as God wanted her to be, a person for her own sake, who discovers herself "by means of a sincere gift of self."

This discovery is connected with a clear awareness of God's gift, of his generosity. From the very "beginning" sin had obscured this awareness, in a sense had stifled it, as is shown in the words of the first temptation by the "father of lies" (cf. *Gen* 3:1–5). At the advent of the "fullness of time" (cf. *Gal* 4:4), when the mystery of Redemption begins to be fulfilled in the history of humanity, this awareness bursts forth in all its power in the words of the biblical "woman" of Nazareth. *In Mary, Eve discovers* the nature of the true dignity of woman, of feminine humanity. This discovery must continually reach the heart of every woman and shape her vocation and her life.

V

JESUS CHRIST

"They marvelled that he was talking with a woman"

12. The words of the Proto-evangelium in the Book of Genesis enable us to move into the context of the Gospel. Man's Redemption, foretold in Genesis, now becomes a reality in the person and mission of Jesus Christ, in which we also recognize *what the reality of the Redemption means* for the dignity and the vocation *of women.* This meaning becomes clearer for us from Christ's words and from his whole attitude towards women, an attitude which is extremely simple, and for this very reason extraordinary, if seen against the background of his time. It is an attitude marked by great clarity and depth. Various women appear along the path of the mission of Jesus of Nazareth, and his meeting with each of them is a confirmation of the evangelical "newness of life" already spoken of.

It is universally admitted – even by people with a critical attitude towards the Christian message – that *in the eyes of his contemporaries Christ became a promotor of women's true dignity* and of the *vocation* corresponding to this dignity. At times this caused wonder, surprise, often to the point of scandal: "They marvelled that he was talking with a woman" (*Jn* 4:27), because this behaviour differed from that of his contemporaries. Even Christ's own disciples "marvelled." The Pharisee to whose house the sinful woman went to anoint Jesus' feet with perfumed oil "said to himself, 'If this man were a prophet, *he would have known who* and what sort of woman this is who is touching him, for she is a sinner'" (*Lk* 7:39). Even greater dismay, or even "holy indignation," must have filled the self-satisfied hearers of Christ's words: "the tax collectors and the harlots go into the Kingdom of God before you" (*Mt* 21:31).

By speaking and acting in this way, Jesus made it clear that "the mysteries of the Kingdom" were known to him in every detail. He also "knew what was in man" (*Jn* 2:25), in his innermost being, in his "heart." He was a witness of God's eternal plan for the human being, created in his own image and likeness as man and woman. He was also perfectly aware of the consequences of sin, of that "mystery of iniquity" working in human hearts as the bitter fruit of the obscuring of the divine image. It is truly significant that in his important discussion about marriage and its indissolubility, in the presence of "the Scribes," who by profession were experts in the Law, Jesus *makes reference to the "beginning."* The question asked concerns a man's right "to divorce one's wife for any cause" (*Mt* 19:3) and therefore also concerns the woman's right, her rightful position in marriage, her dignity. The questioners think they have on their side the Mosaic legislation then followed in Israel: "Why then did Moses command one to give a certificate of divorce, and to put her away?" (*Mt* 19:7). Jesus answers: "For your hardness of heart Moses allowed you to divorce your wives, but from the beginning it was not so" (*Mt* 19:8). Jesus appeals to the "beginning," to the creation of man as male and female and their ordering by God himself, which is based upon the fact that *both were created "in his image and likeness."* Therefore, when "a man shall leave his father and mother and is joined to his wife, so that the two become one flesh," there remains in force the law which comes from God himself: "What therefore God has joined together, let no man put asunder" (*Mt* 19:6).

The principle of this "ethos," which from the beginning marks the reality of creation, is now confirmed by Christ in opposition to that tradition which discriminated against women. In this tradition the male "dominated," without having proper regard for woman and for her dignity, which *the "ethos"* of creation made the basis of the mutual relationships of two people united in marriage. This "ethos" is *recalled and confirmed by Christ's words*; it is the "ethos" of the Gospel and of Redemption.

Women in the Gospel

13. As we scan the pages of the Gospel, *many women, of different ages and conditions*, pass before our eyes. We meet women with illnesses or physical sufferings, such as the one who had "a spirit of infirmity for eighteen years; she was bent over and could not fully straighten herself" (*Lk* 13:11); or Simon's mother-in-law, who "lay sick with a fever" (*Mk* 1:30); or the woman "who had a flow of blood" (cf. *Mk* 5:25–34), who could not touch anyone because it was believed that her touch would make a person "impure." Each of them was healed, and the last-mentioned – the one with a flow of blood, who touched Jesus' garment "in the crowd" (*Mk* 5:27) – was praised by him for her great faith: "Your faith has made you well" (*Mk* 5:34). Then there is *the daughter of Jairus*, whom Jesus brings back to life, saying to her tenderly: "Little girl, I say

to you, arise" (*Mk* 5:41). There also is *the widow of Nain*, whose only son Jesus brings back to life, accompanying his action by an expression of affectionate mercy: "He had compassion on her and said to her, 'Do not weep!'" (*Lk* 7:13). And finally there is the *Canaanite woman*, whom Christ extols for her faith, her humility and for that greatness of spirit of which only a mother's heart is capable. "O woman, great is your faith! Be it done for you as you desire" (*Mt* 15:28). The Canaanite woman was asking for the healing of her daughter.

Sometimes the women whom Jesus met and who received so many graces from him, also accompanied him as he journeyed with the Apostles through the towns and villages, proclaiming the Good News of the Kingdom of God; and they "provided for them out of their means." The Gospel names Joanna, who was the wife of Herod's steward, Susanna and "many others" (cf. *Lk* 8:1–3).

Sometimes *women* appear *in the parables* which Jesus of Nazareth used to illustrate for his listeners the truth about the Kingdom of God. This is the case in the parables of the lost coin (cf. *Lk* 15:8–10), the leaven (cf. *Mt* 13:33), and the wise and foolish virgins (cf. *Mt* 25:1–13). Particularly eloquent is the story of the widow's mite. While "the rich were putting their gifts into the treasury . . . a poor widow put in two copper coins." Then Jesus said: "This poor widow *has put in more than all of* them. . . . She out of her poverty put in all the living that she had" (*Lk* 21:1–4). In this way Jesus presents her as a model for everyone and defends her, for in the socio-juridical system of the time widows were totally defenceless people (cf. also *Lk* 18:1–7).

In all of Jesus' teaching, as well as in his behaviour, one can find nothing which reflects the discrimination against women prevalent in his day. On the contrary, *his words and works always express the respect and honour due to women.* The woman with a stoop is called a "daughter of Abraham" (*Lk* 13:16), while in the whole Bible the title "son of Abraham" is used only of men. Walking the *Via Dolorosa* to Golgotha, Jesus will say to the women: "Daughters of Jerusalem, do not weep for me" (*Lk* 23:28). This way of speaking to and about women, as well as his manner of treating them, clearly constitutes an "innovation" with respect to the prevailing custom at that time.

This becomes even more explicit in regard to women whom popular opinion contemptuously labelled sinners, public sinners and adulteresses. There is the Samaritan woman, to whom Jesus himself says: "For you have had five husbands, and he whom you now have is not your husband." And she, realizing that he knows the secrets of her life, recognizes him as the Messiah and runs to tell her neighbours. The conversation leading up to this realization is one of the most beautiful in the Gospel (cf. *Jn* 4:7–27).

Then there is the public sinner who, in spite of her condemnation by common opinion, enters into the house of the Pharisee to anoint the feet of Jesus with perfumed oil. To his host, who is scandalized by this, he will say: "Her sins, which are many, are forgiven, for she loved much" (cf. *Lk* 7:37–47).

Finally, there is a situation which is perhaps the most eloquent: *a woman caught in adultery* is brought to Jesus. To the leading question "In the law Moses commanded us to stone such. What do you say about her?" Jesus replies: "Let him who is without sin among you be the first to throw a stone at her." The power of truth contained in this answer is so great that "they went away, one by one, beginning with the eldest." Only Jesus and the woman remain. "Woman, where are they? Has no one condemned you?" "No one, Lord." "Neither do I condemn you; go, and do not sin again" (cf. *Jn* 8:3–11).

These episodes provide a very clear picture. Christ is the one who "knows what is in man" (cf. *Jn* 2:25) – in man and woman. He knows *the dignity of man,* his *worth in God's eyes.* He himself, the Christ, is the definitive confirmation of this worth. Everything he says and does is definitively fulfilled in the Paschal Mystery of the Redemption. Jesus' attitude to the women whom he meets in the course of his Messianic service reflects the eternal plan of God, who, in creating each one of them, chooses her and loves her in Christ (cf. *Eph* 1:1–5). Each woman therefore is "the only creature on earth which God willed for its own sake." *Each of them from the "beginning" inherits as a woman the dignity of personhood.* Jesus of Nazareth confirms this dignity, recalls it, renews it, and makes it a part of the Gospel and of the Redemption for which he is sent into the world. Every word and gesture of Christ about women must therefore be brought into the dimension of the Paschal Mystery. In this way everything is completely explained.

The woman caught in adultery

14. Jesus enters *into the concrete and historical situation of women,* a situation which is *weighed down by the inheritance of sin.* One of the ways in which this inheritance is expressed is habitual discrimination against women in favour of men. This inheritance is rooted within women too. From this point of view the episode of the woman "caught in adultery" (cf. *Jn* 8:3–11) is particularly eloquent. In the end Jesus says to her: "*Do not sin again,*" but first he *evokes an awareness* of sin in the men who accuse her in order to stone her, thereby revealing his profound capacity to see human consciences and actions in their true light. Jesus seems to say to the accusers: Is not this woman, for all her sin, above all a confirmation of your own transgressions, of your "male" injustice, your misdeeds?

This truth is *valid for the whole human race.* The episode recorded in the Gospel of John is repeated in countless similar situations in every period of history. A woman is left alone, exposed to public opinion with "her sin," while behind "her" sin there lurks a man – a sinner, guilty "of the other's sin," indeed equally responsible for it. And yet his sin escapes notice, it is passed over in silence: he does not appear to be responsible for "the other's sin"! Sometimes, forgetting his own sin, he even makes himself the accuser, as in the case described. How often, in a similar way, *the woman pays* for her own sin (maybe it is she, in some cases, who is guilty of the "other's sin" – the sin of the man), but she alone pays and she pays *all alone*! How often is she abandoned with her pregnancy, when the man, the child's father, is unwilling to accept responsibility for it? And besides the many "unwed mothers" in our society, we also must consider all those who, as a result of various pressures, even on the part of the guilty man, very often "get rid of" the child before it is born. "They get rid of it": but at what price? Public opinion today tries in various ways to "abolish" the evil of this sin. Normally a *woman's conscience does not let her forget* that she has taken the life of her own child, for she cannot destroy that readiness to accept life which marks her "ethos" from the "beginning."

The attitude of Jesus in the episode described in John 8:3–11 is significant. This is one of the few instances in which his power – the power of truth – is so clearly manifested with regard to human consciences. Jesus is calm, collected and thoughtful. As in the conversation with the Pharisees (cf. *Mt* 19:3–9), is Jesus not aware of being in contact with the mystery of the "beginning," when man was created male and female, and the woman was entrusted to the man with her feminine distinctiveness, and with her potential for motherhood? The man was also entrusted by the Creator to the woman – they were *entrusted to each other as persons* made in the image and likeness of God himself. This entrusting is the test of love, spousal love. In order to become "a sincere gift" to one another, each of them has to feel responsible for the gift. This test is meant for both of them – man and woman – from the "beginning." After original sin, contrary forces are at work in man and woman as a result of the threefold concupiscence, the "stimulus of sin." They act from deep within the human being. Thus Jesus will say in the Sermon on the Mount: "*Every one who looks at a woman lustfully has already committed adultery with her in his heart*" (*Mt* 5:28). These words, addressed directly to man, show the fundamental truth of his responsibility vis-à-vis woman: her dignity, her motherhood, her vocation. But indirectly these words concern the woman. Christ did everything possible to ensure that – in the context of the customs and social relationships of that time – women would find in his teaching and actions their own subjectivity and dignity. On the basis of the eternal "unity of the two," *this dignity directly depends on woman herself, as a subject responsible for herself, and at the same time it is "given as a task" to man*. Christ logically appeals to man's

responsibility. In the present meditation on women's dignity and vocation, it is necessary that we refer to the context which we find in the
Gospel. The dignity and the vocation of women – as well as those of
men – find their eternal source in the heart of God. And in the temporal
conditions of human existence, they are closely connected with the
"unity of the two." Consequently each man must look within himself to
see whether she who was entrusted to him as a sister in humanity, as
a spouse, has not become in his heart an object of adultery; to see
whether she who, in different ways, is the cosubject of his existence in
the world, has not become for him an "object": an object of pleasure,
of exploitation.

Guardians of the Gospel message

15. *Christ's way of acting, the Gospel of his words and deeds,* is
a consistent *protest* against whatever offends the dignity of women.
Consequently, the women who are close to Christ discover themselves
in the truth which he "teaches" and "does," even when this truth concerns their "sinfulness." They feel *"liberated" by this truth,* restored to
themselves: they feel loved with "eternal love," with a love which finds
direct expression in Christ himself.

In Christ's sphere of action their position is transformed. They feel
that Jesus is speaking to them about matters which in those times one
did not discuss with a woman. Perhaps the most significant example of
this is the *Samaritan woman* at the well of Sychar. *Jesus* – who knows
that she is a sinner and speaks to her about this – *discusses the most
profound mysteries of God with her.* He speaks to her of God's infinite
gift of love, which is like a "spring of water welling up to eternal life" (*Jn*
4:14). He speaks to her about God who is Spirit, and about the true
adoration which the Father has a right to receive in spirit and truth (cf.
Jn 4:24). Finally he reveals to her that he is the Messiah promised to
Israel (cf. *Jn* 4:26).

This is an event without precedent: that a *woman,* and what is more
a "sinful woman," becomes a "disciple" of Christ. Indeed, once taught,
she proclaims Christ to the inhabitants of Samaria, so that they too receive him with faith (cf. *Jn* 4:39–42). This is an unprecedented event, if
one remembers the usual way women were treated by those who were
teachers in Israel; whereas in Jesus of Nazareth's way of acting such
an event becomes normal. In this regard, the sisters of Lazarus also
deserve special mention: "Jesus loved Martha and her sister (Mary) and
Lazarus" (cf. *Jn* 11:5). Mary "listened to the teaching" of Jesus: when
he pays them a visit, he calls Mary's behaviour "the good portion" in
contrast to Martha's preoccupation with domestic matters (cf. *Lk* 10:
38–42). On another occasion – *after the death of Lazarus* – Martha is
the one who talks to Christ, and the conversation concerns the most
profound truths of revelation and faith: "Lord, if you had been here, my

brother would not have died." "Your brother will rise again." "I know that he will rise again in the resurrection at the last day." Jesus said to her: "I am the resurrection and the life; he who believes in me, though he die, yet shall he live, and whoever lives and believes in me shall never die. Do you believe this?" "Yes, Lord; I believe that you are the Christ, the Son of God, he who is coming into the world" (*Jn* 11:21–27). After this profession of faith Jesus raises Lazarus. *This conversation with Martha is one of the most important in the Gospel.*

Christ speaks to women about the things of God, and they understand them; there is a true resonance of mind and heart, a response of faith. Jesus expresses appreciation and admiration for this distinctly "feminine" response, as in the case of the Canaanite woman (cf. *Mt* 15:28). Sometimes he presents this lively faith, filled with love, as an example. *He teaches,* therefore, taking *as his starting-point this feminine response of mind and heart.* This is the case with the "sinful" woman in the Pharisee's house, whose way of acting is taken by Jesus as the starting-point for explaining the truth about the forgiveness of sins: "Her sins, which are many, are forgiven, for she loved much; but he who is forgiven little, loves little" (*Lk* 7:47). On the occasion of another anointing, Jesus defends the woman and her action before the disciples, Judas in particular: "Why do you trouble this woman? *For she has done a beautiful thing to me. . . .* In pouring this ointment on my body she has done it to prepare me for burial. Truly, I say to you, wherever this gospel is preached in the whole world, what she has done will be told in memory of her" (*Mt* 26:6–13).

Indeed, the Gospels not only describe what that woman did at Bethany in the house of Simon the Leper; they also highlight the fact that *women were in the forefront at the foot of the Cross*, at the decisive moment in Jesus of Nazareth's whole messianic mission. John was the only Apostle who remained faithful, but there were many faithful women. Not only the Mother of Christ and "his mother's sister, Mary the wife of Clopas and Mary Magdalene" (*Jn* 19:25) were present, but "there were also many women there, looking on from afar, who had followed Jesus from Galilee, ministering to him" (*Mt* 27:55). As we see, in this most arduous test of faith and fidelity the women proved stronger than the Apostles. In this moment of danger, those who love much succeed in overcoming their fear. Before this there were the *women on the Via Dolorosa, "who bewailed and lamented him"* (*Lk* 23:27). Earlier still, there was *Pilate's wife*, who had warned her husband: "Have nothing to do with that righteous man, for I have suffered much over him today in a dream" (*Mt* 27:19).

First witnesses of the Resurrection

16. From the beginning of Christ's mission, women show to him and to his mystery a special *sensitivity which is characteristic* of their

femininity. It must also be said that this is especially confirmed in the Paschal Mystery, not only at the Cross but also at the dawn of the Resurrection. The women *are the first at the tomb*. They are the first to find it empty. They are the first to hear: "He is not here. *He has risen*, as he said" (*Mt* 28:6). They are the first to embrace his feet (cf. *Mt* 28:9). They are also the first to be called to announce this truth to the Apostles (cf. *Mt* 28:1–10; *Lk* 24:8–11). The Gospel of John (cf. also *Mk* 16:9) emphasizes *the special role of Mary Magdalene*. She is the first to meet the Risen Christ. At first she thinks he is the gardener; she recognizes him only when he calls her by name: "Jesus said to her, 'Mary'. She turned and said to him in Hebrew, 'Rabbuni' (which means Teacher). Jesus said to her, 'Do not hold me, for I have not yet ascended to the Father, but go to my brethren and say to them, I am ascending to my Father and to your Father, to my God and your God'. Mary Magdalene went and said to the disciples, 'I have seen the Lord'; and she told them that he had said these things to her" (*Jn* 20:16–18).

Hence she came to be called "the apostle of the Apostles." Mary Magdalene was the first eyewitness of the Risen Christ, and for this reason she was also *the first to bear witness to him before the Apostles*. This event, in a sense, crowns all that has been said previously about Christ entrusting divine truths to women as well as men. One can say that this fulfilled the words of the Prophet: "*I will pour out my spirit* on all flesh; your sons and *your daughters shall prophesy*" (*Jl* 2:28). On the fiftieth day after Christ's Resurrection, these words are confirmed once more in the Upper Room in Jerusalem, at the descent of the Holy Spirit, the Paraclete (cf. *Acts* 2:17).

Everything that has been said so far about Christ's attitude to women confirms and clarifies, in the Holy Spirit, the truth about the equality of man and woman. One must speak of an essential "equality," since both of them – the woman as much as the man – are created in the image and likeness of God. Both of them are equally capable of receiving the outpouring of divine truth and love in the Holy Spirit. Both receive his salvific and sanctifying "visits."

The fact of being a man or a woman involves no limitation here, just as the salvific and sanctifying action of the Spirit in man is in no way limited by the fact that one is a Jew or a Greek, slave or free, according to the well-known words of Saint Paul: "For you are all one in Christ Jesus" (*Gal* 3:28). *This unity does not cancel out diversity*. The Holy Spirit, who brings about this unity in the supernatural order of sanctifying grace, contributes in equal measure to the fact that "your sons will prophesy" and that "your daughters will prophesy." "To prophesy" means to express by one's words and one's life "*the mighty works of God*" (*Acts* 2:11), preserving the truth and originality of each person, whether woman or man. Gospel "equality," the "equality" of women and men in regard to the "mighty works of God" – manifested so clearly in the words and deeds of Jesus of Nazareth – constitutes the most obvious basis for the dignity and vocation of women in the Church and in the world. Every *vocation has* a profoundly *personal and prophetic meaning*. In "vocation" understood in this way, what is personally feminine reaches a new dimension: the dimension of the "mighty works of God," of which the woman becomes the living subject and an irreplaceable witness.

VI

MOTHERHOOD – VIRGINITY

Two dimensions of women's vocation

17. We must now focus our meditation on virginity and motherhood as two particular dimensions of the fulfillment of the female personality. In the light of the Gospel, they acquire their full meaning and value in Mary, who as a Virgin became the Mother of the Son of God. These *two dimensions of the female vocation* were united in her in an exceptional manner, in such a way that one did not exclude the other but wonderfully complemented it. The description of the Annunciation in the Gospel of Luke clearly shows that this seemed impossible to the Virgin of Nazareth. When she hears the words: "You will conceive in your womb and bear a son, and you shall call his name Jesus," she immediately asks: "How can this be, since I have no husband?" (*Lk 1*:31, 34). In the usual order of things motherhood is the result of mutual "knowledge" between a man and woman in the marriage union. Mary, firm in her resolve to preserve her virginity, puts this question to the divine messenger, and obtains from him the explanation: "*The Holy Spirit will come upon you*" – your motherhood will not be the consequence of matrimonial "knowledge," but will be the work of the Holy Spirit; the "power of the Most High" will "overshadow" the mystery of the Son's conception and birth; as the Son of the Most High, he is given to you exclusively by God, in a manner known to God. Mary, therefore, maintained her virginal "I have no husband" (cf. *Lk* 1:34) and at the same time became a Mother. *Virginity and motherhood co-exist in her*: they do not mutually exclude each other or place limits on each other. Indeed, the person of the Mother of God helps everyone – especially women – to see how these two dimensions, these two paths in the vocation of women as persons, explain and complete each other.

Motherhood

18. In order to share in this "vision," we must once again *seek a deeper understanding of the truth about the human person* recalled

by the Second Vatican Council. The human being – both male and female – is the only being in the world which God willed for its own sake. The human being is a person, a subject who decides for himself. At the same time, man "cannot fully find himself except through a sincere gift of self." It has already been said that this description, indeed this definition of the person, corresponds to the fundamental biblical truth about the creation of the human being – man and woman – in the image and likeness of God. This is not a purely theoretical interpretation, nor an abstract definition, for it *gives an essential indication of what it means to be human*, while emphasizing *the value of the gift of self, the gift of the person*. In this vision of the person we also find the essence of that "ethos" which, together with the truth of creation, will be fully developed by the books of Revelation, particularly the Gospels.

This truth about the person also opens up *the path to a full understanding of women's motherhood*. Motherhood is the fruit of the marriage union of a man and woman, of that biblical "knowledge" which corresponds to the "union of the two in one flesh" (cf. *Gen* 2:24). This brings about – on the woman's part – a special "gift of self," as an expression of that spousal love whereby the two are united to each other so closely that they become "one flesh." Biblical "knowledge" is achieved in accordance with the truth of the person only when the mutual self-giving is not distorted either by the desire of the man to become the "master" of his wife ("he shall rule over you") or by the woman remaining closed within her own instincts ("your desire shall be for your husband": *Gen* 3:16).

This *mutual gift of the person in marriage* opens to the gift of a new life, *a new human being*, who is also a person in the likeness of his parents. Motherhood implies from the beginning a special openness to the new person: and this is precisely the woman's "part." In this openness, in conceiving and giving birth to a child, the woman "discovers herself through a sincere gift of self." The gift of interior readiness to accept the child and bring it into the world is linked to the marriage union, which – as mentioned earlier – should constitute a special moment in the mutual self-giving both by the woman and the man. According to the Bible, the conception and birth of a new human being are accompanied by the following words of the woman: "I *have brought a man into being with the help of the Lord*" (*Gen* 4:1).This exclamation of Eve, the "mother of all the living," is repeated every time a new human being comes into the world. It expresses the woman's joy and awareness that she is sharing in the great mystery of eternal generation. The spouses share in the creative power of God!

The woman's motherhood in the period between the baby's conception and birth is a bio-physiological and psychological process which is better understood in our days than in the past, and is the subject of many detailed studies. Scientific analysis fully confirms that the very physical constitution of women is naturally disposed to motherhood – conception, pregnancy and giving birth – which is a consequence of the marriage union with the man. At the same time, this also corresponds to the psycho-physical structure of women. What the different branches of science have to say on this subject is important and useful, provided that it is not limited to an exclusively bio-physiological interpretation of women and of motherhood. Such a *"restricted" picture* would go hand in hand with a materialistic concept of the human being and of the world. In such a case, what is truly essential would unfortunately be lost. Motherhood as a *human* fact and phenomenon, is fully explained on the basis of the truth about the person. Motherhood *is linked to the personal structure of the woman and to the personal dimension of the gift*: "I have brought a man into being with the help of the Lord" (*Gen* 4:1). The Creator grants the parents the gift of a child. On the woman's part, this fact is linked in a special way to "a sincere gift of self." Mary's words at the Annunciation – "Let it be to me according to your word" – signify the woman's readiness for the gift of self and her readiness to accept a new life.

The eternal mystery of generation, which is in God himself, the one and Triune God (cf. *Eph* 3:14–15), is reflected in the woman's motherhood and in the man's fatherhood. Human parenthood is something shared by both the man and the woman. Even if the woman, out of love for her husband, says: "I have given you a child," her words also mean: "This is our child." Although both of them together are parents of their child, *the woman's motherhood constitutes a special "part" in this shared parenthood*, and the most demanding part. Parenthood – even though it belongs to both – is realized much more fully in the woman, especially in the prenatal period. It is the woman who "pays" directly for this shared generation, which literally absorbs the energies of her body and soul. It is therefore necessary that *the man* be fully aware that in their shared parenthood he owes *a special debt to the woman*. No programme of "equal rights" between women and men is valid unless it takes this fact fully into account.

Motherhood involves a special communion with the mystery of life, as it develops in the woman's womb. The mother is filled with wonder at this mystery of life, and "understands" with unique intuition what is happening inside her. In the light of the "beginning," the mother accepts and loves as a person the child she is carrying in her womb. This unique contact with the new human being developing within her gives rise to an attitude towards human beings – not only towards her own child, but every human being – which profoundly marks the woman's personality. It is commonly thought that *women* are more capable than men of paying attention *to another person,* and that motherhood develops this predisposition even more. The man – even with all his sharing in parenthood – always remains "outside" the process of pregnancy and the baby's birth; in many ways he has to *learn* his own *"fatherhood" from the mother.* One can say that this is part of the normal human dimension of parenthood, including the stages that follow the birth of the baby, especially the initial period. The child's upbringing, taken as a whole, should include the contribution of both parents: the maternal and paternal contribution. In any event, the mother's contribution is decisive in laying the foundation for a new human personality.

Motherhood in relation to the Covenant

19. Our reflection returns to *the biblical exemplar of the "woman"* in the Proto-evangelium. The "woman," as mother and first teacher of the human being (education being the spiritual dimension of parent-hood), has a specific precedence over the man. Although motherhood, especially in the bio-physical sense, depends upon the man, it places an essential "mark" on the whole personal growth process of new chil-dren. Motherhood *in the bio-physical sense* appears to be passive: the formation process of a new life "takes place" in her, in her body, which is nevertheless profoundly involved in that process. At the same time, motherhood *in its personal-ethical sense* expresses a very important creativity on the part of the woman, upon whom the very humanity of the new human being mainly depends. In this sense too the woman's motherhood presents a special call and a special challenge to the man and to his fatherhood.

The biblical exemplar of the "woman" finds its culmination *in the motherhood of the Mother of God.* The words of the Proto-evangelium – "I will put enmity between you and the woman" – find here a fresh con-firmation. We see that through Mary – through her maternal "fiat" ("Let it be done to me") – God *begins a New Covenant with humanity.* This is the eternal and definitive Covenant in Christ, in his body and blood, in his Cross and Resurrection. Precisely because this Covenant is to be fulfilled "in flesh and blood" its beginning is in the Mother. Thanks solely to her and to her virginal and maternal "fiat," the "Son of the Most High" can say to the Father: "A body you have prepared for me. Lo, I have come to do your will, O God" (cf. *Heb* 10:5, 7).

Motherhood has been introduced into the order of the Covenant that God made with humanity in Jesus Christ. Each and every time that *motherhood* is repeated in human history, it is always *related to the Covenant* which God established with the human race through the motherhood of the Mother of God.

Does not Jesus bear witness to this reality when he answers the exclamation of that woman in the crowd who blessed him for Mary's motherhood: "Blessed is the womb that bore you, and the breasts that you sucked!" Jesus replies: "Blessed rather are those who hear the word of God and keep it" (*Lk* 11:27–28). Jesus confirms the meaning of motherhood in reference to the body, but at the same time he indicates an even deeper meaning, which is connected with the order of the spirit: it is a sign of the Covenant with God who "is spirit" (*Jn* 4:24). This is true above all for the motherhood of the Mother of God. *The motherhood of every woman, understood in the light of the Gospel, is similarly not only "of flesh and blood"*: it expresses a profound *"listening to the word of the living God"* and a readiness to "safeguard" this Word, which is "the word of eternal life" (cf. *Jn* 6:68). For it is precisely those born of earthly mothers, the sons and daughters of the human race, who receive from the Son of God the power to become "children of God" (*Jn* 1:12). A dimension of the New Covenant in Christ's blood enters into human parenthood, making it a reality and a task for "new creatures" (cf. 2 *Cor* 5:17). The history of every human being passes through the threshold of a woman's motherhood; crossing it conditions "the revelation of the children of God" (cf. *Rom* 8:19).

"When a woman is in travail she has sorrow, because her hour has come; but when she is delivered of the child, *she no longer remembers the anguish*, for joy that a child is born into the world" (*Jn* 16:21). The first part of Christ's words refers to the "pangs of childbirth" which belong to the heritage of original sin; at the same time these words indicate *the link that exists between the woman's motherhood and the Paschal Mystery*. For this mystery also includes the Mother's sorrow at the foot of the Cross – the Mother who through faith shares in the amazing mystery of her Son's "self-emptying": "This is perhaps the deepest 'kenosis' of faith in human history."

As we contemplate this Mother, whose heart "a sword has pierced" (cf. *Lk* 2:35), our thoughts go to *all the suffering women in the world*, suffering either physically or morally. In this suffering a woman's sensitivity plays a role, even though she often succeeds in resisting suffering better than a man. It is difficult to enumerate these sufferings; it is difficult to call them all by name. We may recall her maternal care for her children, especially when they fall sick or fall into bad ways; the death of those most dear to her; the loneliness of mothers forgotten by their grown up children; the loneliness of widows; the sufferings of women who struggle alone to make a living; and women who have been wronged or exploited. Then there are the sufferings of consciences as a result of sin, which has wounded the woman's human or maternal dignity: the wounds of consciences which do not heal easily. With these sufferings too we must place ourselves at the foot of the Cross.

But the words of the Gospel about the woman who suffers when the time comes for her to give birth to her child, immediately afterwards express joy: it is *"the joy that a child is born into the world."* This joy too is referred to the Paschal Mystery, to the joy which is communicated to the Apostles on *the day of Christ's Resurrection*: "So you have sorrow now" (these words were said the day before the Passion); "but I will see you again and your hearts will rejoice, and no one will take your joy from you" (*Jn* 16:22–23).

Virginity for the sake of the Kingdom

20. In the teaching of Christ, *motherhood is connected with virginity*, but also *distinct from it*. Fundamental to this is Jesus' statement in the conversation on the indissolubility of marriage. Having heard the answer given to the Pharisees, the disciples say to Christ: "If such is the case of a man with his wife, it is not expedient to marry" (*Mt* 19:10). Independently of the meaning which "it is not expedient" had at that time in the mind of the disciples, *Christ* takes their mistaken opinion as a starting point for instructing them *on the value of celibacy*. He distinguishes celibacy which results from natural defects – even though they may have been caused by man – from "*celibacy for the sake of the Kingdom of heaven.*" Christ says, "and there are eunuchs who have made themselves eunuchs for the sake of the Kingdom of heaven" (*Mt* 19:12). It is, then, a voluntary celibacy, chosen for the sake of the Kingdom of heaven, in view of man's eschatological vocation to union with God. He then adds: "He who is able to receive this, let him receive it." These words repeat what he had said at the beginning of the discourse on celibacy (cf. *Mt* 19:11). Consequently, *celibacy for the kingdom of heaven results not only from a free choice* on the part of man, but also from a special *grace* on the part of God, who calls a particular person to live celibacy. While this is a special sign of the Kingdom of God to come, it also serves as a way to devote all the energies of soul and body during one's earthly life exclusively for the sake of the eschatological kingdom.

Jesus' words are the answer to the disciples' question. They are addressed directly to those who put the question: in this case they were men. Nevertheless, Christ's answer, in itself, has a *value both for men and for women*. In this context it indicates the evangelical ideal of virginity, an ideal which constitutes a clear "innovation" with respect to the tradition of the Old Testament. Certainly that tradition was connected in some way with Israel's expectation of the Messiah's coming, especially among the women of Israel from whom he was to be born. In fact, the ideal of celibacy and virginity for the sake of greater closeness to God was not entirely foreign to certain Jewish circles, especially in the period immediately preceding the coming of Jesus. Nevertheless, celibacy for the sake of the Kingdom, or rather virginity, is undeniably an innovation connected with the incarnation of God.

From the moment of Christ's coming, the expectation of the People of God has to be directed to the eschatological Kingdom which is coming and to which he must lead "the new Israel." A new awareness of faith is essential for such a turn-about and change of values. Christ emphasizes this twice: "He who is able to receive this, let him receive it." Only "those to whom it is given" understand it (*Mt* 19:11). *Mary* is the first person in whom this *new awareness* is manifested, for she asks the Angel: "How can this be, since I have no husband?" (*Lk* 1:34).Even though she is "betrothed to a man whose name was Joseph" (cf. *Lk* 1:27), she is firm in her resolve to remain a virgin. The motherhood which is accomplished in her comes exclusively from the "power of the Most High," and is the result of the Holy Spirit's coming down upon her (cf. *Lk* 1:35). This divine motherhood, therefore, is an altogether unforeseen response to the human expectation of women in Israel: it comes to Mary as a gift from God himself. This gift is the beginning and the prototype of a new expectation on the part of all. It measures up to the Eternal Covenant, to God's new and definitive promise: it is *a sign of eschatological hope*.

On the basis of the Gospel, the meaning of virginity was developed and better understood as a vocation for women too, one in which their dignity, like that of the Virgin of Nazareth, finds confirmation. The Gospel puts forward *the ideal of the consecration of the person*, that is, the person's exclusive dedication to God by virtue of the evangelical counsels: in particular, chastity, poverty and obedience. Their perfect incarnation is Jesus Christ himself. Whoever wishes to follow him in a radical way chooses to live according to these counsels. They are distinct from the commandments and show the Christian the radical way of the Gospel. From the very beginning of Christianity men and women have set out on this path, since the evangelical ideal is addressed to human beings without any distinction of sex.

In this wider context, *virginity* has to be considered *also as a path for women*, a path on which they realize their womanhood in a way different from marriage. In order to understand this path, it is necessary to refer once more to the fundamental idea of Christian anthropology. By freely choosing virginity, women confirm themselves as persons, as beings whom the Creator from the beginning has willed for their own sake. At the same time they realize the personal value of their own femininity by becoming "a sincere gift" for God who has revealed himself in Christ, a gift for Christ, the Redeemer of humanity and the Spouse of souls: a "spousal" gift. *One cannot correctly understand virginity* – a woman's consecration in virginity – *without referring to spousal love*. It is through this kind of love that a person becomes a gift for the other. Moreover, a man's consecration in priestly celibacy or in the religious state is to be understood analogously.

The naturally spousal predisposition of the feminine personality finds a response in virginity understood in this way. Women, called from the very "beginning" to be loved and to love, in a vocation to virginity *find Christ* first of all as the Redeemer who "loved until the end" through his total gift of self; *and they respond to this gift with a "sincere gift"* of their whole lives. They thus give themselves to the divine Spouse, and this personal gift tends to union, which is properly spiritual in character.

Through the Holy Spirit's action a woman becomes "one spirit" with Christ the Spouse (cf. 1 *Cor* 6:17).

This is the evangelical ideal of virginity, in which both the dignity and the vocation of women are realized in a special way. In virginity thus understood the so-called *radicalism of the Gospel* finds expression: "Leave everything and follow Christ" (cf. *Mt* 19:27). This cannot be compared to remaining simply unmarried or single, because virginity is not restricted to a mere "no," but contains a profound "yes" in the spousal order: the gift of self for love in a total and undivided manner.

Motherhood according to the Spirit

21. Virginity according to the Gospel means *renouncing marriage and thus physical motherhood*. Nevertheless, the renunciation of this kind of motherhood, a renunciation that can involve great sacrifice for a woman, makes possible a different kind of motherhood: motherhood *"according to the Spirit"* (cf. *Rom* 8:4). For virginity does not deprive a woman of her prerogatives. Spiritual motherhood takes on many different forms. In the life of consecrated women, for example, who live according to the charism and the rules of the various apostolic Institutes, it can express itself as concern for people, especially the most needy: the sick, the handicapped, the abandoned, orphans, the elderly, children, young people, the imprisoned and, in general, people on the edges of society. *In this way a consecrated woman finds her Spouse*, different and the same in each and every person, according to his very words: "As you did it to one of the least of these my brethren, you did it to me" (*Mt* 25:40). Spousal love always involves a special readiness to be poured out for the sake of those who come within one's range of activity. In marriage this readiness, even though open to all, consists mainly in the love that parents give to their children. In virginity this readiness is open *to all people, who are embraced by the love of Christ the Spouse*.

Spousal love – with its maternal potential hidden in the heart of the woman as a virginal bride – when joined to Christ, the Redeemer of each and every person, is also predisposed to being open to each and every person. This is confirmed in the religious communities of apostolic life, and in a different way in communities of contemplative life, or the cloister. There exist still other forms of a vocation to virginity for the sake of the Kingdom; for example, the Secular Institutes, or the communities of consecrated persons which flourish within Movements, Groups and Associations. In all of these *the same truth about the spiritual motherhood* of virgins is confirmed in various ways. However, it is not only a matter of communal forms but also of non-communal forms. In brief, virginity as a woman's vocation is always the vocation of a person – of a unique, individual person. Therefore the spiritual motherhood which makes itself felt in this vocation is also profoundly personal.

This is also the basis of a specific *convergence between the virginity* of the unmarried woman and *the motherhood* of the married woman. This convergence moves not only from motherhood towards virginity, as emphasized above; it also moves from virginity towards marriage, the form of woman's vocation in which she becomes a mother by giving birth to her children. The starting point of this second analogy is *the meaning of marriage*. A woman is "married" either through the sacrament of marriage or spiritually through marriage to Christ. *In both cases marriage* signifies the "sincere gift of the person" of the bride to the groom. In this way, one can say that the profile of marriage is found spiritually in virginity. And does not physical motherhood also have to be a spiritual motherhood, in order to respond to the whole truth about the human being who is a unity of body and spirit? Thus there exist many reasons for discerning in these two different paths – the two different vocations of women – a profound complementarity, and even a profound union within a person's being. . . .

The dignity of women and the order of love

29. The passage from the Letter to the Ephesians already quoted (5:21–33), in which the relationship between Christ and the Church is presented as the link between the Bridegroom and the Bride, also makes reference to the institution of marriage as recorded in the Book of Genesis (cf. 2:24). This passage connects the truth about marriage as a primordial sacrament with the creation of man and woman in the image and likeness of God (cf. *Gen* 1:27; 5:1). The significant comparison in the Letter to the Ephesians gives perfect clarity to *what is decisive for the dignity of women both in the eyes of God* – the Creator and Redeemer – *and in the eyes of human beings* – men and women. In God's eternal plan, woman is the one in whom the order of love in the created world of persons takes first root. The order of love belongs to the intimate life of God himself, the life of the Trinity. In the intimate life of God, the Holy Spirit is the personal hypostasis of love. Through the Spirit, Uncreated Gift, love becomes a gift for created persons. *Love, which is of God, communicates itself to creatures*: "God's love has been poured into our hearts through the Holy Spirit who has been given to us" (*Rom* 5:5).

The calling of woman into existence at man's side as "a helper fit for him" (*Gen* 2:18) in the "unity of the two," provides the visible world of creatures with particular conditions so that "the love of God may be poured into the hearts" of the beings created in his image. When the author of the Letter to the Ephesians calls Christ "the Bridegroom" and the Church "the Bride," he indirectly confirms through this analogy *the truth about woman as bride*. The Bridegroom is the one who loves. The Bride is loved: *it is she who receives love, in order to love in return*.

Rereading Genesis in light of the spousal symbol in the Letter to the Ephesians enables us to grasp a truth which seems to determine in an essential manner the question of women's dignity, and, subsequently, also the question of their vocation: *the dignity of women is measured by the order of love*, which is essentially the order of justice and charity.

Only a person can love and only a person can be loved. This statement is primarily ontological in nature, and it gives rise to an ethical affirmation. Love is an ontological and ethical requirement of the person. The person must be loved, since love alone corresponds to what the person is. This explains *the commandment of love*, known already in the Old Testament (cf. *Deut* 6:5; *Lev* 19:18) and placed by Christ at the very centre of the Gospel "*ethos*" (cf. *Mt* 22:36–40; *Mk* 12:28–34). This also explains the *primacy of love* expressed by Saint Paul in the First Letter to the Corinthians: "the greatest of these is love" (cf. 13:13).

Unless we refer to this order and primacy we cannot give a complete and adequate answer to the question about women's dignity and vocation. When we say that the woman is the one who receives love in order to love in return, this refers not only or above all to the specific spousal relationship of marriage. It means something more universal, based on the very fact of her being a woman within all the interpersonal relationships which, in the most varied ways, shape society and structure the interaction between all persons – men and women. In this broad and diversified context, a *woman represents a particular value by the fact that she is a human person*, and, at the same time, this particular person, *by the fact of her femininity*. This concerns each and every woman, independently of the cultural context in which she lives, and independently of her spiritual, psychological and physical characteristics, as for example, age, education, health, work, and whether she is married or single.

The passage from the Letter to the Ephesians which we have been considering enables us to think of a special kind of "prophetism" that belongs to women in their femininity. The analogy of the Bridegroom and the Bride speaks of the love with which every human being – man and woman – is loved by God in Christ. But in the context of the biblical analogy and the text's interior logic, it is precisely the woman – the bride – who manifests this truth to everyone. This "*prophetic*" *character of women in their femininity* finds its highest expression in the Virgin Mother of God. She emphasizes, in the fullest and most direct way, the intimate linking of the order of love – which enters the world of human persons through a Woman – with the Holy Spirit. At the Annunciation Mary hears the words: "The Holy Spirit will come upon you" (*Lk* 1:35).

Awareness of a mission

30. A woman's dignity is closely connected with the love which she receives by the very reason of her femininity; it is likewise connected

with the love which she gives in return. The truth about the person and about love is thus confirmed. With regard to the truth about the person, we must turn again to the Second Vatican Council: "Man, who is the only creature on earth that God willed for its own sake, cannot fully find himself except through a sincere gift of self." This applies to every human being, as a person created in God's image, whether man or woman. This ontological affirmation also indicates the ethical dimension of a person's vocation. *Woman can only hand herself by giving love to others.*

From the "beginning," woman – like man – was created and "placed" by God in this order of love. The sin of the first parents did not destroy this order, nor irreversibly cancel it out. This is proved by the words of the Proto-evangelium (cf. *Gen* 3:15). Our reflections have focused on *the particular place occupied by the "woman"* in this key text of revelation. It is also to be noted how the same Woman, who attains the position of a biblical "exemplar," also appears within the eschatological perspective of the world and of humanity given in the Book of Revelation. She is "a *woman clothed with the sun*," with the moon under her feet, and on her head a crown of stars (cf. *Rev* 12:1). One can say she is a Woman of cosmic scale, on a scale with the whole work of creation. At the same time she is "suffering the pangs and anguish of childbirth" (*Rev* 12:2) like Eve "the mother of all the living" (*Gen* 3:20). She also suffers because "before the woman who is about to give birth" (cf. *Rev* 12:4) there stands "the great dragon . . . that ancient serpent" (*Rev* 12:9), already known from the Proto-evangelium: the Evil One, the "father of lies" and of sin (cf. *Jn* 8:44). The "ancient serpent" wishes to devour "the child." While we see in this text an echo of the Infancy Narrative (cf. *Mt* 2:13,16), we can also see that the struggle with evil and the Evil One marks the biblical exemplar of the "woman" from the beginning to the end of history. It is also a *struggle for man, for his true good, for his salvation.* Is not the Bible trying to tell us that it is precisely in the "woman" – Eve-Mary – that history witnesses a dramatic struggle for every human being, the struggle for his or her fundamental "yes" or "no" to God and God's eternal plan for humanity?

While the dignity of woman witnesses to the love which she receives in order to love in return, the biblical "exemplar" of the Woman also seems to reveal *the true order of love which constitutes woman's own vocation.* Vocation is meant here in its fundamental, and one may say universal significance, a significance which is then actualized and expressed in women's many different "vocations" in the Church and the world.

The moral and spiritual strength of a woman is joined to her awareness that *God entrusts the human being to her in a special way.* Of course, God entrusts every human being to each and every other human being. But this entrusting concerns women in a special way – precisely by reason of their femininity – and this in a particular way determines their vocation.

The moral force of women, which draws strength from this awareness and this entrusting, expresses itself in a great number of figures
of the Old Testament, of the time of Christ, and of later ages right up
to our own day.

A woman is strong because of her awareness of this entrusting,
strong because of the fact that God "entrusts the human being to her,"
always and in every way, even in the situations of social discrimination in which she may find herself. This awareness and this fundamental vocation speak to women of the dignity which they receive
from God himself, and this makes them "strong" and strengthens
their vocation.

Thus the "perfect woman" (cf. *Prov* 31:10) becomes an irreplaceable
support and source of spiritual strength for other people, who perceive
the great energies of her spirit. These "perfect women" are owed much
by their families, and sometimes by whole nations.

In our own time, the successes of science and technology make it
possible to attain material well-being to a degree hitherto unknown.
While this favours some, it pushes others to the edges of society. In this
way, unilateral progress can also lead to a gradual *loss of sensitivity
for man, that is, for what is essentially human*. In this sense, our time
in particular *awaits the manifestation* of that "genius" which belongs to
women, and which can ensure sensitivity for human beings in every
circumstance: because they are human! – and because "the greatest
of these is love" (cf. 1 *Cor* 13:13).

Thus a careful reading of the biblical exemplar of the Woman – from
the Book of Genesis to the Book of Revelation – confirms that which
constitutes women's dignity and vocation, as well as that which is unchangeable and ever relevant in them, because it has its "ultimate foundation in Christ, who is the same yesterday and today, yes and forever."
If the human being is entrusted by God to women in a particular way,
does not this mean that *Christ looks to them for the accomplishment
of the "royal priesthood"* (1 *Pt* 2:9), which is the treasure he has given
to every individual? Christ, as the supreme and only priest of the New
and Eternal Covenant, and as the Bridegroom of the Church, does not
cease to submit this same inheritance to the Father through the Spirit,
so that God may be "everything to everyone" (1 *Cor* 15:28).

Then the truth that "the greatest of these is love" (cf. 1 *Cor* 13:13)
will have its definitive fulfillment.

IX

CONCLUSION

If you knew the gift of God

31. "If you knew the gift of God" (*Jn* 4:10), Jesus says to the Samaritan woman during one of those remarkable conversations which show his great esteem for the dignity of women and for the vocation which enables them to share in his messianic mission.

The present reflections, now at an end, have sought to recognize, within the "gift of God," what he, as Creator and Redeemer, entrusts to women, to every woman. In the Spirit of Christ, in fact, women can discover the entire meaning of their femininity and thus be disposed to making a "sincere gift of self" to others, thereby finding themselves.

During the Marian Year *the Church desires to give thanks to the Most Holy Trinity* for the "mystery of woman" and for every woman – for that which constitutes the eternal measure of her feminine dignity, for the "great works of God," which throughout human history have been accomplished in and through her. After all, was it not in and through her that the greatest event in human history – the incarnation of God himself – was accomplished?

Therefore *the Church gives thanks for each and every woman*: for mothers, for sisters, for wives; for women consecrated to God in virginity; for women dedicated to the many human beings who await the gratuitous love of another person; for women who watch over the human persons in the family, which is the fundamental sign of the human community; for women who work professionally, and who at times are burdened by a great social responsibility; for *"perfect"* women and for "weak" women – for all women as they have come forth from the heart of God in all the beauty and richness of their femininity; as they have been embraced by his eternal love; as, together with men, they are pilgrims on this earth, which is the temporal "homeland" of all people and is transformed sometimes into a "valley of tears"; as they assume, together with men, *a common responsibility for the destiny of humanity* according to daily necessities and according to that definitive destiny which the human family has in God himself, in the bosom of the ineffable Trinity.

The Church gives thanks *for all the manifestations of the feminine "genius"* which have appeared in the course of history, in the midst of all peoples and nations; she gives thanks for all the charisms which the Holy Spirit distributes to women in the history of the People of God, for all the victories which she owes to their faith, hope and charity: she gives thanks for all *the fruits of feminine holiness*.

The Church asks at the same time that these invaluable "manifestations of the Spirit" (cf. 1 *Cor* 12:4ff.), which with great generosity are poured forth upon the "daughters" of the eternal Jerusalem, may be attentively recognized and appreciated so that they may return for the common good of the Church and of humanity, especially in our times. Meditating on the biblical mystery of the "woman," the Church prays that in this mystery all women may discover themselves and their "supreme vocation."

May *Mary*, who "is a model of the Church in the matter of faith, charity, and perfect union with Christ," obtain for all of us *this same "grace,"* in the Year which we have dedicated to her as we approach the third millennium from the coming of Christ.

With these sentiments, I impart the Apostolic Blessing to all the faithful, and in a special way to women, my sisters in Christ.

Given in Rome, at Saint Peter's, on 15 August, the Solemnity of the Assumption of the Blessed Virgin Mary, in the year 1988, the tenth of my Pontificate.

Chapter 4

THE 1990s

Of all of the decades since the 1960s, the Roman Catholic Church in the 1990s probably produced the most documents that commented on the position of women, even though many did so only as reaffirmations of previous positions laid out in other documents. This chapter addresses eight documents, although only half of them are reprinted here. The most significant documents in this chapter in terms of women are *Evangelium vitae* and *Ordinatio sacerdotalis*. Nevertheless, all of these eight documents reassert the Roman Catholic Church's theology of womanhood in relationship to two main themes: gender complementarity and gender difference. In other words, women are different from men in many ways, including in their theological importance, but at the same time they complement men in biological and social ways.

CENTESIMUS ANNUS

Before turning to an in-depth examination of theological additions, let us look at some of the documents that reaffirm the theological position of women within the Roman Catholic Church already laid out in this book. Pope John Paul II, in *Centesimus annus*, released on May 1, 1991, for the one hundredth anniversary of the social encyclical *Rerum novarum*, confirms workers' rights and the struggle for fair and justice conditions for workers and all human beings. The pope also reaffirms Pope Leo XIII's conclusion about women and their relationship to the labor force: women should do work that takes into account their nature, circumstances, and abilities (7). Men should be provided a wage that allows them to support their wife and children (8). Finally, in a world quite different from that of Pope Leo XIII's day, one must recognize worker's rights as part of the larger human struggle for human rights across the globe (26). Within the document the church affirms human rights and supports movements for justice, equality, and freedom while recognizing that they do not exist everywhere. *Centesimus annus* recognizes that within contemporary society it is often women who suffer, along with the young and the elderly, in situations of injustice, inequality, and restricted freedom (33).

GRATISSIMAM SANE

Another document that confirms these conclusions about the place and status of women in the world is *Gratissimam sane*. Promulgated on February 2, 1994, this document specifically addresses families and their role in the world. It is from this perspective that the role of women within the family is discussed. The document reaffirms the traditional Christian understanding of human beings, their nature, and their creation. It states that women's work in the home should be valued more. Raising children should be held in the same esteem that other work is.

While confirming older notions, the document also lays out some new ideas about human nature and its development. In the biological sense, because humans develop within women, women shape not only their babies' bodies but their personalities (16). Unlike some of the previous documents, the pope is somewhat suspicious of the modern notion of human rights, saying that rights neither imply respect nor necessarily acknowledge the individual as a human being (15). They are insufficient in and of themselves, and in this regard, humanity suffers.

ORDINATIO SACERDOTALIS

During the 1990s the church also released an apostolic letter affirming the male-only priesthood entitled *Ordinatio sacerdotalis*, or *On Reserving Priestly Ordination to Men Alone*. Pope John Paul II published this document on May 22, 1994. It mentions the traditional arguments against women's ordination, yet it also makes one of the strongest statements against women's ordination in the history of the church (one to be surpassed only by *Responsum ad propositum dubium,* published on October 28, 1995, by the SCDF).

Pope John Paul II begins *Ordinatio sacerdotalis* by affirming tradition. Throughout the entire history of the Roman Catholic Church, the church has never ordained women. This is true of the Eastern Church as well, the document reminds the faithful.

Next, the pope traces the contemporary history of the question of women's ordination in modern theological writings. When discussion of women's ordination took place within the Anglican Church, the document reminds its readers how Pope Paul VI responded. He affirmed the traditional

Catholic stance saying, "It is not admissible to ordain women to the priest-hood, for very fundamental reasons. These reasons include: the example recorded in the Sacred Scriptures of Christ choosing his apostles only from among men; the constant practice of the church, which has imitated Christ in choosing only men; and her living teaching authority which has consistently held that the exclusion of women from the priesthood is in accordance with God's plan for the church" (1). The document also reaf-firms *Inter insigniores*, stating that these same reasons—Jesus chose only men and the church imitates Jesus' example—were given in this document as proof as well.

Another theological argument against women's ordination concerns the Roman Catholic Church's concept of its own authority. The document highlights the idea that the church does not think it has any authority on the tradition of a male-only priesthood. According to *Ordinatio sacerdotalis*, the church is only following its founder's example. It recalls *Inter insigniores*, which declared that Jesus' treatment of women was quite contrary to soci-etal standards of the time, which only reaffirms his choice of men only for the priesthood. Pope John Paul II, through *Ordinatio sacerdotalis*, reminds the readers of his own statements in *Mulieris dignitatem*. In that document he concluded two things about Jesus as his life and ministry relate to wom-en. First, Jesus' treatment of women shows women's dignity; and second, Jesus chose only men to be his apostles, therefore relegating women to a different role. Because Jesus did not treat women the way society expected, but rather with dignity and respect, his choice of a male-only apostolate is free of any and all societal pressure or influence (*Ordinatio sacerdotalis*, 2).

Even though Jesus did not choose women to serve in the role of priest, the pope, in *Ordinatio sacerdotalis*, insists that women have a very impor-tant role to play in the divine plan. This role includes motivating society to change for the better. Reserving the priesthood to men does not denigrate women in the least. It is not discriminatory, nor does it create a situation in which women should be considered lesser in dignity than men. Rather, women have a complementary role to play in society, in the family, and in the church. This complementary role was defined and designed by God from the creation of the first human beings, Adam and Eve.

Yet, within current feminist rights movements, especially those that show liberal tendencies, many argue that different roles imply varying degrees of value. Given the significance of the Eucharist within the life of the Roman Catholic Church and its efficacy in terms of salvation for Roman Catho-lics, would it not be true that women, because they cannot consecrate the sacrament, have less worth, dignity, and holiness than men? Many feminist men and women would not agree with the notion of "separate but equal." In order for men and women truly to be equal, they need to have access to the same roles, vocations, and opportunities. This is referred to in feminist terminology as *gender equality as sameness* and is often viewed as contrary to gender complementarity.

This is one example of a feminist argument used to support women's entrance into the priesthood. In fact, within the document the pope acknowledges contemporary debates that question whether women's roles can include or should include the priesthood. He responds to such questions concerning women's roles in the church: "I declare that the church has no authority whatsoever to confer priestly ordination on women and that this judgment is to be definitely held by all the church's faithful" (4). In many ways this judgment of the church has nothing to do with the question of gender sameness or gender difference but is rather a question of church understanding of its own authority. The pope is fully convinced that no matter what the argument, the church has no choice but to continue its tradition of a male-only priesthood.

There are three important reasons why this declaration is significant regarding church authority above and beyond the declaration itself. First, the church is claiming a certain kind of authority: the authority to make an authoritative pronouncement. Second, this declaration of "a lack of authority" is worded in such a way that it seems intended to be interpreted as an infallible document. Third, the pope says that all faithful must agree with the statement (another testament to its infallible nature).

Given these three reasons, *Ordinatio sacerdotalis* contains one of the most important developments regarding the theology of womanhood created by the Roman Catholic Church during the 1990s. The document appears to settle the question of women's ordination once and for all. In doing so, the church explains what women are called to do within the life of the church.

WOMEN BEAR AN EFFECTIVE WITNESS TO FAITH

On July 6, 1994, the pope addressed the crowd gathered outside of Saint Peter's Basilica in his general audience for the day with a short speech entitled "Women Bear an Effective Witness to Faith." According to the document, Mary offers a good example of what God intends for women and their roles in the world. Jesus' treatment of women with respect and dignity also shows God's will for women in the world. Jesus also treated women well by healing them, praising them often for their strong faith, and forgiving them when they sinned. Jesus said that women were included in the kingdom of God that he wished to help bring about. Jesus also had women accompany him in his ministry, letting them follow him and assist him and his disciples. Women were the first to see that Jesus' body was no longer in the tomb and were entrusted with the news of his resurrection.

In these many ways the document argues that Jesus' attitude and treatment of women were contrary to his society's established notions, laws, and understanding. They also show that Jesus wanted women to be part of the new community he was establishing. Jesus sought to end the inequality between men and women as well as the unjust way in which society treated women at the time.

The document concludes that women have, throughout the history of the church, been good witnesses of faith. This is one of the things women are encouraged to do for the betterment of society and the family. Women should also assist the church, as did those first women who traveled with and assisted the first apostles.

This brief address to the people gathered for the papal audience explains the role of women as Jesus' helpers, faithful individuals, and witnesses to the power and mystery of Jesus. The Christian community, based on Jesus' atypical treatment of women, should also treat women with respect, dignity, forgiveness, and goodness. The document concentrates on women's roles as transmitters of the faith. This is one important role, but more will be encountered as well.

EVANGELIUM VITAE

The next document that addresses women's roles in society and in the church is *Evangelium vitae*, or *On the Value and Inviolability of Human Life,* released by Pope John Paul II on March 25, 1995. The document begins by looking at what is happening in contemporary society, especially its understanding of a culture of death or at the very least an anti-life mentality (3). This culture of death is closely connected to a lack of relationship between humans and God.

There are many aspects of this culture of death that hurt modern human beings and their relationships to one another and to God. First, modern society misunderstands attacks against life as rights, such as the "right" to abortion (55–58). There also exists a "structure of sin" in the world that opposes life from its very beginning, that gives reasons and justifications to those seeking and securing abortions (59). The pope says, "I declare that direct abortion, that is, abortion willed as an end or as a means, always constitutes a grave moral disorder, since it is the deliberate killing of an innocent human being" (62). The pope uses the same declarative language he used about the priesthood being accessible only to men. These theological declarations are highly significant in that they are intended to resolve any debate over the issues; they clearly and once and for all define the church's official position on the theological question at hand. For the church, all human beings from their initial conception in the womb have a right to life.

This right cannot be violated by any other human being without grave sin and threat to the moral order.

According to the church, modern notions of rights do, even though they should not, revolve around mistaken concepts of freedom and individualism or overt selfishness. This culture of death sees the goods in life as material possessions, pleasure, and the depersonalization of many aspects of life. It is often women, along with their children, the elderly, and the sick, who suffer the most when this occurs.

In order to follow God's teachings, modern culture needs to build and foster a culture of life. Modern people need to become more attuned to their consciences and engaged in more moral activity. Likewise, society should focus on rights that increase human dignity; align with respect; do not discriminate by sex/gender, race, class, or ethnicity; and that instill a moral standard. The world needs to value love, service, and Christian charity to become a better place. God created all people to love one another, and that is humanity's first and main vocation. Jesus' life and death show us what love means and how to be love to one another (25–35).

This culture of life and love includes respect for human beings and love for life, whether it is life in the womb; planetary life in the forms of plants, animals, and ecological soundness; or other human beings, according to the pope. Humans in marriage respect life in sexual relations when they are open to procreation. More than anything else, respecting life must begin with the child in the womb. This is one of the most fundamental ways humans can show respect to life in all its forms. Motherhood should be more respected and valued (59, 81). Another way to cultivate a culture of life is cherishing and caring for the elderly. Finally, life comes when we practice justice and respect one another's human dignity (48, 74, 81). Those who work in the public sector should focus on these concerns and promote these values in their work (88–91). One of the ways this is accomplished is through consciousness-raising in ways that promote life and see its inviolable value as a gift from God (96).

The pope focuses the discussion in sections 86 and 99 on the place, position, and roles of women. Section 86 blames modern society for its devaluation of motherhood, pointing out that mothers have shown the world the best models of Christian values. These values include fidelity, chastity, sacrifice, love, trust in God, and suffering for others. Women suffer in childbirth. They also give of themselves for the good of their families. Women give their lives to others in lives of service apart from and in addition to physical motherhood. Likewise, women should also be praised for raising children on their own when they must. Society should help women who answer the call to motherhood all alone (87).

According to the document, women also play an important role in promoting a culture of life. Section 99 begins by describing how women can best accomplish this responsibility. The pope calls for a "new feminism which rejects the temptation of imitating male models of 'male domination,' in order to acknowledge and affirm the true genius of women in every aspect of the life of society, and overcome all discrimination, violence and exploitation." In other words, women have to show the world what love means and what it means to practice love in the ways that are appropriate to their nature, using their special gifts and talents. One of the ways women learn about love is through having children and that special connection they establish with their children while they are still in the womb.

It is up to women who have been mothers to teach others what that connection to life means. Women must also teach how to accept others as human beings and creations of God and not value them for other reasons that modern society uses to determine worthiness. The document says, "This is the fundamental contribution which the church and humanity expect from women. And it is the indispensable prerequisite for an authentic cultural change" (99). On women's shoulders is placed the burden for true and authentic cultural change, one that the church does not think can be accomplished through the modern feminist movement because it does not rely at all on women's special nature and gifts as mothers. The church believes that true cultural change can only happen if feminism changes in a way that values this "true genius" of women. Feminism will not create a culture of life if it continues to utilize male forms of domination to make change.

This interpretation of feminism and how it works is a misunderstanding of feminism. The church believes, quite mistakenly, that feminism relies on male models of domination to further societal change when, in fact, the feminist movement critiques these models. While liberal feminism has pushed for women to have equal access to traditionally male-only occupations (like the priesthood), much of feminism has approached a revaluing of traditionally feminine values while at the same time removing the cultural demand that women continuously sacrifice themselves, their dreams, their wants, and their lives for others. Feminism has often said that women are often asked to be more self-sacrificing than men to the detriment of their personal development. Many feminists argue that feminine values are not necessarily natural to women but are taught social constructions that inhibit personal growth and development of both men and women. Instead, all individuals should be allowed to develop into mature human beings who balance the needs of the self with the needs of the other. Everyone should cultivate feminine values like listening, loving, giving, caring, and the like. Too often, women have been called upon to ignore themselves for the other. In this way feminism does clash in some respects with church teaching.

Nevertheless, this misunderstanding of feminism by the church is what prompts the church to ask for a new kind of feminism, one that values women's self-sacrificing and those gifts that are particularly feminine gifts. Some Catholic women and men have heeded this call. A few good examples of a Roman Catholic Vatican-inspired form of feminism can be seen in *Women in Christ: Toward a New Feminism,* edited by Michele M. Schumacher, and in Genevieve Kineke's *The Authentic Catholic Woman.* Both of these books cite the call in *Evangelium vitae* to create a new kind of feminism based on the Vatican theology of womanhood, especially its loving, caring, mothering, and self-sacrificing dimensions. This new kind of feminism specifically reflects the Vatican's call to a male-only priesthood as one of its basic tenets as well as the complementarity of the sexes and its refusal of contraception and choice regarding abortion. In these ways this new feminism sets itself off in quite a fundamental way from traditional feminists and many Roman Catholic feminist men and women, laity and theologians as well.

LETTER TO WOMEN

Pope John Paul II's "Letter to Women" was released on June 29, 1995, as an explicit precursor to the Fourth World Conference on Women to be held in September of 1995 in Beijing. The document's expressed purpose is to offer the world "the church's teachings with regard to women's issues" (1). According to the document, the church's main goal is to support the dignity and rights of women in the world, and it is written with that theme in mind.

The document begins by thanking women for all they have done in the different roles they play in the world. Mothers are thanked for bearing children and being their first teachers. Wives are thanked for their love, commitment, and service. Women who are daughters and sisters are thanked for the way in which they bring sensitivity, intuitiveness, generosity, and fidelity to their families and the larger society as well. Working women are thanked for showing the world how to bring feelings into a rational world view and their striving to make the world a better place. Women who live their lives as consecrated virgins are thanked for being faithful to their calling and showing humans how to live in close relationship to God.

Finally, all women, no matter what their roles, are thanked for "being *a woman*! Through the insight which is so much a part of your womanhood you enrich the world's understanding and help to make human relations more honest and authentic" (2). What women are thanked for is important because these gifts, while something fostered by women, also seem to come naturally to women. The church is convinced that God created women to be a certain way and that they show their natural gifts of fidelity, teaching, caring, honesty, authenticity, love, and service to the world as they interact with it. Just by being themselves, as God created them, the world is a better place and is continually becoming better through women's participation in it.

In line with this thinking the document considers women to be naturally good at relationships and the promotion and living out of ethical and spiritual values (9). Women naturally excel at the same time that they find fulfillment by devoting their lives to serving others. This can be done within their own families or as participants in larger society.

According to the pope, women's service done out of love is what separates women from men and women's roles from men's roles in theological terms as well. As the document puts it:

Perhaps more than men, women *acknowledge the person*, because they see persons with their hearts. They see them independently of various ideological or political systems. They see others in their greatness and limitations; they try to go out to them and *help them*. In this way the basic plan of the Creator takes flesh in the history of humanity and there is constantly revealed, in the variety of vocations, that *beauty*—not merely physical, but above all spiritual—which God bestowed from the very beginning on all, and in a particular way on women. (12)

Women see people as human beings regardless of whatever other labels or situations these individuals may have or be in, and women, by using what God created within them, are always seeking to help other human beings. In other words, women's true self and true beauty can be found when women dedicate themselves to serving others.

The best example of this gift of self in the service of others is Mary (11). The document explains that Mary served God by freely choosing to be the mother of Jesus and that Mary then served Jesus. Mary is the quintessential woman whose service done out of love made this world a better place.

In the document the church also defends its traditional teachings concerning the priesthood. It reaffirms previous statements saying that Jesus specifically did not choose women to be priests. This is part of the mystery of the church, because Jesus treated women without prejudice. His treatment of women deserves special recognition because the contemporary society did not treat women the way he did. Therefore, his choice for a male-only priesthood was free of social influence. Nevertheless, while women cannot be priests in the church, women's roles are extremely important and women deserve the same dignity men have because both sexes/ genders were created by God.

No matter what women may give the world or should give the world based on their God-given abilities, the document asserts that their gifts are being stifled (4) and their ability to find fulfillment in life is also being hindered. All of this is because society has discriminated against women and put many obstacles in place that do not let women be themselves. Women continue to face oppression, objectification, devaluing, disrespect, discrimination, and injustice. The pope acknowledges that the Roman Catholic Church has to accept some responsibility for the present oppressive situation of women around the globe.

One example the document gives in support of the position it is laying out is abortion. Some women seem to have no other choice than to have an abortion because of societal situations. In this way, while women are guilty of the sin, some of this guilt of abortion also lies with men and the larger society as a whole (5).

The document also acknowledges the strides made by women to change their situation, and the document points out that the church views the feminist struggle for economic, political, and social rights for women somewhat differently than it did in the past, when it called it "extremely inappropriate, the sign of a lack of femininity, a manifestation of exhibitionism, and even a sin!" (6). It now believes this struggle has always been a fight for women's dignity. The mission of feminism to restore women's dignity as creations of God is not over, according to the document, because women still face oppression and the like in societies across the globe. The church ends the document by expressing its hope that the Beijing meeting will help the world better appreciate women and their principal vocation of service.

RESPONSUM AD PROPOSITUM DUBIUM

The next document centers again on the question of women's ordination. It is the shortest document in this anthology. *Responsum ad propositum dubium* was published on October 28, 1995, by the SCDF. It confirms in one short paragraph the definitive nature of the teachings concerning women's ordination in *Ordinatio sacerdotalis*. In fact, it considers the pope's declaration in *Ordinatio sacerdotalis*—that the church has no authority to ordain women—to be an infallible statement. It bases the infallible nature of the declaration on the church's understanding of the papal office, the longstanding tradition within the Roman Catholic Church not to ordain women, and the evidence of the Bible. It ends by reminding the faithful that infallible statements require the assent of all.

THE TRUTH AND MEANING OF HUMAN SEXUALITY

The final document of this decade that relates to women is the Pontifical Council of the Family's (PCF) "The Truth and Meaning of Human Sexuality," published on December 8, 1995. The document, like many of the documents explored in this chapter, reiterates much of what has already been said concerning human nature, women's roles, human sexuality, and the like. However, the document does add a few novel ideas to the Roman Catholic Church's understanding of womanhood. Of course, this occurs within the context of an understanding of human sexuality and how to best approach teaching children.

When it comes to raising children, the document argues that strict obedience to gender stereotyping is not appropriate. It offers the examples that girls should be allowed to play sports and boys should not be discouraged from expressing their emotions. Likewise, chastity should be taught to boys and girls and not required only of girls (111).

However, the document believes that total disregard for gender stereotyping is also problematic because sex/gender difference also exists. It offers the reader some examples of this difference in family roles. For example, between the age of five to right before puberty, "girls will generally be developing a maternal interest in babies, motherhood and homemaking" (81). This femininity should be valued and promoted in developing girls. During puberty, girls should be taught to value the changes that are taking place in their bodies and gain some understanding about what fertility means. They should also be taught to put a high value on motherhood and bearing children (90, 92). However, parents should also use caution with very realistic portrayals of giving birth so that daughters are not scared by the idea (126).

Some of these differences in girls' development are more clearly understood if one examines the same time period with regard to boys and their development. From age five to puberty, there is little change, according to the PCF. Boys should be taught not to be too aggressive or power hungry and to learn that their "masculinity is not a sign of superiority with regard to women, but a call from God to take on certain roles and responsibilities" (82). Yet, sometime before puberty, boys need to be taught about changes to their genitals and how that fits within the context of married life. They also need to be educated about how their sexual drives will increase during puberty and how to avoid misuing that instinct so that they will afford women all the respect that they are due (93).

One can better see what the church understands by girls' education when what is required of boys is also explained. There is a certain God-given naturalness to sex/gender characteristics: boys are inherently more physical, while girls naturally develop interests in babies and homemaking. Boys have a stronger sex drive than girls. Boys are naturally more aggressive than girls, which can lead them to think themselves better than girls. In summary, the different roles boys and girls play in family life are dependent on the physical realities of human biological development perhaps more than emotional and spiritual growth.

The 1990s repeated much of the theology laid out in earlier documents. Women play different roles than men, even though as creations of God men and women are equal in dignity and respect. As workers, women should be given jobs that conform with their nature and ability. Women's rights should be respected. Injustice, inequality, unjust discrimination, and the oppression of women should be stopped with effort from all groups and nations across the globe. Women's roles as mothers should be respected more. Both as mothers and through other roles within and outside of family life, women fulfill themselves through service to others. One of the roles not assigned to women is the priesthood. Given Jesus' treatment of women, his choice to have only men lead the community he founded is sound and shows no signs of discrimination or cultural bias. Women show the world how to be a better place.

At the same time, the documents of the 1990s also explore some new territory regarding its development of a theology of womanhood. One of the main ideas is that women are to be promoters of a culture of life. Women are called to create a kind of feminism that centers on feminine qualities. Women are naturally nurturers, caregivers, concerned with relationships, and faithful, honest, and loving. A feminism that makes the most of these feminine ideals will make the world a better place, a more humane one tuned to a culture of life rather than death.

In addition, women make the world a better place just by cultivating the nature that is within them. Even little girls at the age of five take an interest in caring for their dolls and their pretend homes. By nature, women have a feminine "genius" that centers on love, service, and human relations. If women were free from societal oppression and discrimination, they could develop fully in the way God created them, and then the world would become a better place. Women's faith testimony is just one example of how women make the world better—they pass on their faith to their children and to others they encounter. Women are also natural helpers whose beauty radiates when they are free to be themselves.

Related to all of these ideas is the church declaration that it has no authority to ordain women to the priesthood. In the 1990s two documents confirmed this position: *Ordinatio sacerdotalis* declared that the church lacked the authority and that it required the full assent of the faithful to this declaration, while *Responsum ad propositum dubium* ingrained as infallible what had been declared in *Ordinatio sacerdotalis*.

The new millennium offers little shift from this chain of thought. In the 1990s the prefect of the Sacred Congregation of the Doctrine of the Faith, the main producers of the documents along with Pope John Paul II, was Cardinal Joseph Ratzinger. In 2005 Cardinal Ratzinger became Pope Benedict XVI. For the most part, his position regarding women during his papacy has been quite clear. Nonetheless, there were some significant developments in the first decade of the new century regarding women, including an explicit definition of femininity and an explanation of how men and women should work together to make the world a better place. For these reasons alone the decade at the beginning of the third millennium after Christ is worth examining in depth. We will do so in the next chapter, following sections of four important documents from the 1990s.

ORDINATIO SACERDOTALIS

APOSTOLIC LETTER OF JOHN PAUL II
TO THE BISHOPS
OF THE CATHOLIC CHURCH
ON RESERVING PRIESTLY ORDINATION
TO MEN ALONE

22 MAY 1994

Venerable Brothers in the Episcopate,

1. Priestly ordination, which hands on the office entrusted by Christ to his Apostles of teaching, sanctifying and governing the faithful, has in the Catholic Church from the beginning always been reserved to men alone. This tradition has also been faithfully maintained by the Oriental Churches.

When the question of the ordination of women arose in the Anglican Communion, Pope Paul VI, out of fidelity to his office of safeguarding the Apostolic Tradition, and also with a view to removing a new obstacle placed in the way of Christian unity, reminded Anglicans of the position of the Catholic Church: "She holds that it is not admissible to ordain women to the priesthood, for very fundamental reasons. These reasons include: the example recorded in the Sacred Scriptures of Christ choosing his Apostles only from among men; the constant practice of the Church, which has imitated Christ in choosing only men; and her living teaching authority which has consistently held that the exclusion of women from the priesthood is in accordance with God's plan for his Church."

But since the question had also become the subject of debate among theologians and in certain Catholic circles, Paul VI directed the Congregation for the Doctrine of the Faith to set forth and expound the teaching of the Church on this matter. This was done through the Declaration *Inter Insigniores*, which the Supreme Pontiff approved and ordered to be published.

2. The Declaration recalls and explains the fundamental reasons for this teaching, reasons expounded by Paul VI, and concludes that the Church "does not consider herself authorized to admit women to priestly ordination." To these fundamental reasons the document adds other

theological reasons which illustrate the appropriateness of the divine provision, and it also shows clearly that Christ's way of acting did not proceed from sociological or cultural motives peculiar to his time. As Paul VI later explained: "The real reason is that, in giving the Church her fundamental constitution, her theological anthropology – hereafter always followed by the Church's Tradition – Christ established things in this way."

In the Apostolic Letter *Mulieris Dignitatem*, I myself wrote in this regard: "In calling only men as his Apostles, Christ acted in a completely free and sovereign manner. In doing so, he exercised the same freedom with which, in all his behavior, he emphasized the dignity and the vocation of women, without conforming to the prevailing customs and to the traditions sanctioned by the legislation of the time."

In fact the Gospels and the Acts of the Apostles attest that this call was made in accordance with God's eternal plan; Christ chose those whom he willed (cf. Mk 3:13–14; Jn 6:70), and he did so in union with the Father, "through the Holy Spirit" (Acts 1:2), after having spent the night in prayer (cf. Lk 6:12). Therefore, in granting admission to the ministerial priesthood, the Church has always acknowledged as a perennial norm her Lord's way of acting in choosing the twelve men whom he made the foundation of his Church (cf. Rv 21:14). These men did not in fact receive only a function which could thereafter be exercised by any member of the Church; rather they were specifically and intimately associated in the mission of the Incarnate Word himself (cf. Mt 10:1, 7–8; 28:16–20; Mk 3:13–16; 16:14–15). The Apostles did the same when they chose fellow workers who would succeed them in their ministry. Also included in this choice were those who, throughout the time of the Church, would carry on the Apostles' mission of representing Christ the Lord and Redeemer.

3. Furthermore, the fact that the Blessed Virgin Mary, Mother of God and Mother of the Church, received neither the mission proper to the Apostles nor the ministerial priesthood clearly shows that the non-admission of women to priestly ordination cannot mean that women are of lesser dignity, nor can it be construed as discrimination against them. Rather, it is to be seen as the faithful observance of a plan to be ascribed to the wisdom of the Lord of the universe.

The presence and the role of women in the life and mission of the Church, although not linked to the ministerial priesthood, remain absolutely necessary and irreplaceable. As the Declaration *Inter Insigniores* points out, "the Church desires that Christian women should become fully aware of the greatness of their mission: today their role is of capital importance both for the renewal and humanization of society and for the rediscovery by believers of the true face of the Church."

The New Testament and the whole history of the Church give ample evidence of the presence in the Church of women, true disciples,

witnesses to Christ in the family and in society, as well as in total consecration to the service of God and of the Gospel. "By defending the
dignity of women and their vocation, the Church has shown honor and
gratitude for those women who – faithful to the Gospel – have shared
in every age in the apostolic mission of the whole People of God. They
are the holy martyrs, virgins and mothers of families, who bravely bore
witness to their faith and passed on the Church's faith and tradition by
bringing up their children in the spirit of the Gospel."

Moreover, it is to the holiness of the faithful that the hierarchical
structure of the Church is totally ordered. For this reason, the Declaration *Inter Insigniores* recalls: "the only better gift, which can and must
be desired, is love (cf. 1 Cor 12 and 13). The greatest in the Kingdom
of Heaven are not the ministers but the saints."

4. Although the teaching that priestly ordination is to be reserved to
men alone has been preserved by the constant and universal Tradition
of the Church and firmly taught by the Magisterium in its more recent
documents, at the present time in some places it is nonetheless considered still open to debate, or the Church's judgment that women are not
to be admitted to ordination is considered to have a merely disciplinary
force.

Wherefore, in order that all doubt may be removed regarding a matter
of great importance, a matter which pertains to the Church's divine constitution itself, in virtue of my ministry of confirming the brethren (cf. Lk
22:32) I declare that the Church has no authority whatsoever to confer
priestly ordination on women and that this judgment is to be definitively
held by all the Church's faithful.

Invoking an abundance of divine assistance upon you, venerable
brothers, and upon all the faithful, I impart my apostolic blessing.

*From the Vatican, on May 22, the Solemnity of Pentecost, in the year
1994, the sixteenth of my Pontificate.*

EVANGELIUM VITAE

ENCYCLICAL LETTER TO THE BISHOPS
PRIESTS AND DEACONS
MEN AND WOMEN RELIGIOUS
LAY FAITHFUL
AND ALL PEOPLE OF GOOD WILL
ON THE VALUE AND INVIOLABILITY
OF HUMAN LIFE

25 MARCH 1995

* * *

11. Here though we shall concentrate particular attention on another category of attacks, affecting life in its earliest and in its final stages, attacks which present new characteristics with respect to the past and which raise questions of extraordinary seriousness. It is not only that in generalized opinion these attacks tend no longer to be considered as "crimes"; paradoxically they assume the nature of "rights," to the point that the State is called upon to give them legal recognition and to make them available through the free services of health-care personnel. Such attacks strike human life at the time of its greatest frailty, when it lacks any means of self-defence. Even more serious is the fact that, most often, those attacks are carried out in the very heart of and with the complicity of the family – the family which by its nature is called to be the "sanctuary of life."

How did such a situation come about? Many different factors have to be taken into account. In the background there is the profound crisis of culture, which generates skepticism in relation to the very foundations of knowledge and ethics, and which makes it increasingly difficult to grasp clearly the meaning of what man is, the meaning of his rights and his duties. Then there are all kinds of existential and interpersonal difficulties, made worse by the complexity of a society in which individuals, couples and families are often left alone with their problems. There are situations of acute poverty, anxiety or frustration in which the struggle to make ends meet, the presence of unbearable pain, or instances of violence, especially against women, make the choice to defend and promote life so demanding as sometimes to reach the point of heroism.

All this explains, at least in part, how the value of life can today undergo a kind of "eclipse," even though conscience does not cease to point to it as a sacred and inviolable value, as is evident in the tendency to disguise certain crimes against life in its early or final stages by using innocuous medical terms which distract attention from the fact that what is involved is the right to life of an actual human person.

12. In fact, while the climate of widespread moral uncertainty can in some way be explained by the multiplicity and gravity of today's social problems, and these can sometimes mitigate the subjective responsibility of individuals, it is no less true that we are confronted by an even larger reality, which can be described as a veritable structure of sin. This reality is characterized by the emergence of a culture which denies solidarity and in many cases takes the form of a veritable "culture of death." This culture is actively fostered by powerful cultural, economic and political currents which encourage an idea of society excessively concerned with efficiency. Looking at the situation from this point of view, it is possible to speak in a certain sense of a war of the powerful against the weak: a life which would require greater acceptance, love and care is considered useless, or held to be an intolerable burden, and is therefore rejected in one way or another. A person who, because of illness, handicap or, more simply, just by existing, compromises the well-being or life-style of those who are more favoured tends to be looked upon as an enemy to be resisted or eliminated. In this way a kind of "conspiracy against life" is unleashed. This conspiracy involves not only individuals in their personal, family or group relationships, but goes far beyond, to the point of damaging and distorting, at the international level, relations between peoples and States.

13. In order to facilitate the spread of abortion, enormous sums of money have been invested and continue to be invested in the production of pharmaceutical products which make it possible to kill the fetus in the mother's womb without recourse to medical assistance. On this point, scientific research itself seems to be almost exclusively preoccupied with developing products which are ever more simple and effective in suppressing life and which at the same time are capable of removing abortion from any kind of control or social responsibility.

It is frequently asserted that contraception, if made safe and available to all, is the most effective remedy against abortion. The Catholic Church is then accused of actually promoting abortion, because she obstinately continues to teach the moral unlawfulness of contraception. When looked at carefully, this objection is clearly unfounded. It may be that many people use contraception with a view to excluding the subsequent temptation of abortion. But the negative values inherent in the "contraceptive mentality" – which is very different from responsible parenthood, lived in respect for the full truth of the conjugal act – are such that they in fact strengthen this temptation when an unwanted life is conceived. Indeed, the pro-abortion culture is especially strong precisely where the Church's teaching on contraception is rejected. Certainly, from the moral point of view contraception and abortion are specifically different evils: the former contradicts the full truth of the sexual act as the proper expression of conjugal love, while the latter destroys the life of a human being; the former is opposed to the virtue of chastity in marriage, the latter is opposed to the virtue of justice and directly violates the divine commandment "You shall not kill."

But despite their differences of nature and moral gravity, contraception and abortion are often closely connected, as fruits of the same tree. It is true that in many cases contraception and even abortion are practised under the pressure of real-life difficulties, which nonetheless can never exonerate from striving to observe God's law fully. Still, in very many other instances such practices are rooted in a hedonistic mentality unwilling to accept responsibility in matters of sexuality, and they imply a self-centered concept of freedom, which regards procreation as an obstacle to personal fulfilment. The life which could result from a sexual encounter thus becomes an enemy to be avoided at all costs, and abortion becomes the only possible decisive response to failed contraception.

The close connection which exists, in mentality, between the practice of contraception and that of abortion is becoming increasingly obvious. It is being demonstrated in an alarming way by the development of chemical products, intrauterine devices and vaccines which, distributed with the same ease as contraceptives, really act as abortifacients in the very early stages of the development of the life of the new human being. . . .

"Am I my brother's keeper?" (Gen 4:9): a perverse idea of freedom

18. The panorama described needs to be understood not only in terms of the phenomena of death which characterize it but also in the variety of causes which determine it. The Lord's question: "What have you done?" (Gen 4:10), seems almost like an invitation addressed to Cain to go beyond the material dimension of his murderous gesture, in order to recognize in it all the gravity of the motives which occasioned it and the consequences which result from it.

Decisions that go against life sometimes arise from difficult or even tragic situations of profound suffering, loneliness, a total lack of economic prospects, depression and anxiety about the future. Such circumstances can mitigate even to a notable degree subjective responsibility and the consequent culpability of those who make these choices which in themselves are evil. But today the problem goes far beyond the necessary recognition of these personal situations. It is a problem which exists at the cultural, social and political level, where it reveals its more sinister and disturbing aspect in the tendency, ever more widely shared, to interpret the above crimes against life as legitimate expressions of individual freedom, to be acknowledged and protected as actual rights.

In this way, and with tragic consequences, a long historical process is reaching a turning-point. The process which once led to discovering the idea of "human rights" – rights inherent in every person and prior to any Constitution and State legislation – is today marked by a surprising contradiction. Precisely in an age when the inviolable rights of the person are solemnly proclaimed and the value of life is publicly affirmed, the very right to life is being denied or trampled upon, especially at the more significant moments of existence: the moment of birth and the moment of death.

On the one hand, the various declarations of human rights and the many initiatives inspired by these declarations show that at the global level there is a growing moral sensitivity, more alert to acknowledging the value and dignity of every individual as a human being, without any distinction of race, nationality, religion, political opinion or social class.

On the other hand, these noble proclamations are unfortunately contradicted by a tragic repudiation of them in practice. This denial is still more distressing, indeed more scandalous, precisely because it is occurring in a society which makes the affirmation and protection of human rights its primary objective and its boast. How can these repeated affirmations of principle be reconciled with the continual increase and widespread justification of attacks on human life? How can we reconcile these declarations with the refusal to accept those who are weak and needy, or elderly, or those who have just been conceived? These attacks go directly against respect for life and they represent a direct threat to the entire culture of human rights. It is a threat capable, in the end, of jeopardizing the very meaning of democratic coexistence: rather than societies of "people living together," our cities risk becoming societies of people who are rejected, marginalized, uprooted and oppressed. If we then look at the wider worldwide perspective, how can we fail to think that the very affirmation of the rights of individuals and peoples made in distinguished international assemblies is a merely futile exercise of rhetoric, if we fail to unmask the selfishness of the rich countries which exclude poorer countries from access to development or make such access dependent on arbitrary prohibitions against procreation, setting up an opposition between development and man himself? Should we not question the very economic models often adopted by States which, also as a result of international pressures and forms of conditioning, cause and aggravate situations of injustice and violence in which the life of whole peoples is degraded and trampled upon? . . .

22. Consequently, when the sense of God is lost, the sense of man is also threatened and poisoned, as the Second Vatican Council concisely states: "Without the Creator the creature would disappear. . . . But when God is forgotten the creature itself grows unintelligible." Man is no longer able to see himself as "mysteriously different" from other earthly creatures; he regards himself merely as one more living being, as an organism which, at most, has reached a very high stage of perfection. Enclosed in the narrow horizon of his physical nature, he is somehow reduced to being "a thing," and no longer grasps the "transcendent" character of his "existence as man." He no longer considers life as a splendid gift of God, something "sacred" entrusted to his responsibility and thus also to his loving care and "veneration." Life itself becomes a mere "thing," which man claims as his exclusive property, completely subject to his control and manipulation.

Thus, in relation to life at birth or at death, man is no longer capable of posing the question of the truest meaning of his own existence, nor can he assimilate with genuine freedom these crucial moments of his own history. He is concerned only with "doing," and, using all kinds of technology, he busies himself with programming, controlling and dominating birth and death. Birth and death, instead of being primary experiences demanding to be "lived," become things to be merely "possessed" or "rejected."

Moreover, once all reference to God has been removed, it is not surprising that the meaning of everything else becomes profoundly distorted. Nature itself, from being "mater" (mother), is now reduced to being "matter," and is subjected to every kind of manipulation. This is the direction in which a certain technical and scientific way of thinking, prevalent in present-day culture, appears to be leading when it rejects the very idea that there is a truth of creation which must be acknowledged, or a plan of God for life which must be respected. Something similar happens when concern about the consequences of such a "freedom without law" leads some people to the opposite position of a "law without freedom," as for example in ideologies which consider it unlawful to interfere in any way with nature, practically "divinizing" it. Again, this is a misunderstanding of nature's dependence on the plan of the Creator. Thus it is clear that the loss of contact with God's wise design is the deepest root of modern man's confusion, both when this loss leads to a freedom without rules and when it leaves man in "fear" of his freedom.

By living "as if God did not exist," man not only loses sight of the mystery of God, but also of the mystery of the world and the mystery of his own being.

23. The eclipse of the sense of God and of man inevitably leads to a practical materialism, which breeds individualism, utilitarianism and hedonism. Here too we see the permanent validity of the words of the

Apostle: "And since they did not see fit to acknowledge God, God gave them up to a base mind and to improper conduct" (Rom 1:28). The values of being are replaced by those of having. The only goal which counts is the pursuit of one's own material well-being. The so-called "quality of life" is interpreted primarily or exclusively as economic efficiency, inordinate consumerism, physical beauty and pleasure, to the neglect of the more profound dimensions – interpersonal, spiritual and religious – of existence.

In such a context suffering, an inescapable burden of human existence but also a factor of possible personal growth, is "censored," rejected as useless, indeed opposed as an evil, always and in every way to be avoided. When it cannot be avoided and the prospect of even some future well-being vanishes, then life appears to have lost all meaning and the temptation grows in man to claim the right to suppress it.

Within this same cultural climate, the body is no longer perceived as a properly personal reality, a sign and place of relations with others, with God and with the world. It is reduced to pure materiality: it is simply a complex of organs, functions and energies to be used according to the sole criteria of pleasure and efficiency. Consequently, sexuality too is depersonalized and exploited: from being the sign, place and language of love, that is, of the gift of self and acceptance of another, in all the other's richness as a person, it increasingly becomes the occasion and instrument for self-assertion and the selfish satisfaction of personal desires and instincts. Thus the original import of human sexuality is distorted and falsified, and the two meanings, unitive and procreative, inherent in the very nature of the conjugal act, are artificially separated: in this way the marriage union is betrayed and its fruitfulness is subjected to the caprice of the couple. Procreation then becomes the "enemy" to be avoided in sexual activity: if it is welcomed, this is only because it expresses a desire, or indeed the intention, to have a child "at all costs," and not because it signifies the complete acceptance of the other and therefore an openness to the richness of life which the child represents.

In the materialistic perspective described so far, interpersonal relations are seriously impoverished. The first to be harmed are women, children, the sick or suffering, and the elderly. The criterion of personal dignity – which demands respect, generosity and service – is replaced by the criterion of efficiency, functionality and usefulness: others are considered not for what they "are," but for what they "have, do and produce." This is the supremacy of the strong over the weak.

24. It is at the heart of the moral conscience that the eclipse of the sense of God and of man, with all its various and deadly consequences for life, is taking place. It is a question, above all, of the individual conscience, as it stands before God in its singleness and uniqueness. But it is also a question, in a certain sense, of the "moral conscience" of

society: in a way it too is responsible, not only because it tolerates or fosters behaviour contrary to life, but also because it encourages the "culture of death," creating and consolidating actual "structures of sin" which go against life. The moral conscience, both individual and social, is today subjected, also as a result of the penetrating influence of the media, to an extremely serious and mortal danger: that of confusion between good and evil, precisely in relation to the fundamental right to life. A large part of contemporary society looks sadly like that humanity which Paul describes in his Letter to the Romans. It is composed "of men who by their wickedness suppress the truth" (1:18): having denied God and believing that they can build the earthly city without him, "they became futile in their thinking" so that "their senseless minds were darkened" (1:21); "claiming to be wise, they became fools" (1:22), carrying out works deserving of death, and "they not only do them but approve those who practise them" (1:32). When conscience, this bright lamp of the soul (cf. Mt 6:22–23), calls "evil good and good evil" (Is 5:20), it is already on the path to the most alarming corruption and the darkest moral blindness.

And yet all the conditioning and efforts to enforce silence fail to stifle the voice of the Lord echoing in the conscience of every individual: it is always from this intimate sanctuary of the conscience that a new journey of love, openness and service to human life can begin. . . .

41. The commandment "You shall not kill," included and more fully expressed in the positive command of love for one's neighbour, is re-affirmed in all its force by the Lord Jesus. To the rich young man who asks him: "Teacher, what good deed must I do, to have eternal life?," Jesus replies: "If you would enter life, keep the commandments" (Mt 19:16,17). And he quotes, as the first of these: "You shall not kill" (Mt 19:18). In the Sermon on the Mount, Jesus demands from his disciples a righteousness which surpasses that of the Scribes and Pharisees, also with regard to respect for life: "You have heard that it was said to the men of old, 'You shall not kill; and whoever kills shall be liable to judgment.' But I say to you that every one who is angry with his brother shall be liable to judgment" (Mt 5:21–22).

By his words and actions Jesus further unveils the positive requirements of the commandment regarding the inviolability of life. These requirements were already present in the Old Testament, where legislation dealt with protecting and defending life when it was weak and threatened: in the case of foreigners, widows, orphans, the sick and the poor in general, including children in the womb (cf. Ex 21:22; 22:20–26). With Jesus these positive requirements assume new force and urgency, and are revealed in all their breadth and depth: they range from caring for the life of one's brother (whether a blood brother, someone belonging to the same people, or a foreigner living in the land of Israel) to showing concern for the stranger, even to the point of loving one's enemy.

A stranger is no longer a stranger for the person who must become a neighbour to someone in need, to the point of accepting responsibility for his life, as the parable of the Good Samaritan shows so clearly (cf. Lk 10:25–37). Even an enemy ceases to be an enemy for the person who is obliged to love him (cf. Mt 5:38–48; Lk 6:27–35), to "do good" to him (cf. Lk 6:27, 33, 35) and to respond to his immediate needs promptly and with no expectation of repayment (cf. Lk 6:34–35). The height of this love is to pray for one's enemy. By so doing we achieve harmony with the providential love of God: "But I say to you, love your enemies and pray for those who persecute you, so that you may be children of your Father who is in heaven; for he makes his sun rise on the evil and on the good and sends rain on the just and on the unjust" (Mt 5:44–45; cf. Lk 6:28, 35).

Thus the deepest element of God's commandment to protect human life is the requirement to show reverence and love for every person and the life of every person. This is the teaching which the Apostle Paul, echoing the words of Jesus, addressed to the Christians in Rome: "The commandments, 'You shall not commit adultery, You shall not kill, You shall not steal, You shall not covet,' and any other commandment, are summed up in this sentence, 'You shall love your neighbour as yourself.' Love does no wrong to a neighbour; therefore love is the fulfilling of the law" (Rom 13:9–10).

"Be fruitful and multiply, and fill the earth and subdue it" (Gen 1:28): man's responsibility for life

42. To defend and promote life, to show reverence and love for it, is a task which God entrusts to every man, calling him as his living image to share in his own lordship over the world: "God blessed them, and God said to them, 'Be fruitful and multiply, and fill the earth and subdue it; and have dominion over the fish of the sea and over the birds of the air and over every living thing that moves upon the earth'" (Gen 1:28).

The biblical text clearly shows the breadth and depth of the lordship which God bestows on man. It is a matter first of all of dominion over the earth and over every living creature, as the Book of Wisdom makes clear: "O God of my fathers and Lord of mercy . . . by your wisdom you have formed man, to have dominion over the creatures you have made, and rule the world in holiness and righteousness" (Wis 9:1, 2–3). The Psalmist too extols the dominion given to man as a sign of glory and honour from his Creator: "You have given him dominion over the works of your hands; you have put all things under his feet, all sheep and oxen, and also the beasts of the field, the birds of the air, and the fish of the sea, whatever passes along the paths of the sea" (Ps 8:6–8).

As one called to till and look after the garden of the world (cf. Gen 2:15), man has a specific responsibility towards the environment in which he lives, towards the creation which God has put at the service of his personal dignity, of his life, not only for the present but also for future generations. It is the ecological question – ranging from the preservation of the natural habitats of the different species of animals and of other forms of life to "human ecology" properly speaking – which finds in the Bible clear and strong ethical direction, leading to a solution which respects the great good of life, of every life. In fact, "the dominion granted to man by the Creator is not an absolute power, nor can one speak of a freedom to 'use and misuse,' or to dispose of things as one pleases. The limitation imposed from the beginning by the Creator himself and expressed symbolically by the prohibition not to 'eat of the fruit of the tree' (cf. Gen 2:16–17) shows clearly enough that, when it comes to the natural world, we are subject not only to biological laws but also to moral ones, which cannot be violated with impunity."

43. A certain sharing by man in God's lordship is also evident in the specific responsibility which he is given for human life as such. It is a responsibility which reaches its highest point in the giving of life through procreation by man and woman in marriage. As the Second Vatican Council teaches: "God himself who said, 'It is not good for man to be alone' (Gen 2:18) and 'who made man from the beginning male and female' (Mt 19:4), wished to share with man a certain special participation in his own creative work. Thus he blessed male and female saying: 'Increase and multiply' (Gen 1:28)."

By speaking of "a certain special participation" of man and woman in the "creative work" of God, the Council wishes to point out that having a child is an event which is deeply human and full of religious meaning, insofar as it involves both the spouses, who form "one flesh" (Gen 2:24), and God who makes himself present. As I wrote in my *Letter to Families*: "When a new person is born of the conjugal union of the two, he brings with him into the world a particular image and likeness of God himself: the genealogy of the person is inscribed in the very biology of generation. In affirming that the spouses, as parents, cooperate with God the Creator in conceiving and giving birth to a new human being, we are not speaking merely with reference to the laws of biology. Instead, we wish to emphasize that God himself is present in human fatherhood and motherhood quite differently than he is present in all other instances of begetting 'on earth.' Indeed, God alone is the source of that 'image and likeness' which is proper to the human being, as it was received at Creation. Begetting is the continuation of Creation."

This is what the Bible teaches in direct and eloquent language when it reports the joyful cry of the first woman, "the mother of all the living" (Gen 3:20). Aware that God has intervened, Eve exclaims: "I have begotten a man with the help of the Lord" (Gen 4:1). In procreation therefore, through the communication of life from parents to child, God's own image and likeness is transmitted, thanks to the creation of the immortal soul. The beginning of the "book of the genealogy of Adam" expresses it in this way: "When God created man, he made him in the likeness of God. Male and female he created them, and he blessed them and called them man when they were created. When Adam had lived a hundred and thirty years, he became the father of a son in his own likeness, after his image, and named him Seth" (Gen 5:1–3). It is precisely in their role as co-workers with God who transmits his image to the new creature that we see the greatness of couples who are ready "to cooperate with the love of the Creator and the Saviour, who through them will enlarge and enrich his own family day by day." This is why the Bishop Amphilochius extolled "holy matrimony, chosen and elevated above all other earthly gifts" as "the begetter of humanity, the creator of images of God."

Thus, a man and woman joined in matrimony become partners in a divine undertaking: through the act of procreation, God's gift is accepted and a new life opens to the future.

But over and above the specific mission of parents, the task of accepting and serving life involves everyone; and this task must be fulfilled above all towards life when it is at its weakest. It is Christ himself who reminds us of this when he asks to be loved and served in his brothers and sisters who are suffering in any way: the hungry, the thirsty, the foreigner, the naked, the sick, the imprisoned ... Whatever is done to each of them is done to Christ himself (cf. Mt 25:31–46).

"For you formed my inmost being" (Ps 139:13): the dignity of the unborn child

44. Human life finds itself most vulnerable when it enters the world and when it leaves the realm of time to embark upon eternity. The word of God frequently repeats the call to show care and respect, above all where life is undermined by sickness and old age. Although there are no direct and explicit calls to protect human life at its very beginning, specifically life not yet born, and life nearing its end, this can easily be explained by the fact that the mere possibility of harming, attacking, or actually denying life in these circumstances is completely foreign to the religious and cultural way of thinking of the People of God.

In the Old Testament, sterility is dreaded as a curse, while numerous offspring are viewed as a blessing: "Sons are a heritage from the Lord, the fruit of the womb a reward" (Ps 127:3; cf. Ps 128:3–4). This belief is also based on Israel's awareness of being the people of the Covenant, called to increase in accordance with the promise made to Abraham: "Look towards heaven, and number the stars, if you are able to number them . . . so shall your descendants be" (Gen 15:5). But more than anything else, at work here is the certainty that the life which parents transmit has its origins in God. We see this attested in the many biblical passages which respectfully and lovingly speak of conception, of the forming of life in the mother's womb, of giving birth and of the intimate connection between the initial moment of life and the action of God the Creator.

"Before I formed you in the womb I knew you, and before you were born I consecrated you" (Jer 1:5): the life of every individual, from its very beginning, is part of God's plan. Job, from the depth of his pain, stops to contemplate the work of God who miraculously formed his body in his mother's womb. Here he finds reason for trust, and he expresses his belief that there is a divine plan for his life: "You have fashioned and made me; will you then turn and destroy me? Remember that you have made me of clay; and will you turn me to dust again? Did you not pour me out like milk and curdle me like cheese? You clothed me with skin and flesh, and knit me together with bones and sinews. You have granted me life and steadfast love; and your care has preserved my spirit" (Job 10:8–12). Expressions of awe and wonder at God's intervention in the life of a child in its mother's womb occur again and again in the Psalms.

How can anyone think that even a single moment of this marvellous process of the unfolding of life could be separated from the wise and loving work of the Creator, and left prey to human caprice? Certainly the mother of the seven brothers did not think so; she professes her faith in God, both the source and guarantee of life from its very conception, and the foundation of the hope of new life beyond death: "I do not know how you came into being in my womb. It was not I who gave you life and breath, nor I who set in order the elements within each of you. Therefore the Creator of the world, who shaped the beginning of man and devised the origin of all things, will in his mercy give life and breath back to you again, since you now forget yourselves for the sake of his laws" (2 Mac 7:22–23). . . .

"Your eyes beheld my unformed substance" (Ps 139:16): the unspeakable crime of abortion

58. Among all the crimes which can be committed against life, procured abortion has characteristics making it particularly serious and deplorable. The Second Vatican Council defines abortion, together with infanticide, as an "unspeakable crime."

But today, in many people's consciences, the perception of its gravity has become progressively obscured. The acceptance of abortion in the popular mind, in behaviour and even in law itself, is a telling sign of an extremely dangerous crisis of the moral sense, which is becoming more and more incapable of distinguishing between good and evil, even when the fundamental right to life is at stake. Given such a grave situation, we need now more than ever to have the courage to look the truth in the eye and to call things by their proper name, without yielding to convenient compromises or to the temptation of self-deception. In this regard the reproach of the Prophet is extremely straightforward: "Woe to those who call evil good and good evil, who put darkness for light and light for darkness" (Is 5:20). Especially in the case of abortion there is a widespread use of ambiguous terminology, such as "interruption of pregnancy," which tends to hide abortion's true nature and to attenuate its seriousness in public opinion. Perhaps this linguistic phenomenon is itself a symptom of an uneasiness of conscience. But no word has the power to change the reality of things: procured abortion is the deliberate and direct killing, by whatever means it is carried out, of a human being in the initial phase of his or her existence, extending from conception to birth.

The moral gravity of procured abortion is apparent in all its truth if we recognize that we are dealing with murder and, in particular, when we consider the specific elements involved. The one eliminated is a human being at the very beginning of life. No one more absolutely innocent could be imagined. In no way could this human being ever be considered an aggressor, much less an unjust aggressor! He or she is weak, defenceless, even to the point of lacking that minimal form of defence consisting in the poignant power of a newborn baby's cries and tears. The unborn child is totally entrusted to the protection and care of the woman carrying him or her in the womb. And yet sometimes it is precisely the mother herself who makes the decision and asks for the child to be eliminated, and who then goes about having it done.

It is true that the decision to have an abortion is often tragic and painful for the mother, insofar as the decision to rid herself of the fruit of conception is not made for purely selfish reasons or out of convenience, but out of a desire to protect certain important values such as her own health or a decent standard of living for the other members of the family. Sometimes it is feared that the child to be born would live in such conditions that it would be better if the birth did not take place. Nevertheless, these reasons and others like them, however serious and tragic, can never justify the deliberate killing of an innocent human being.

59. As well as the mother, there are often other people too who decide upon the death of the child in the womb. In the first place, the father of the child may be to blame, not only when he directly pressures the woman to have an abortion, but also when he indirectly encourages such a decision on her part by leaving her alone to face the problems of pregnancy: in this way the family is thus mortally wounded and profaned in its nature as a community of love and in its vocation to be the "sanctuary of life." Nor can one overlook the pressures which sometimes come from the wider family circle and from friends. Sometimes the woman is

subjected to such strong pressure that she feels psychologically forced to have an abortion: certainly in this case moral responsibility lies particularly with those who have directly or indirectly obliged her to have an abortion. Doctors and nurses are also responsible, when they place at the service of death skills which were acquired for promoting life.

But responsibility likewise falls on the legislators who have promoted and approved abortion laws, and, to the extent that they have a say in the matter, on the administrators of the health-care centres where abortions are performed. A general and no less serious responsibility lies with those who have encouraged the spread of an attitude of sexual permissiveness and a lack of esteem for motherhood, and with those who should have ensured – but did not – effective family and social policies in support of families, especially larger families and those with particular financial and educational needs. Finally, one cannot overlook the network of complicity which reaches out to include international institutions, foundations and associations which systematically campaign for the legalization and spread of abortion in the world. In this sense abortion goes beyond the responsibility of individuals and beyond the harm done to them, and takes on a distinctly social dimension. It is a most serious wound inflicted on society and its culture by the very people who ought to be society's promoters and defenders. As I wrote in my Letter to Families, "we are facing an immense threat to life: not only to the life of individuals but also to that of civilization itself." We are facing what can be called a "structure of sin" which opposes human life not yet born.

60. Some people try to justify abortion by claiming that the result of conception, at least up to a certain number of days, cannot yet be considered a personal human life. But in fact, "from the time that the ovum is fertilized, a life is begun which is neither that of the father nor the mother; it is rather the life of a new human being with his own growth. It would never be made human if it were not human already. This has always been clear, and ... modern genetic science offers clear confirmation. It has demonstrated that from the first instant there is established the programme of what this living being will be: a person, this individual person with his characteristic aspects already well determined. Right from fertilization the adventure of a human life begins, and each of its capacities requires time – a rather lengthy time – to find its place and to be in a position to act." Even if the presence of a spiritual soul cannot be ascertained by empirical data, the results themselves of scientific research on the human embryo provide "a valuable indication for discerning by the use of reason a personal presence at the moment of the first appearance of a human life: how could a human individual not be a human person?"

Furthermore, what is at stake is so important that, from the standpoint of moral obligation, the mere probability that a human person is involved would suffice to justify an absolutely clear prohibition of any intervention aimed at killing a human embryo. Precisely for this reason, over and above all scientific debates and those philosophical affirmations to which the Magisterium has not expressly committed itself, the Church has always taught and continues to teach that the result of human procreation, from the first moment of its existence, must be guaranteed that unconditional respect which is morally due to the human being in his or her totality and unity as body and spirit: "The human being is to be respected and treated as a person from the moment of conception; and therefore from that same moment his rights as a person must be recognized, among which in the first place is the inviolable right of every innocent human being to life."

61. The texts of Sacred Scripture never address the question of deliberate abortion and so do not directly and specifically condemn it. But they show such great respect for the human being in the mother's womb that they require as a logical consequence that God's commandment "You shall not kill" be extended to the unborn child as well.

Human life is sacred and inviolable at every moment of existence, including the initial phase which precedes birth. All human beings, from their mothers' womb, belong to God who searches them and knows them, who forms them and knits them together with his own hands, who gazes on them when they are tiny shapeless embryos and already sees in them the adults of tomorrow whose days are numbered and whose vocation is even now written in the "book of life" (cf. Ps 139:1, 13–16). There too, when they are still in their mothers' womb – as many passages of the Bible bear witness – they are the personal objects of God's loving and fatherly providence.

Christian Tradition – as the Declaration issued by the Congregation for the Doctrine of the Faith points out so well – is clear and unanimous, from the beginning up to our own day, in describing abortion as a particularly grave moral disorder. From its first contacts with the Greco-Roman world, where abortion and infanticide were widely practised, the first Christian community, by its teaching and practice, radically opposed the customs rampant in that society, as is clearly shown by the Didache mentioned earlier. Among the Greek ecclesiastical writers, Athenagoras records that Christians consider as murderesses women who have recourse to abortifacient medicines, because children, even if they are still in their mother's womb, "are already under the protection of Divine Providence." Among the Latin authors, Tertullian affirms: "It is anticipated murder to prevent someone from being born; it makes little difference whether one kills a soul already born or puts it to death at birth. He who will one day be a man is a man already."

Throughout Christianity's two thousand year history, this same doctrine has been constantly taught by the Fathers of the Church and by her Pastors and Doctors. Even scientific and philosophical discussions about the precise moment of the infusion of the spiritual soul have never given rise to any hesitation about the moral condemnation of abortion.

62. The more recent Papal Magisterium has vigorously reaffirmed this common doctrine. Pius XI in particular, in his Encyclical *Casti Connubii*, rejected the specious justifications of abortion. Pius XII excluded all direct abortion, i.e., every act tending directly to destroy human life in the womb "whether such destruction is intended as an end or only as a means to an end." John XXIII reaffirmed that human life is sacred because "from its very beginning it directly involves God's creative activity." The Second Vatican Council, as mentioned earlier, sternly condemned abortion: "From the moment of its conception life must be guarded with the greatest care, while abortion and infanticide are unspeakable crimes."

The Church's canonical discipline, from the earliest centuries, has inflicted penal sanctions on those guilty of abortion. This practice, with more or less severe penalties, has been confirmed in various periods of history. The 1917 Code of Canon Law punished abortion with excommunication. The revised canonical legislation continues this tradition when it decrees that "a person who actually procures an abortion incurs automatic *(latae sententiae)* excommunication." The excommunication affects all those who commit this crime with knowledge of the penalty attached, and thus includes those accomplices without whose help the crime would not have been committed. By this reiterated sanction, the Church makes clear that abortion is a most serious and dangerous crime, thereby encouraging those who commit it to seek without delay the path of conversion. In the Church the purpose of the penalty of excommunication is to make an individual fully aware of the gravity of a certain sin and then to foster genuine conversion and repentance.

Given such unanimity in the doctrinal and disciplinary tradition of the Church, Paul VI was able to declare that this tradition is unchanged and unchangeable. Therefore, by the authority which Christ conferred upon Peter and his Successors, in communion with the Bishops – who on various occasions have condemned abortion and who in the aforementioned consultation, albeit dispersed throughout the world, have shown unanimous agreement concerning this doctrine – I declare that direct abortion, that is, abortion willed as an end or as a means, always constitutes a grave moral disorder, since it is the deliberate killing of an innocent human being. This doctrine is based upon the natural law and upon the written Word of God, is transmitted by the Church's Tradition and taught by the ordinary and universal Magisterium.

No circumstance, no purpose, no law whatsoever can ever make licit an act which is intrinsically illicit, since it is contrary to the Law of God which is written in every human heart, knowable by reason itself, and proclaimed by the Church. . . .

81. This involves above all proclaiming the core of this Gospel. It is the proclamation of a living God who is close to us, who calls us to profound communion with himself and awakens in us the certain hope of eternal life. It is the affirmation of the inseparable connection between the person, his life and his bodiliness. It is the presentation of human life as a life of relationship, a gift of God, the fruit and sign of his love. It is the proclamation that Jesus has a unique relationship with every person, which enables us to see in every human face the face of Christ. It is the call for a "sincere gift of self" as the fullest way to realize our personal freedom.

It also involves making clear all the consequences of this Gospel. These can be summed up as follows: human life, as a gift of God, is sacred and inviolable. For this reason procured abortion and euthanasia are absolutely unacceptable. Not only must human life not be taken, but it must be protected with loving concern. The meaning of life is found in giving and receiving love, and in this light human sexuality and pro- creation reach their true and full significance. Love also gives meaning to suffering and death; despite the mystery which surrounds them, they can become saving events. Respect for life requires that science and technology should always be at the service of man and his integral de- velopment. Society as a whole must respect, defend and promote the dignity of every human person, at every moment and in every condition of that person's life. . . .

85. In celebrating the Gospel of life we also need to appreciate and make good use of the wealth of gestures and symbols present in the traditions and customs of different cultures and peoples. There are special times and ways in which the peoples of different nations and cultures express joy for a newborn life, respect for and protection of individual human lives, care for the suffering or needy, closeness to the elderly and the dying, participation in the sorrow of those who mourn, and hope and desire for immortality.

In view of this and following the suggestion made by the Cardinals in the Consistory of 1991, I propose that a Day for Life be celebrated each year in every country, as already established by some Episcopal Conferences. The celebration of this Day should be planned and carried out with the active participation of all sectors of the local Church. Its pri- mary purpose should be to foster in individual consciences, in families, in the Church and in civil society a recognition of the meaning and value of human life at every stage and in every condition. Particular attention should be drawn to the seriousness of abortion and euthanasia, without neglecting other aspects of life which from time to time deserve to be given careful consideration, as occasion and circumstances demand.

86. As part of the spiritual worship acceptable to God (cf. Rom 12:1), the Gospel of life is to be celebrated above all in daily living, which should be filled with self-giving love for others. In this way, our lives will

become a genuine and responsible acceptance of the gift of life and a heartfelt song of praise and gratitude to God who has given us this gift. This is already happening in the many different acts of selfless generosity, often humble and hidden, carried out by men and women, children and adults, the young and the old, the healthy and the sick.

It is in this context, so humanly rich and filled with love, that heroic actions too are born. These are the most solemn celebration of the Gospel of life, for they proclaim it by the total gift of self. They are the radiant manifestation of the highest degree of love, which is to give one's life for the person loved (cf. Jn 15:13). They are a sharing in the mystery of the Cross, in which Jesus reveals the value of every person, and how life attains its fullness in the sincere gift of self. Over and above such outstanding moments, there is an everyday heroism, made up of gestures of sharing, big or small, which build up an authentic culture of life. A particularly praiseworthy example of such gestures is the donation of organs, performed in an ethically acceptable manner, with a view to offering a chance of health and even of life itself to the sick who sometimes have no other hope.

Part of this daily heroism is also the silent but effective and eloquent witness of all those "brave mothers who devote themselves to their own family without reserve, who suffer in giving birth to their children and who are ready to make any effort, to face any sacrifice, in order to pass on to them the best of themselves." In living out their mission "these heroic women do not always find support in the world around them. On the contrary, the cultural models frequently promoted and broadcast by the media do not encourage motherhood. In the name of progress and modernity the values of fidelity, chastity, sacrifice, to which a host of Christian wives and mothers have borne and continue to bear outstanding witness, are presented as obsolete. . . . We thank you, heroic mothers, for your invincible love! We thank you for your intrepid trust in God and in his love. We thank you for the sacrifice of your life. . . . In the Paschal Mystery, Christ restores to you the gift you gave him. Indeed, he has the power to give you back the life you gave him as an offering." . . .

99. In transforming culture so that it supports life, women occupy a place, in thought and action, which is unique and decisive. It depends on them to promote a "new feminism" which rejects the temptation of imitating models of "male domination," in order to acknowledge and affirm the true genius of women in every aspect of the life of society, and overcome all discrimination, violence and exploitation.

Making my own the words of the concluding message of the Second Vatican Council, I address to women this urgent appeal: "Reconcile people with life." You are called to bear witness to the meaning of genuine love, of that gift of self and of that acceptance of others which are present in a special way in the relationship of husband and wife, but which ought also to be at the heart of every other interpersonal relationship. The experience of motherhood makes you acutely aware of the other person and, at the same time, confers on you a particular task: "Motherhood involves a special communion with the mystery of life, as it develops in the woman's womb. . . . This unique contact with the new human being developing within her gives rise to an attitude towards human beings not only towards her own child, but every human being, which profoundly marks the woman's personality." A mother welcomes and carries in herself another human being, enabling it to grow inside her, giving it room, respecting it in its otherness. Women first learn and then teach others that human relations are authentic if they are open to accepting the other person: a person who is recognized and loved because of the dignity which comes from being a person and not from other considerations, such as usefulness, strength, intelligence, beauty or health. This is the fundamental contribution which the Church and humanity expect from women. And it is the indispensable prerequisite for an authentic cultural change.

I would now like to say a special word to women who have had an abortion. The Church is aware of the many factors which may have influenced your decision, and she does not doubt that in many cases it was a painful and even shattering decision. The wound in your heart may not yet have healed. Certainly what happened was and remains terribly wrong. But do not give in to discouragement and do not lose hope. Try rather to understand what happened and face it honestly. If you have not already done so, give yourselves over with humility and trust to repentance. The Father of mercies is ready to give you his forgiveness and his peace in the Sacrament of Reconciliation. To the same Father and his mercy you can with sure hope entrust your child. With the friendly and expert help and advice of other people, and as a result of your own painful experience, you can be among the most eloquent defenders of everyone's right to life. Through your commitment to life, whether by accepting the birth of other children or by welcoming and caring for those most in need of someone to be close to them, you will become promoters of a new way of looking at human life. . . .

LETTER OF POPE JOHN PAUL II TO WOMEN

29 JUNE 1995

I greet you all most cordially,
women throughout the world!

1. I am writing this letter to each one of you as a sign of solidarity and gratitude on the eve of the Fourth World Conference on Women, to be held in Beijing this coming September.

Before all else, I wish to express my *deep appreciation* to the United Nations Organization for having sponsored this very significant event. The Church desires for her part to contribute to upholding the dignity, role and rights of women, not only by the specific work of the Holy See's official Delegation to the Conference in Beijing, but also by speaking directly to the heart and mind of every woman. Recently, when *Mrs Gertrude Mongella,* the Secretary General of the Conference, visited me in connection with the Peking meeting, I gave her a *written Message* which stated some basic points of the Church's teaching with regard to women's issues. That message, apart from the specific circumstances of its origin, was concerned with a broader vision of the situation and problems of *women in general*, in an attempt to promote the *cause* of women in the Church and in today's world. For this reason, I arranged to have it forwarded to every Conference of Bishops, so that it could be circulated as widely as possible.

Taking up the themes I addressed in that document, I would now like to *speak directly to every woman*, to reflect with her on the problems and the prospects of what it means to be a woman in our time. In particular I wish to consider the essential issue of the *dignity* and *rights* of women, as seen in the light of the word of God.

This "dialogue" really needs to begin with a word of thanks. As I wrote in my Apostolic Letter *Mulieris Dignitatem*, the Church "desires to give thanks to the Most Holy Trinity for the 'mystery of woman' and for every woman – for all that constitutes the eternal measure of her feminine dignity, for the 'great works of God,' which throughout human history have been accomplished in and through her" (no. 31).

2. This word of thanks to the Lord for his mysterious plan regarding the vocation and mission of women in the world is at the same time a

concrete and direct word of thanks to women, to every woman, for all that they represent in the life of humanity.

Thank you, *women who are mothers*! You have sheltered human beings within yourselves in a unique experience of joy and travail. This experience makes you become God's own smile upon the newborn child, the one who guides your child's first steps, who helps it to grow, and who is the anchor as the child makes its way along the journey of life.

Thank you, *women who are wives*! You irrevocably join your future to that of your husbands, in a relationship of mutual giving, at the service of love and life.

Thank you, *women who are daughters* and *women who are sisters*! Into the heart of the family, and then of all society, you bring the richness of your sensitivity, your intuitiveness, your generosity and fidelity.

Thank you, *women who work*! You are present and active in every area of life – social, economic, cultural, artistic and political. In this way you make an indispensable contribution to the growth of a culture which unites reason and feeling, to a model of life ever open to the sense of "mystery," to the establishment of economic and political structures ever more worthy of humanity.

Thank you, *consecrated women*! Following the example of the greatest of women, the Mother of Jesus Christ, the Incarnate Word, you open yourselves with obedience and fidelity to the gift of God's love. You help the Church and all mankind to experience a "spousal" relationship to God, one which magnificently expresses the fellowship which God wishes to establish with his creatures.

Thank you, *every woman*, for the simple fact of being *a woman*! Through the insight which is so much a part of your womanhood you enrich the world's understanding and help to make human relations more honest and authentic.

3. I know of course that simply saying thank you is not enough. Unfortunately, we are heirs to a history which has *conditioned* us to a remarkable extent. In every time and place, this conditioning has been an obstacle to the progress of women. Women's dignity has often been unacknowledged and their prerogatives misrepresented; they have often been relegated to the margins of society and even reduced to servitude. This has prevented women from truly being themselves and it has resulted in a spiritual impoverishment of humanity. Certainly it is no easy task to assign the blame for this, considering the many kinds of cultural conditioning which down the centuries have shaped ways of thinking and acting. And if objective blame, especially in particular historical contexts, has belonged to not just a few members of the Church, for this I am truly sorry. May this regret be transformed, on the part of the whole Church, into a renewed commitment of fidelity to the Gospel

vision. When it comes to setting women free from every kind of exploitation and domination, the Gospel contains an ever relevant message which goes back to the *attitude of Jesus Christ himself.* Transcending the established norms of his own culture, Jesus treated women with openness, respect, acceptance and tenderness. In this way he honoured the dignity which women have always possessed according to God's plan and in his love. As we look to Christ at the end of this Second Millennium, it is natural to ask ourselves: how much of his message has been heard and acted upon?

Yes, it is time to *examine the past with courage*, to assign responsibility where it is due in a review of the long history of humanity. Women have contributed to that history as much as men and, more often than not, they did so in much more difficult conditions. I think particularly of those women who loved culture and art, and devoted their lives to them in spite of the fact that they were frequently at a disadvantage from the start, excluded from equal educational opportunities, underestimated, ignored and not given credit for their intellectual contributions. Sadly, very little of women's achievements in history can be registered by the science of history. But even though time may have buried the documentary evidence of those achievements, their beneficent influence can be felt as a force which has shaped the lives of successive generations, right up to our own. To this great, immense feminine "tradition" humanity owes a debt which can never be repaid. Yet how many women have been and continue to be valued more for their physical appearance than for their skill, their professionalism, their intellectual abilities, their deep sensitivity; in a word, the very dignity of their being!

4. And what shall we say of the obstacles which in so many parts of the world still keep women from being fully integrated into social, political and economic life? We need only think of how the gift of motherhood is often penalized rather than rewarded, even though humanity owes its very survival to this gift. Certainly, much remains to be done to prevent discrimination against those who have chosen to be wives and mothers. As far as personal rights are concerned, there is an urgent need to achieve *real equality* in every area: equal pay for equal work, protection for working mothers, fairness in career advancements, equality of spouses with regard to family rights and the recognition of everything that is part of the rights and duties of citizens in a democratic State.

This is a matter of justice but also of necessity. Women will increasingly play a part in the solution of the serious problems of the future: leisure time, the quality of life, migration, social services, euthanasia, drugs, health care, the ecology, etc. In all these areas a greater presence of women in society will prove most valuable, for it will help to manifest the contradictions present when society is organized solely according to the criteria of efficiency and productivity, and it will force systems to be redesigned in a way which favours the processes of humanization which mark the "civilization of love."

5. Then too, when we look at one of the most sensitive aspects of the situation of women in the world, how can we not mention the long and degrading history, albeit often an "underground" history, of violence against women in the area of sexuality? At the threshold of the Third Millennium we cannot remain indifferent and resigned before this phenomenon. The time has come to condemn vigorously the types of *sexual violence* which frequently have women for their object and to pass laws which effectively defend them from such violence. Nor can we fail, in the name of the respect due to the human person, to condemn the widespread hedonistic and commercial culture which encourages the systematic exploitation of sexuality and corrupts even very young girls into letting their bodies be used for profit.

In contrast to these sorts of perversion, what great appreciation must be shown to those women who, with a heroic love for the child they have conceived, proceed with a pregnancy resulting from the injustice of rape. Here we are thinking of atrocities perpetrated not only in situations of war, still so common in the world, but also in societies which are blessed by prosperity and peace and yet are often corrupted by a culture of hedonistic permissiveness which aggravates tendencies to aggressive male behaviour. In these cases the choice to have an abortion always remains a grave sin. But before being something to blame on the woman, it is a crime for which guilt needs to be attributed to men and to the complicity of the general social environment.

6. My word of thanks to women thus becomes a *heartfelt appeal* that everyone, and in a special way States and international institutions, should make every effort to ensure that women regain full respect for their dignity and role. Here I cannot fail to express my admiration for those women of good will who have devoted their lives to defending the dignity of womanhood by fighting for their basic social, economic and political rights, demonstrating courageous initiative at a time when this was considered extremely inappropriate, the sign of a lack of femininity, a manifestation of exhibitionism, and even a sin!

In this year's *World Day of Peace Message*, I noted that when one looks at the great process of women's liberation, "the journey has been a difficult and complicated one and, at times, not without its share of mistakes. But it has been substantially a positive one, even if it is still unfinished, due to the many obstacles which, in various parts of the world, still prevent women from being acknowledged, respected, and appreciated in their own special dignity."

This journey must go on! But I am convinced that the secret of making speedy progress in achieving full respect for women and their identity involves more than simply the condemnation of discrimination and injustices, necessary though this may be. Such respect must first and foremost be won through an effective and intelligent *campaign for the promotion of women*, concentrating on all areas of women's life and beginning with a *universal recognition of the dignity of women*. Our ability to recognize this dignity, in spite of historical conditioning, comes from the use of reason itself, which is able to understand the law of God written in the heart of every human being. More than anything else, the word of God enables us to grasp clearly the ultimate *anthropological basis* of the dignity of women, making it evident as a part of God's plan for humanity.

7. Dear sisters, together let us reflect anew on the magnificent passage in Scripture which describes the creation of the human race and which has so much to say about your dignity and mission in the world.

The Book of Genesis speaks of creation in summary fashion, in language which is poetic and symbolic, yet profoundly true: "God created man in his own image, in the image of God he created him; *male and female he created them*" (*Gen* 1:27). The creative act of God takes place according to a precise plan. First of all, we are told that the human being is created "in the image and likeness of God" (cf. *Gen* 1:26). This expression immediately makes clear *what is distinct about the human being with regard to the rest of creation*.

We are then told that, from the very beginning, man has been created "male and female" (*Gen* 1:27). Scripture itself provides the interpretation of this fact: even though man is surrounded by the innumerable creatures of the created world, he realizes that *he is alone* (cf. *Gen* 2:20). God intervenes in order to help him escape from this situation of solitude: "*It is not good that the man should be alone; I will make him a helper fit for him*" (*Gen* 2:18). The creation of woman is thus marked from the outset by *the principle of help*: a help which is not one-sided but *mutual*. Woman complements man, just as man complements woman: men and women are *complementary*. Womanhood expresses the "human" as much as manhood does, but in a different and complementary way.

When the Book of Genesis speaks of "help," it is not referring merely to *acting,* but also to *being.* Womanhood and manhood are complementary *not only from the physical and psychological points of view*, but also from the *ontological*. It is only through the duality of the "masculine" and the "feminine" that the "human" finds full realization.

8. After creating man male and female, God says to both: "*Fill the earth and subdue it*" (*Gen* 1:28). Not only does he give them the power to procreate as a means of perpetuating the human species throughout time, *he also gives them the earth, charging them with the responsible use of its resources*. As a rational and free being, man is called to transform the face of the earth. In this task, which is essentially that of culture, *man and woman alike* share equal responsibility from the start.

In their fruitful relationship as husband and wife, in their common task of exercising dominion over the earth, woman and man are marked neither by a static and undifferentiated equality nor by an irreconcilable and inexorably conflictual difference. Their most natural relationship, which corresponds to the plan of God, is the "unity of the two," a relational "uni-duality," which enables each to experience their interpersonal and reciprocal relationship as a gift which enriches and which confers responsibility.

To this "unity of the two" God has entrusted not only the work of procreation and family life, but the creation of history itself. *While the 1994 International Year of the Family* focused attention on *women as mothers*, the Beijing Conference, which has as its theme "Action for Equality, Development and Peace," provides an auspicious occasion for heightening awareness of *the many contributions made by women to the life of whole societies and nations*. This contribution is primarily spiritual and cultural in nature, but socio-political and economic as well. The various sectors of society, nations and states, and the progress of all humanity, are certainly deeply indebted to the contribution of women!

9. Progress usually tends to be measured according to the criteria of science and technology. Nor from this point of view has the contribution of women been negligible. Even so, this is not the only measure of progress, nor in fact is it the principal one. Much more important is *the social and ethical dimension*, which deals with human relations and spiritual values. In this area, which often develops in an inconspicuous way beginning with the daily relationships between people, especially within the family, society certainly owes much to the *"genius of women."*

Here I would like to express particular appreciation to those women who are involved in the various *areas of education* extending well beyond the family: nurseries, schools, universities, social service agencies, parishes, associations and movements. Wherever the work of education is called for, we can note that women are ever ready and willing to give themselves generously to others, especially in serving the weakest and most defenceless. In this work they exhibit a kind of *affective, cultural and spiritual motherhood* which has inestimable value for the development of individuals and the future of society. At this point how can I fail to mention the witness of so many Catholic women and Religious Congregations of women from every continent who have made education, particularly the education of boys and girls, their principal apostolate? How can I not think with gratitude of all the women who have worked and continue to work in the area of health care, not only in highly organized institutions, but also in very precarious circumstances, in the poorest countries of the world, thus demonstrating a spirit of service which not infrequently borders on martyrdom?

10. It is thus my hope, dear sisters, that you will reflect carefully on what it means to speak of the *"genius of women,"* not only in order to

be able to see in this phrase a specific part of God's plan which needs to be accepted and appreciated, but also in order to let this genius be more fully expressed in the life of society as a whole, as well as in the life of the Church. This subject came up frequently during *the Marian Year* and I myself dwelt on it at length in my Apostolic Letter *Mulieris Dignitatem* (1988). In addition, this year in the Letter which I customarily send to priests for Holy Thursday, I invited them to reread *Mulieris Dignitatem* and reflect on the important roles which women have played in their lives as mothers, sisters and co-workers in the apostolate. This is another aspect – different from the conjugal aspect, but also important – of that "help" which women, according to the Book of Genesis, are called to give to men.

The Church sees in Mary the highest expression of the "feminine genius" and she finds in her a source of constant inspiration. Mary called herself the "handmaid of the Lord" (*Lk* 1:38). Through obedience to the Word of God she accepted her lofty yet not easy vocation as wife and mother in the family of Nazareth. Putting herself at God's service, she also put herself at the service of others: a *service of love.* Precisely through this service Mary was able to experience in her life a mysterious, but authentic "reign." It is not by chance that she is invoked as "Queen of heaven and earth." The entire community of believers thus invokes her; many nations and peoples call upon her as their "Queen." *For her, "to reign" is to serve! Her service is "to reign"!*

This is the way in which authority needs to be understood, both in the family and in society and the Church. Each person's fundamental vocation is revealed in this "reigning," for each person has been created in the "image" of the One who is Lord of heaven and earth and called to be his adopted son or daughter in Christ. Man is the only creature on earth "which God willed for its own sake," as the Second Vatican Council teaches; it significantly adds that man "cannot fully find himself except through a sincere gift of self" (*Gaudium et Spes*, 24).

The maternal "reign" of Mary consists in this. She who was, in all her being, a gift for her Son, *has also become a gift for the sons and daughters of the whole human race*, awakening profound trust in those who seek her guidance along the difficult paths of life on the way to their definitive and transcendent destiny. Each one reaches this *final goal* by fidelity to his or her own vocation; this goal provides meaning and direction for the earthly labours of men and women alike.

11. In this perspective of "service" – which, when it is carried out with freedom, reciprocity and love, expresses the truly "royal" nature of mankind – one can also appreciate that the presence of *a certain diversity of roles* is in no way prejudicial to women, provided that this diversity is not the result of an arbitrary imposition, but is rather an expression of what is specific to being male and female. This issue also has a particular application within the Church. If Christ – by his

free and sovereign choice, clearly attested to by the Gospel and by the Church's constant Tradition – entrusted only to men the task of being an *"icon" of his countenance as "shepherd" and "bridegroom" of the Church through the exercise of the ministerial priesthood*, this in no way detracts from the role of women, or for that matter from the role of the other members of the Church who are not ordained to the sacred ministry, since *all* share equally in the dignity proper to the *"common priesthood"* based on Baptism. These role distinctions should not be viewed in accordance with the criteria of functionality typical in human societies. Rather they must be understood according to the particular criteria of the *sacramental economy*, i.e. the economy of "signs" which God freely chooses in order to become present in the midst of humanity.

Furthermore, precisely in line with this economy of signs, even if apart from the sacramental sphere, there is great significance to that "womanhood" which was lived in such a sublime way by Mary. In fact, there is present in the "womanhood" of a woman who believes, and especially in a woman who is "consecrated," a kind of inherent "prophecy" (cf. *Mulieris Dignitatem*, 29), a powerfully evocative symbolism, a highly significant "iconic character," which finds its full realization in Mary and which also aptly expresses the very essence of the Church as a community consecrated with the integrity of a *"virgin"* heart to become the *"bride"* of Christ and *"mother"* of believers. When we consider the "iconic" complementarity of male and female roles, two of the Church's essential dimensions are seen in a clearer light: the "Marian" principle and the Apostolic-Petrine principle (cf. *ibid.*, 27).

On the other hand – as I wrote to priests in this year's Holy Thursday Letter – the ministerial priesthood, according to Christ's plan, "is an expression not of domination but of service" (No. 7). The Church urgently needs, in her daily self-renewal in the light of the Word of God, to emphasize this fact ever more clearly, both by developing the spirit of communion and by carefully fostering all those means of participation which are properly hers, and also by showing respect for and promoting the diverse personal and communal charisms which the Spirit of God bestows for the building up of the Christian community and the service of humanity.

In this vast domain of service, the Church's two-thousand-year history, for all its historical conditioning, has truly experienced the "genius of woman"; from the heart of the Church there have emerged women of the highest calibre who have left an impressive and beneficial mark in history. I think of the great line of woman martyrs, saints and famous mystics. In a particular way I think of Saint Catherine of Siena and of Saint Teresa of Avila, whom Pope Paul VI of happy memory granted the title of Doctors of the Church. And how can we overlook the many women, inspired by faith, who were responsible for initiatives of extraordinary social importance, especially in serving the poorest of the poor? The life of the Church in the Third Millennium will certainly not be lacking in new and surprising manifestations of "the feminine genius."

12. You can see then, dear sisters, that the Church has many reasons for hoping that the forthcoming United Nations Conference in Beijing *will bring out the full truth about women*. Necessary emphasis should be placed on the "*genius of women*," not only by considering great and famous women of the past or present, but also those *ordinary* women who reveal the gift of their womanhood by placing themselves at the service of others in their everyday lives. For in giving themselves to others each day women fulfil their deepest vocation. Perhaps more than men, women *acknowledge the person*, because they see persons with their hearts. They see them independently of various ideological or political systems. They see others in their greatness and limitations; they try to go out to them and *help them*. In this way the basic plan of the Creator takes flesh in the history of humanity and there is constantly revealed, in the variety of vocations, that *beauty* – not merely physical, but above all spiritual – which God bestowed from the very beginning on all, and in a particular way on women.

While I commend to the Lord in prayer the success of the important meeting in Beijing, I invite *Ecclesial Communities* to make this year an occasion of heartfelt thanksgiving to the Creator and Redeemer of the world for the gift of *this great treasure* which is womanhood. In all its expressions, womanhood is part of the essential heritage of mankind and of the Church herself.

May Mary, Queen of Love, watch over women and their mission in service of humanity, of peace, of the spread of God's Kingdom!

With my Blessing.

From the Vatican, 29 June 1995, the Solemnity of Saints Peter and Paul.

RESPONSUM AD PROPOSITUM DUBIUM

CONCERNING THE TEACHING
CONTAINED IN "ORDINATIO SACERDOTALIS"

28 OCTOBER 1995

Dubium: Whether the teaching that the Church has no authority whatsoever to confer priestly ordination on women, which is presented in the Apostolic Letter *Ordinatio Sacerdotalis* to be held definitively, is to be understood as belonging to the deposit of faith.

Responsum: Affirmative.

This teaching requires definitive assent, since, founded on the written Word of God, and from the beginning constantly preserved and applied in the Tradition of the Church, it has been set forth infallibly by the ordinary and universal Magisterium (cf. Second Vatican Council, Dogmatic Constitution on the Church *Lumen Gentium* 25, 2). Thus, in the present circumstances, the Roman Pontiff, exercising his proper office of confirming the brethren (cf. Lk 22:32), has handed on this same teaching by a formal declaration, explicitly stating what is to be held always, everywhere, and by all, as belonging to the deposit of the faith.

The Sovereign Pontiff John Paul II, at the Audience granted to the undersigned Cardinal Prefect, approved this Reply, adopted in the Ordinary Session of this Congregation, and ordered it to be published.

Rome, from the offices of the Congregation for the Doctrine of the Faith, on the Feast of the Apostles SS. Simon and Jude, October 28, 1995.

Chapter 5

THE 2000s

The dawn of the new millennium signified an important event for the Roman Catholic Church. Not only was it two thousand years after the birth of Jesus Christ, it also marked for many within the church the dawn of a new era within church history: the beginning of its third millennium. In many ways this historical change signified reflection on the past and new aspirations and goals for the future. Pope John Paul II opened the new millennium with a year-long celebration called the Great Jubilee Year of 2000.

The Great Jubilee Year began on December 24, 1999 with the opening of the holy door at Saint Peter's Basilica in Rome and the subsequent opening of the holy doors of the three other patriarchal basilicas in Rome over the next month; it ended January 6, 2001 with the closing of Saint Peter's holy door. The church recommitted itself to justice in the world centered on a strong commitment to acceptance, freedom, forgiveness of debts, and solidarity with the poor.[1] In addition, the church also focused its energy on deepening its faith, recognizing God's grace, and asking for forgiveness of sins committed by the church. The pope made it a special feature of this Great Jubilee Year to renew the church's commitment to Christian unity, which was given considerable visible representation when the Greek patriarch, the pope, and the archbishop of Canterbury jointly opened the holy door of Saint Paul Outside the Wall and prayed together while kneeling on its threshold on January 18, 2000.

Another significant historical event and decisive moment in the Roman Catholic Church also occurred in this decade—the death of Pope John Paul II on April 2, 2005. Pope John Paul II, who occupied the papal office from October 16, 1978 until his death, has often been referred to as the church's first modern pope. He traveled extensively outside Italy, was born and raised in Poland, worked fiercely for interreligious dialogue, and sought

---

[1] Pope John Paul II's "Jubilee Commitment to Freedom and Justice" can be found on the vatican.va website.

an end to communism. While he accepted many aspects of the modern world and sought intensive interaction and dialogue with the world, he remained committed to traditional church teachings on sexuality and contraception. For example, he has often been criticized for mishandling the clergy sex abuse scandal and failing to address the church's conceptions of sexuality and authority that supported such heinous crimes. Nevertheless, Pope John Paul II was the first pope that many people had the opportunity to meet in person, and his humanity, faith, and constant devotion to Mary made him a very popular pope and has, since his death, put him on the fast track for sainthood.

Pope John Paul II was succeeded by Cardinal Joseph Ratzinger, who chose the name Benedict XVI. He was consecrated on April 24, 2005. Educated as a theologian, Pope Benedict XVI is a prolific author writing on many theological topics. He spent some years as a professional academic teaching at various universities in Germany and became an archbishop of Munich and Freising in 1977. Beginning in 1981 and continuing to his election to the papacy, he also led the SCDF as its prefect, one of the highest positions within the Roman Curia.

With regard to the Roman Catholic Church's construction of a theology of womanhood, Pope Benedict XVI continues many of Pope John Paul II's teachings. There has not been much new documentation or specifically new teachings regarding the role, position, and status of women. Nevertheless, there are three significant documents that enrich, more by nuances than by broader concepts, the church's teachings concerning women. They include Pope John Paul II's "On the Collaboration of Men and Women in the Church and in the Modern World" and two short documents by papal nuncio H. E. Msg. Celestino Migliore to international councils on gender equality and women's empowerment. All three of these documents are included at the end of this chapter. This chapter also examines two other important documents: the PCF's "Family, Marriage and 'De Facto' Unions," and Pope Benedict XVI's encyclical *Deus caritas est*, or *God Is Love*.

FAMILY, MARRIAGE, AND "DE FACTO" UNIONS

Chronologically, the first document of the 2000s is the Pontifical Council for the Family's (PCF) "Family, Marriage and 'De Facto' Unions," published on November 9, 2000. The PCF had been working on its construction through study groups throughout 1999 as well. Probably the most significant contribution to a construction of a theology of womanhood contained in the document is the church's discussion of the feminist conception of gender and sex as social constructions (8). While the church believes that these mistaken theories have hurt humanity and threaten the family, the church understands that they are part of contemporary society, having been used by the larger society to justify some of the current trends toward accepting homosexual activity, various types of cohabitation, and changes in women's roles and responsibilities.

Of all of the cultural factors that have affected the family recently, the church is convinced that a corrupted, mistaken understanding of gender as a social construction has had a powerful and damaging influence on modern society, especially family life, marriage, and gender roles. In the document the church says modern society is wrong to think that gender and gender roles come from culture and are constructions that do not have any origin in nature or biology. The problem with this idea comes from its insistence on the ability to separate one's gender from one's self, which can lead to justifying homosexuality, the creation of multiple genders, and the separation of masculinity and femininity from their biological origin in men and women.

The church argues that, contrary to this idea, one's biological sex and an acknowledgment of the difference between the sexes are part of human development and personality creation. The church argues that a return to the gospel truth regarding human beings' physical and spiritual makeup will better society. Gender "corresponds to and is harmonious with sexual identity of a psycho-biological nature when the integration of the personality is achieved as recognition of the fullness of the person's inner truth, the unity of body and soul" (8). In other words, a woman is a feminine being in her soul, in her body, and in her mind/personality. The same relationship exists between men and masculinity. A woman is naturally feminine, and a man is naturally masculine. The two sexes therefore complement each other in obviously biological ways as well as in other ways. Biologically, only the sexual union of a woman and a man can create children. Men and women, according to the document, need each other to bring about new generations of humans both literally and in terms of support and mutual support (6).

Men and women do this by entering into marriage. Marriage has a different significance and purpose in the world than other unions. Marriage as an institution should be the only publicly recognized union of two people because society has an interest in it for the generation of future humans. It should be the *only* union of two people to be publicly recognized as valid; families should be promoted and protected because they provide society many goods, including the birthing and raising of children who, within and because of family life, are instilled with a moral system, nonviolent values, and a spirit of cooperation to become responsible, good members of society (17). In this way the family works toward society's common good and welfare.

If other unions are also given public recognition, marriages are hurt (11). Public recognition gives other unions equivalency to marriage, even though they cannot accomplish for society what marriages do. Likewise, public recognition would go against truth and justice. Cohabitating heterosexual couples lack the commitment to each other that marriage and the raising of children require (20 and 35). Same-sex couples lack the complementarity of the sexes, are unable to conceive children, and commit sin in their sexual unions as well. Since homosexual couples are not families, they should not be allowed to adopt children. Allowing them to adopt will only hurt families (23).

The idea of the socially constructed nature of sex and gender also hurts women. If women must work outside the home, they need to have jobs that align with and honor their commitments to family life and the care of the home (29). Sex/gender as a social construction also degrades the notion of gender complementarity because it separates femininity from femaleness and masculinity from maleness. And gender as a social construction fails to recognize that men and women are equal "in different ways" (19, 22). The document believes that women also have a strong biological bond with their children even within the womb that needs to be supported within a family.

Finally, an ontological change happens to men and women within marriage. Becoming a husband or a wife is a change in one's being through a mutual commitment to join one's life with another. This ontological change of status affects one's whole future (26). Marriage and family life take this real change in humans seriously, as it should. This does not take place in de facto and homosexual unions.

While this document does not focus exclusively on women, it comments on women in so much as it discusses notions of gender and sex and how they have affected marriage as an institution. It says little about women's roles but says much about what marriage should be and the ontological change that takes place with marriage. Given that most women enter into marriages, this is significant for all women and the church's theology of womanhood. In fact, the church believes that women fulfill their divine purpose through motherhood, of which physical motherhood should (ideally) be experienced only within the context of a marriage. Thus, the document's significance for a theology of womanhood seems clear.

ON THE COLLABORATION OF MEN AND WOMEN IN THE CHURCH AND IN THE WORLD

The next document concentrates more specifically on women and women's roles and also defines femininity. This is an extremely important development. Of course, one can see these developments and a construction of femininity within earlier documents, but there had never been an explicit definition of femininity.

"On the Collaboration" was written by the SCDF and released on May 31, 2004. It opens with the question of women's roles, status, and position in society, and how best to better women's position within society. Given the changing place of women, the church uses this document to explain how women and men, who are different by nature, should work together in light of women's advances and women's changing place in society to build up the world and the church.

"On the Collaboration" begins by arguing that two current trends in society are problematic regarding gender and a correct understanding of it: first, ignoring differences between the sexes; and second, overemphasizing women's oppression in such a way that women seek power to set themselves up in opposition to men. Both of these ideas deny or at least seek to minimize as much as possible the differences between the sexes, that is, gender complementarity or, in this document, gender "duality" (8).

Modern society also falls into trouble when it tries to end biological determinism in order to liberate women. Biological determinism is the idea that biology (being able to bear children) defines a woman's role in life: motherhood. When society denies the realities of the body in an effort to end biological determinism, the church argues in this document, modern society fundamentally questions the basis of the family, marriage, and the significance of sexuality. Women cannot be dissociated from their biological nature because it is part of who they are. Likewise, it is problematic to deny biological determinism because this can lead to strong criticism of the Bible and deny the significance of Jesus assuming a male form. In light of all of this, the church calls for *"active collaboration* between the sexes precisely in the recognition of the difference between man and woman" (4).

"On the Collaboration," as has been already noted in other works, considers human beings to be essentially equal, given their creation in the image and likeness of God. But it also draws out the point that God created man and woman for different purposes. "On the Collaboration" cites Genesis 1:27—"male and female God created them"—to discuss the fundamental and complementary relationship between men and women. It refers to Genesis 2 to describe woman as man's helpmate, according to God's creation. Likewise, it is argued within the document that this creation story supports the idea that women exist for others. This idea is also found in 1 Corinthians. Women are not the only human beings called to serve, but they are understood to fulfill their destiny better through service. Yet, since humans are at their core relational beings, men, in order to be part of that relationship, must serve women and give of themselves in order to create a community (6).

"On the Collaboration" also describes human anthropology. The Roman Catholic concept of gender/sex is not only a physical or biological concept, but it is also psychological and spiritual. The document says:

> Sexuality characterizes man and woman not only on the physical level, but also on the psychological and spiritual, making its mark on each of their expressions." It cannot be reduced to a pure and insignificant biological fact, but rather "is a fundamental component of personality, one of its modes of being, of manifestation, of communicating with others, of feeling, of expressing and of living human love.". . . The human dimension of sexuality is inseparable from the theological dimension. The human creature, in its unity of soul and body, is characterized therefore, from the very beginning, by the relationship with the other-beyond-the-self. (8)

In other words, not only are people gendered, but so too are souls. One cannot escape being a sexed/gendered human being because that is how God created humanity and being sexed/gendered also describes how humanity relates to the world. This fact is "the immutable *basis of all Christian anthropology*" (8), which one can see has been repeated and defended time and again.

Referring to Christian anthropology, "On the Collaboration" focuses on the differences between men and women. Women are feminine, and femininity is "the fundamental human capacity to live for the other and because of the other" (14). Living for and because of the other, according to the document, entails procreation, maturation at a young age, being responsible, the ability to survive, remembering to cherish the sacredness of life, and focusing on and solving problems in specific situations (13). Likewise, "women are called to be unique examples and witnesses for all Christians of how the Bride is to respond in love to the love of the Bridegroom" (16). Women respond to the bridegroom's love through Mary's characteristics: "listening, welcoming, humility, faithfulness, praise and waiting" (16). Men should learn from women how to be better listeners, more welcoming, more humble, more faithful, give more praise, and be more patient.[2]

---

[2] It is interesting to note that men should cultivate feminine traits, yet Pope John Paul's *Ordinatio sacerdotalis* specifically warns women not to become like men. In other words, women are not supposed to imitate what men are known for.

This document also reaffirms that a woman's main social role is motherhood, whether physical or spiritual (13). However, whatever women choose to do, their primary responsibility and "fundamental vocation" is the family. Women's work should be valued higher and accommodations should be made so that women can prioritize family life over their working life. Femininity should also be valued more because femininity represents human values as much as masculinity represents them. In addition, both men and women are called to live by these values, even though women are more closely connected to them and they come more naturally to women because of their biological makeup (14).

The document also warns society about some conceptions of women that can be taken too far. Focusing solely on the procreative powers of women can reduce women's role to childbearing only; that mentality can be very dangerous because it can lead to women's disregard and may deny the importance of celibacy and consecrated female virgins (13). Thinking that women should be passive is not acceptable either (16). That conception of women should no longer exist in our modern society, according to the document. Serving out of love is not passive, a wholesale acceptance of anything life throws at one. Rather, women's service in love is a form of active participation in and interaction with the world.

This fundamental reality of the different but complementary natures of the sexes is part of salvation history (9–10). In the Old Testament, Israel is frequently depicted as the bride of God, the faithful husband. The book of Isaiah describes the savior as a male figure coming to save his wife from suffering and torment. There are many other examples of the relationship between humans and God portrayed as the marital bond. God, the jealous yet faithful husband, responds to Israel, who often plays the whore, sometimes with anger, rage, and destruction, but more often out of love, forgiveness, acceptance, and mercy.

This nuptial relationship as part of salvation history can also be seen in the life of Jesus and the witness of the Gospels (15–16). Jesus is often understood to be the bridegroom and the church his bride; Jesus loves the church as a husband loves his wife. This idea relates directly to male-only ordination. Women are not priests because women's role in the world is to show the world how to respond to Jesus' love. Men represent Jesus in a bodily way; men are Jesus the bridegroom, and women are the brides.

The document concludes with a picture of how men and women should collaborate to make the world better. Christian theology believes that Jesus' life, death, and resurrection have given humanity the power to transform human relationships. Because of Jesus, humans can break free of sin and live in mutual relationships with one another. They do this by first reclaiming proudly who they are as gendered beings. They have to realize that they are dependent beings as well, dependent on one another for help, support, love, and the like (17). Their married life should be peaceful, happy, and full of love. Without this, they cannot come together in collaboration to make the world a better place. One of the main focuses of transforming the world should be a transformation in the relationship between men and women and an end to ideas of "self-sufficiency, dreams of power, and the drama of violence" (17). In addition, men and women should come together to overcome women's long history of oppression, devaluation, inequality, and disrespect (14).

DEUS CARITAS EST

The relationship between husband and wife is part of the concern of *Deus caritas est* as well. In his first papal encyclical, promulgated on December 25, 2005, Benedict XVI explains God's love and what it means for the world. The concept of God as love is fundamentally different from other images and concepts of God that exist in the world. Humans should respond to God's love for humanity by showing love to their neighbor. This seems to be very similar to Ignatius of Loyola's concept of charity, whereby we serve others in love in gratitude for God's love of us.

God's love for us is best understood as the love that exists between husband and wife; that is, as Pope Benedict XVI writes, "love between man and woman, where body and soul are inseparably joined and human beings glimpse an apparently irresistible promise of happiness. This would seem to be the very epitome of love; all other kinds of love immediately seem to fade in comparison" (2). At the same time, humans must give love in order to be good recipients of it (7, 10, 14). True love, as well as God's love for us, is both *eros* (love between a man and a woman) and *agape* (the kind of love that inspires service to others and care of neighbor).

In this encyclical Benedict XVI also discusses the role of the church in relationship to love and politics. The church does not think its social justice teachings should be imposed on the world; rather, the church should use its teachings to better humanity and human consciences in such a way that they are more attuned to justice and how to better implement it within society. The church cannot be a political institution. Benedict writes, "A just society must be the achievement of politics, not of the church. Yet the promotion of justice through efforts to bring about openness of mind and will to the demands of the common good is something which concerns the church deeply" (28a). In this regard the church guides the laity, whose primary responsibility is to help create a more just world through their work in the world (29). In this same vein people who work for the church's charitable organizations need to be guided by faith and love and not by some political ideology that claims to have a picture of a just world (33).

This papal notion of love and its relationship to the world, social justice, and politics is extremely important in regard to the role and position of women in society. Women's roles, status, and rights are intimately connected with politics. The church says it should not get involved directly in political institutions; this implies that the reverse is also true, that political institutions should have little influence on church practices. For example, all church-related charitable decisions should be made out of love. Such decisions include Catholic adoption services not allowing gay couples to adopt, Catholic hospitals not performing abortions, and the Catholic Church reserving access to the priesthood to men. The church can maintain these policies in spite of political rights and realities to the contrary. This is important to understand because many of the changes of the position of women in society are political, and whether the church admits it or not, it is involved in the political process when it supports or denies political rights women have earned within a given society.[3] Thus, politics is an important consideration in the theology of womanhood the Roman Catholic Church has developed. The church's theology of womanhood chooses sides in politics by denying some political rights women have gained in various societies that do not align with church teaching and supporting other rights which do.

INTERVENTION BY THE HOLY SEE AT THE 61st SESSION OF THE GENERAL ASSEMBLY OF THE UNITED NATIONS ON THE PROMOTION OF GENDER EQUALITY AND THE EMPOWERMENT OF WOMEN

On March 8, 2007, H. E. Msgr. Celestino Migliore addressed the United Nations in New York in a talk entitled "Intervention by the Holy See at the 61st Session of the General Assembly of the United Nations on the Promotion of Gender Equality and the Empowerment of Women." The document bases its argument for women's advancement in society and gender equality on the need for recognition of the difference between the sexes as well as equal access to opportunities. This address sounds very much like "On the Collaboration."

---

[3] The author is not choosing a side here but describing the relationship between the church and politics. Even if the church does not think it can or should have power over political arenas, the truth is that the church is intimately connected with politics, especially social issues. This is the reality, whether we like it or not.

First, the only way that women are ever going to advance in society and become equal with men is if their appropriate role in society is recognized and valued. Men need to value and respect women's roles, and women need to do the same with men's. Recognizing the different roles of men and women underscores equality because without difference any acknowledgment of equality would be false.

In addition to understanding the different roles that are proper to men and women, society must work on women's empowerment. This can be accomplished through education; removing whatever obstacles may be in their way; tackling racism, classism, and religious and social discrimination, which only serve to heighten those obstacles; giving women equal pay for equal work; granting equality of rights within families; ending discriminatory practices regarding promotions; and finally, finding ways to incorporate women into larger networks of societal decision-making. For its part, the Roman Catholic Church has helped promote women's dignity, equality, and advancement through its educational institutions. Catholic charities have also helped women financially by beginning micro-financing projects that grant small loans to help women start their own businesses. On the whole, the Roman Catholic Church believes that women's empowerment and gender equality are important for a just society, but society will only achieve them by heeding the differences and complementarity between men and women. Without gender difference and complementarity, any advancement in the position or status of women will not be authentic change and will only lead to more problems.

STATEMENT OF THE HOLY SEE DELEGATION TO THE ECONOMIC AND SOCIAL COUNCIL ON GENDER EQUALITY AND EMPOWERMENT OF WOMEN

The next address of Msgr. Migliore on women that is being examined here took place on July 1, 2010. This address concerns economic development and is titled "Statement of the Holy See Delegation to the Economic and Social Council on Gender Equality and Empowerment of Women." This too sounds much like "On the Collaboration," but it emphasizes women's social role of mothering, which Migliore's previous document did not.

This address begins by saying that women's dignity needs to be recognized more fully, but this can happen only if women's and men's proper roles in society are understood. Equality is grounded in difference. Migliore states, "Equality is not sameness, and difference is not inequality." In other words, men and women hold different roles within society, and it is the recognition of this difference that shows the true equal and complementary nature of men and women.

In regard to different roles, women's role as mother needs to be valued more. When motherhood is respected the way it should be, women will gain more personal dignity and empowerment through being mothers. Since motherhood is a natural, biological fact of womanhood, women show the "capacity to serve and devote themselves to society and to the family through motherhood which entails a self-giving love and care-giving." Women fulfill themselves at the same time that they help society when they fulfill their role as mothers.

In addition to the need to value motherhood more, the church also sees that some things about society need to change for it to promote women, their dignity, and their empowerment. Women need health-care services, access to education, equal opportunities, better nutrition, the right to be able to own land (or better access to it if that right already exists), adequate financial resources, and the opportunity to borrow money. Women also need to be protected from violence. Discrimination against women in economic situations, in immigration, in access to education and health care, in the workplace, and in civil and social rights also needs to end. Women cannot advance when they still face oppression and exploitation on a daily basis. Therefore, women need to be both "protected and promoted [if] . . . the family, the community and society will truly be fostered."

A key element of the theology of womanhood throughout the 2000s is the need to recognize gender complementarity. Only when grounded in the difference between the sexes does the equality of men and women function well and speak to the truth of the situation as God intended it to be. Theories that minimize gender difference or try to separate men and women from their masculinity and femininity only serve to hurt humanity, especially the institution of marriage. In life, men and women have different, complementary roles to perform. To make society a better place, men and women must work alongside one another.

Another key concept of the decade was the explicit definition of femininity. Women are made to live for others. God created Eve to be Adam's helper; women are called to help men. Women excel at caring, being honest, listening, being sensitive, valuing life, and cultivating relationships. Biologically women are also domestic at heart. The biological fact that women's bodies can bear children makes them more fit for raising, caring for, and educating children. The home should really be their first priority, and whatever work they do outside the home should respect their commitment to home life above all else.

Another concern of the decade was the promotion or advancement of women as well as their dignity. One of the first ways women can gain dignity is if their role as mothers is valued more. Since motherhood is naturally fulfilling for women, supporting women in motherhood helps them gain in personal dignity and self-worth. Women also need better access to various areas of life, from health care to education, to financial resources, to the securing of basic human rights. Without such access, it makes little sense to speak of women's equality, dignity, and respect in society. Violence done to women also needs to end, whether that violence is overtly physical or more subtle, like discrimination and oppression. The dignity of women is extremely important to the Roman Catholic Church. Moreover, women's dignity cannot be secured if women are denied access to opportunities for advancement.

In summary, the 2000s add little new in terms of the theological concept of womanhood. Topics include gender complementarity, gender equality, motherhood, women's dignity, opportunity, and access. Women can only become fully human if they recognize the relationship between their biological constitution and their social, political, and cultural life. Ignoring biology hurts women and the larger society. Society too must recognize biological determinism if it is ever to achieve a just society based on truth.

LETTER TO THE BISHOPS
OF THE CATHOLIC CHURCH
ON THE COLLABORATION OF MEN AND
WOMEN IN THE CHURCH AND IN THE WORLD

31 MAY 2004

INTRODUCTION

1. The Church, expert in humanity, has a perennial interest in whatever concerns men and women. In recent times, much reflection has been given to the question of the dignity of women and to women's rights and duties in the different areas of civil society and the Church. Having contributed to a deeper understanding of this fundamental question, in particular through the teaching of John Paul II, the Church is called today to address certain currents of thought which are often at variance with the authentic advancement of women.

After a brief presentation and critical evaluation of some current conceptions of human nature, this document will offer reflections – inspired by the doctrinal elements of the biblical vision of the human person that are indispensable for safeguarding his or her identity – on some of the essentials of a correct understanding of active collaboration, in recognition of the difference between men and women in the Church and in the world. These reflections are meant as a starting point for further examination in the Church, as well as an impetus for dialogue with all men and women of good will, in a sincere search for the truth and in a common commitment to the development of ever more authentic relationships.

I. THE QUESTION

2. Recent years have seen new approaches to women's issues. A first tendency is to emphasize strongly conditions of subordination in order to give rise to antagonism: women, in order to be themselves, must make themselves the adversaries of men. Faced with the abuse

of power, the answer for women is to seek power. This process leads to opposition between men and women, in which the identity and role of one are emphasized to the disadvantage of the other, leading to harmful confusion regarding the human person, which has its most immediate and lethal effects in the structure of the family.

A second tendency emerges in the wake of the first. In order to avoid the domination of one sex or the other, their differences tend to be denied, viewed as mere effects of historical and cultural conditioning. In this perspective, physical difference, termed *sex*, is minimized, while the purely cultural element, termed *gender*, is emphasized to the maximum and held to be primary. The obscuring of the difference or duality of the sexes has enormous consequences on a variety of levels. This theory of the human person, intended to promote prospects for equality of women through liberation from biological determinism, has in reality inspired ideologies which, for example, call into question the family, in its natural two-parent structure of mother and father, and make homosexuality and heterosexuality virtually equivalent, in a new model of polymorphous sexuality.

3. While the immediate roots of this second tendency are found in the context of reflection on women's roles, its deeper motivation must be sought in the human attempt to be freed from one's biological conditioning. According to this perspective, human nature in itself does not possess characteristics in an absolute manner: all persons can and ought to constitute themselves as they like, since they are free from every predetermination linked to their essential constitution.

This perspective has many consequences. Above all it strengthens the idea that the liberation of women entails criticism of Sacred Scripture, which would be seen as handing on a patriarchal conception of God nourished by an essentially male-dominated culture. Second, this tendency would consider as lacking in importance and relevance the fact that the Son of God assumed human nature in its male form.

4. In the face of these currents of thought, the Church, enlightened by faith in Jesus Christ, speaks instead of *active collaboration* between the sexes precisely in the recognition of the difference between man and woman.

To understand better the basis, meaning and consequences of this response it is helpful to turn briefly to the Sacred Scriptures, rich also in human wisdom, in which this response is progressively manifested thanks to God's intervention on behalf of humanity.

II. BASIC ELEMENTS OF THE BIBLICAL VISION OF THE HUMAN PERSON

5. The first biblical texts to examine are the first three chapters of Genesis. Here we "enter into the setting of the biblical 'beginning.' In it the revealed truth concerning the human person as 'the image

and likeness' of God constitutes the immutable *basis of all Christian anthropology.*"

The first text (*Gn* 1:1—2:4) describes the creative power of the Word of God, which makes distinctions in the original chaos. Light and darkness appear, sea and dry land, day and night, grass and trees, fish and birds, "each according to its kind." An ordered world is born out of differences, carrying with them also the promise of relationships. Here we see a sketch of the framework in which the creation of the human race takes place: "God said 'Let us make man in our image, after our likeness'" (*Gn* 1:26). And then: "God created man in his own image, in the image of God he created him; male and female he created them" (Gn 1:27). From the very beginning therefore, humanity is described as articulated in the male-female relationship. This is the humanity, sexually differentiated, which is explicitly declared "the image of God."

6. The second creation account (*Gn* 2:4–25) confirms in a definitive way the importance of sexual difference. Formed by God and placed in the garden which he was to cultivate, the man, who is still referred to with the generic expression *Adam,* experienced a loneliness which the presence of the animals is not able to overcome. He needs a *helpmate* who will be his partner. The term here does not refer to an inferior, but to a vital helper. This is so that *Adam's* life does not sink into a sterile and, in the end, baneful encounter with himself. It is necessary that he enter into relationship with another being on his own level. Only the woman, created from the same "flesh" and cloaked in the same mystery, can give a future to the life of the man. It is therefore above all on the ontological level that this takes place, in the sense that God's creation of woman characterizes humanity as a relational reality. In this encounter, the man speaks words for the first time, expressive of his wonderment: "This at last is bone of my bones and flesh of my flesh" (*Gn* 2:23).

As the Holy Father has written with regard to this text from Genesis, "woman is another 'I' in a common humanity. From the very beginning they appear as a 'unity of the two,' and this signifies that the original solitude is overcome, the solitude in which man does not find 'a helper fit for him' (*Gn* 2:20). Is it only a question here of a 'helper' in activity, in 'subduing the earth' (cf. *Gn* 1:28)? Certainly it is a matter of a life's companion with whom, as a wife, the man can unite himself, becoming with her 'one flesh' and for this reason leaving 'his father and his mother' (cf. *Gn* 2:24)."

This vital difference is oriented toward communion and was lived in peace, expressed by their nakedness: "And the man and his wife were both naked, yet they felt no shame" (*Gn* 2:25). In this way, the human body, marked with the sign of masculinity or femininity, "includes right from the beginning the nuptial attribute, that is, *the capacity of expressing love, that love in which the person becomes a gift* and – by means of this gift – fulfils the meaning of his being and his existence." Continuing his commentary on these verses of Genesis, the Holy Father writes: "In this peculiarity, the body is the expression of the spirit and is called, in the mystery of creation, to exist in the communion of persons in the image of God."

Through this same spousal perspective, the ancient Genesis narrative allows us to understand how woman, in her deepest and original being, exists "for the other" (cf. *1 Cor* 11:9): this is a statement which, far from any sense of alienation, expresses a fundamental aspect of the similarity with the Triune God, whose Persons, with the coming of Christ, are revealed as being in a communion of love, each for the others. "In the 'unity of the two,' man and woman are called from the beginning not only to exist 'side by side' or 'together,' but they are also called to exist mutually 'one for the other'. . . . The text of Genesis 2:18–25 shows that marriage is the first and, in a sense, the fundamental dimension of this call. But it is not the only one. The whole of human history unfolds within the context of this call. In this history, on the basis of the principle of mutually being 'for' the other in interpersonal 'communion,' there develops in humanity itself, in accordance with God's will, the integration of what is 'masculine' and what is 'feminine.'"

The peaceful vision which concludes the second creation account recalls the "indeed it was very good" (*Gn* 1:31) at the end of the first account. Here we find the heart of God's original plan and the deepest truth about man and woman, as willed and created by him. Although God's original plan for man and woman will later be upset and darkened by sin, it can never be abrogated.

7. Original sin changes the way in which the man and the woman receive and live the Word of God as well as their relationship with the Creator. Immediately after having given them the gift of the garden, God gives them a positive command (cf. *Gn* 2:16), followed by a negative one (cf. *Gn* 2:17), in which the essential difference between God and humanity is implicitly expressed. Following enticement by the serpent, the man and the woman deny this difference. As a consequence, the way in which they live their sexual difference is also upset. In this way, the Genesis account establishes a relationship of cause and effect between the two differences: when humanity considers God its enemy, the relationship between man and woman becomes distorted. When this relationship is damaged, their access to the face of God risks being compromised in turn.

God's decisive words to the woman after the first sin express the kind of relationship which has now been introduced between man and woman: "your desire shall be for your husband, and he shall rule over you" (*Gn* 3:16). It will be a relationship in which love will frequently be debased into pure self-seeking, in a relationship which ignores and kills love and replaces it with the yoke of domination of one sex over the other. Indeed the story of humanity is continuously marked by this situation, which recalls the three-fold concupiscence mentioned by Saint

John: the concupiscence of the flesh, the concupiscence of the eyes and the pride of life (cf. *1 Jn* 2:16). In this tragic situation, the equality, respect and love that are required in the relationship of man and woman according to God's original plan, are lost.

8. Reviewing these fundamental texts allows us to formulate some of the principal elements of the biblical vision of the human person.

Above all, the fact that human beings are persons needs to be underscored: "*Man is a person, man and woman equally so*, since both were created in the image and likeness of the personal God." Their equal dignity as persons is realized as physical, psychological and ontological complementarity, giving rise to a harmonious relationship of "uni-duality," which only sin and "the structures of sin" inscribed in culture render potentially conflictual. The biblical vision of the human person suggests that problems related to sexual difference, whether on the public or private level, should be addressed by a relational approach and not by competition or retaliation.

Furthermore, the importance and the meaning of sexual difference, as a reality deeply inscribed in man and woman, needs to be noted. "Sexuality characterizes man and woman not only on the physical level, but also on the psychological and spiritual, making its mark on each of their expressions." It cannot be reduced to a pure and insignificant biological fact, but rather "is a fundamental component of personality, one of its modes of being, of manifestation, of communicating with others, of feeling, of expressing and of living human love." This capacity to love – reflection and image of God who is Love – is disclosed in the spousal character of the body, in which the masculinity or femininity of the person is expressed.

The human dimension of sexuality is inseparable from the theological dimension. The human creature, in its unity of soul and body, is characterized therefore, from the very beginning, by the relationship with the other-beyond-the-self. This relationship is presented as still good and yet, at the same time, changed. It is good from its original goodness, declared by God from the first moment of creation. It has been changed however by the disharmony between God and humanity introduced by sin. This alteration does not correspond to the initial plan of God for man and woman, nor to the truth of the relationship between the sexes. It follows then that the relationship is good, but wounded and in need of healing.

What might be the ways of this healing? Considering and analyzing the problems in the relationship between the sexes solely from the standpoint of the situation marked by sin would lead to a return to the errors mentioned above. The logic of sin needs to be broken and a way forward needs to be found that is capable of banishing it from the hearts of sinful humanity. A clear orientation in this sense is provided in the third chapter of Genesis by God's promise of a Saviour, involving the "woman" and her "offspring" (cf. *Gn* 3:15). It is a promise which will be preceded by a long preparation in history before it is realized.

9. An early victory over evil is seen in the story of Noah, the just man, who guided by God, avoids the flood with his family and the various species of animals (cf. *Gn* 6—9). But it is above all in God's choice of Abraham and his descendants (cf. *Gn* 12:1ff) that the hope of salvation is confirmed. God begins in this way to unveil his countenance so that, through the chosen people, humanity will learn the path of divine like-ness, that is, the way of holiness, and thus of transformation of heart. Among the many ways in which God reveals himself to his people (cf. *Heb* 1:1), in keeping with a long and patient pedagogy, there is the recurring theme of the covenant between man and woman. This is paradoxical if we consider the drama recounted in Genesis and its concrete repetition in the time of the prophets, as well as the mixing of the sacred and the sexual found in the religions which surrounded Israel. And yet this symbolism is indispensable for understanding the way in which God loves his people: God makes himself known as the Bridegroom who loves Israel his Bride.

If, in this relationship, God can be described as a "jealous God" (cf. *Ex* 20:5; *Nah* 1:2) and Israel denounced as an "adulterous" bride or "prostitute" (cf. *Hos* 2:4–15; *Ez* 16:15–34), it is because of the hope, reinforced by the prophets, of seeing Jerusalem become the perfect bride: "For as a young man marries a virgin so shall your creator marry you, and as the bridegroom rejoices over the bride, so shall your God rejoice over you" (*Is* 62:5). Recreated "in righteousness and in justice, in steadfast love and in mercy" (*Hos* 2:21), she who had wandered far away to search for life and happiness in false gods will return, and "shall respond as in the days of her youth" (*Hos* 2:17) to him who will speak to her heart; she will hear it said: "Your bridegroom is your Creator" (*Is* 54:5). It is substantially the same reality which is expressed when, paral-lel to the mystery of God's action through the male figure of the suffering Servant, the Book of the prophet Isaiah evokes the feminine figure of Zion, adorned with a transcendence and a sanctity which prefigure the gift of salvation destined for Israel.

The Song of Songs is an important moment in the use of this form of revelation. In the words of a most human love, which celebrate the beauty of the human body and the joy of mutual seeking, God's love for his people is also expressed. The Church's recognition of her relation-ship to Christ in this audacious conjunction of language about what is most human with language about what is most divine, cannot be said to be mistaken.

In the course of the Old Testament, a story of salvation takes shape which involves the simultaneous participation of male and female. While having an evident metaphorical dimension, the terms bridegroom and bride – and covenant as well – which characterize the dynamic of sal-vation, are much more than simple metaphors. This spousal language touches on the very nature of the relationship which God establishes with his people, even though that relationship is more expansive than human spousal experience. Likewise, the same concrete conditions of redemption are at play in the way in which prophetic statements, such as those of Isaiah, associate masculine and feminine roles in proclaiming and prefiguring the work of salvation which God is about to undertake. This salvation orients the reader both toward the male figure of the suffering Servant as well as to the female figure of Zion. The prophetic utterances of Isaiah in fact alternate between this figure and the Servant of God, before culminating at the end of the book with the mystical vision of Jerusalem, which gives birth to a people in a single day (cf. *Is* 66:7–14), a prophecy of the great new things which God is about to do (cf. *Is* 48:6–8).

10. All these prefigurations find their fulfillment in the New Testament. On the one hand, Mary, the chosen daughter of Zion, in her femininity, sums up and transfigures the condition of Israel/Bride waiting for the day of her salvation. On the other hand, the masculinity of the Son shows how Jesus assumes in his person all that the Old Testament symbolism had applied to the love of God for his people, described as the love of a bridegroom for his bride. The figures of Jesus and Mary his mother not only assure the continuity of the New Testament with the Old, but go beyond it, since – as Saint Irenaeus wrote – with Jesus Christ "all newness" appears.

This aspect is particularly evident in the Gospel of John. In the scene of the wedding feast at Cana, for example, Jesus is asked by his mother, who is called "woman," to offer, as a sign, the new wine of the future wedding with humanity (cf. *Jn* 2:1–12). This messianic wedding is accomplished on the Cross when, again in the presence of his mother, once again called "woman," the blood/wine of the New Covenant pours forth from the open heart of the crucified Christ (cf. *Jn* 19:25–27, 34). It is therefore not at all surprising that John the Baptist, when asked who he is, describes himself as "the friend of the bridegroom," who rejoices to hear the bridegroom's voice and must be eclipsed by his coming: "He who has the bride is the bridegroom; the friend of the bridegroom, who stands and hears him, rejoices greatly at the bridegroom's voice; therefore this joy of mine is now full. He must increase, but I must decrease" (*Jn* 3:29–30).

In his apostolic activity, Paul develops the whole nuptial significance of the redemption by seeing Christian life as a nuptial mystery. He writes to the Church in Corinth, which he had founded: "I feel a divine jealousy for you, for I betrothed you to Christ to present you as a chaste virgin to her one husband" (*2 Cor* 11:2).

In the Letter to the Ephesians, the spousal relationship between Christ and the Church is taken up again and deepened in its implications. In the New Covenant, the beloved bride is the Church, and as the Holy Father teaches in his *Letter to Families:* "This bride, of whom the

Letter to the Ephesians speaks, is present in each of the baptized and is like one who presents herself before her Bridegroom: 'Christ loved the Church and gave himself up for her . . . that he might present the Church to himself in splendour, without spot or wrinkle or any such thing, that she might be holy and without blemish' (*Eph* 5:25–27)."

Reflecting on the unity of man and woman as described at the moment of the world's creation (cf. *Gn* 2:24), the Apostle exclaims: "this mystery is a profound one, and I am saying that it refers to Christ and the Church" (*Eph* 5:32). The love of a man and a woman, lived out in the power of baptismal life, now becomes the sacrament of the love between Christ and his Church, and a witness to the mystery of fidelity and unity from which the "New Eve" is born and by which she lives in her earthly pilgrimage toward the fullness of the eternal wedding.

11. Drawn into the Paschal mystery and made living signs of the love of Christ and his Church, the hearts of Christian spouses are renewed and they are able to avoid elements of concupiscence in their relationship, as well as the subjugation introduced into the life of the first married couple by the break with God caused by sin. For Christian spouses, the goodness of love, for which the wounded human heart has continued to long, is revealed with new accents and possibilities. It is in this light that Jesus, faced with the question about divorce (cf. *Mt* 19:3–9), recalls the demands of the covenant between man and woman as willed by God at the beginning, that is, before the eruption of sin which had justified the later accommodations found in the Mosaic Law. Far from being the imposition of a hard and inflexible order, these words of Jesus are actually the proclamation of the "good news" of that faithfulness which is stronger than sin. The power of the resurrection makes possible the victory of faithfulness over weakness, over injuries and over the couple's sins. In the grace of Christ which renews their hearts, man and woman become capable of being freed from sin and of knowing the joy of mutual giving.

12. "For all of you who have been baptized into Christ have put on Christ... there is neither male nor female," writes Saint Paul to the Galatians (3:27–28). The Apostle Paul does not say that the distinction between man and woman, which in other places is referred to the plan of God, has been erased. He means rather that in Christ the rivalry, enmity and violence which disfigured the relationship between men and women can be overcome and have been overcome. In this sense, the distinction between man and woman is reaffirmed more than ever; indeed, it is present in biblical revelation up to the very end. In the final hour of present history, the Book of Revelation of Saint John, speaking of "a new heaven and a new earth" (*Rev* 21:1), presents the vision of a feminine Jerusalem "prepared as a bride adorned for her husband" (*Rev* 21:2). Revelation concludes with the words of the Bride and the

Spirit who beseech the coming of the Bridegroom, "Come, Lord Jesus!" (*Rev* 22:20).

Male and female are thus revealed as *belonging ontologically to creation* and destined therefore *to outlast the present time*, evidently in a transfigured form. In this way, they characterize the "love that never ends" (*1 Cor* 13:8), although the temporal and earthly expression of sexuality is transient and ordered to a phase of life marked by procreation and death. Celibacy for the sake of the Kingdom seeks to be the prophecy of this form of future existence of male and female. For those who live it, it is an anticipation of the reality of a life which, while remaining that of a man and a woman, will no longer be subject to the present limitations of the marriage relationship (cf. *Mt* 22:30). For those in married life, celibacy becomes the reminder and prophecy of the completion which their own relationship will find in the face-to-face encounter with God.

From the first moment of their creation, man and woman are distinct, and will remain so for all eternity. Placed within Christ's Paschal mystery, they no longer see their difference as a source of discord to be overcome by denial or eradication, but rather as the possibility for collaboration, to be cultivated with mutual respect for their difference. From here, new perspectives open up for a deeper understanding of the dignity of women and their role in human society and in the Church.

III. THE IMPORTANCE OF FEMININE VALUES IN THE LIFE OF SOCIETY

13. Among the fundamental values linked to women's actual lives is what has been called a "capacity for the other." Although a certain type of feminist rhetoric makes demands "for ourselves," women preserve the deep intuition of the goodness in their lives of those actions which elicit life, and contribute to the growth and protection of the other.

This intuition is linked to women's physical capacity to give life. Whether lived out or remaining potential, this capacity is a reality that structures the female personality in a profound way. It allows her to acquire maturity very quickly, and gives a sense of the seriousness of life and of its responsibilities. A sense and a respect for what is concrete develop in her, opposed to abstractions which are so often fatal for the existence of individuals and society. It is women, in the end, who even in very desperate situations, as attested by history past and present, possess a singular capacity to persevere in adversity, to keep life going even in extreme situations, to hold tenaciously to the future, and finally to remember with tears the value of every human life.

Although motherhood is a key element of women's identity, this does not mean that women should be considered from the sole perspective of physical procreation. In this area, there can be serious distortions, which extol biological fecundity in purely quantitative terms and are often accompanied by dangerous disrespect for women. The existence of the Christian vocation of virginity, radical with regard to both the Old Testament tradition and the demands made by many societies, is of the greatest importance in this regard. Virginity refutes any attempt to enclose women in mere biological destiny. Just as virginity receives from physical motherhood the insight that there is no Christian vocation except in the concrete gift of oneself to the other, so physical motherhood receives from virginity an insight into its fundamentally spiritual dimension: it is in not being content only to give physical life that the other truly comes into existence. This means that motherhood can find forms of full realization also where there is no physical procreation.

In this perspective, one understands the irreplaceable role of women in all aspects of family and social life involving human relationships and caring for others. Here what John Paul II has termed *the genius of women* becomes very clear. It implies first of all that women be significantly and actively present in the family, "the primordial and, in a certain sense sovereign society," since it is here above all that the features of a people take shape; it is here that its members acquire basic teachings. They learn to love inasmuch as they are unconditionally loved, they learn respect for others inasmuch as they are respected, they learn to know the face of God inasmuch as they receive a first revelation of it from a father and a mother full of attention in their regard. Whenever these fundamental experiences are lacking, society as a whole suffers violence and becomes in turn the progenitor of more violence. It means also that women should be present in the world of work and in the organization of society, and that women should have access to positions of responsibility which allow them to inspire the policies of nations and to promote innovative solutions to economic and social problems.

In this regard, it cannot be forgotten that the interrelationship between these two activities – family and work – has, for women, characteristics different from those in the case of men. The harmonization of the organization of work and laws governing work with the demands stemming from the mission of women within the family is a challenge. The question is not only legal, economic and organizational; it is above all a question of mentality, culture, and respect. Indeed, a just valuing of the work of women within the family is required. In this way, women who freely desire will be able to devote the totality of their time to the work of the household without being stigmatized by society or penalized financially, while those who wish also to engage in other work may be able to do so with an appropriate work-schedule, and not have to choose between relinquishing their family life or enduring continual stress, with negative consequences for one's own equilibrium and the harmony of the family. As John Paul II has written, "it will redound to the credit of society to make it possible for a mother – without inhibiting her freedom, without psychological or practical discrimination and without penalizing her as compared with other women – to devote herself to taking care of her children and educating them in accordance with their needs, which vary with age."

14. It is appropriate however to recall that the feminine values mentioned here are above all human values: the human condition of man and woman created in the image of God is one and indivisible. It is only because women are more immediately attuned to these values that they are the reminder and the privileged sign of such values. But, in the final analysis, every human being, man or woman, is destined to be "for the other." In this perspective, that which is called "femininity" is more than simply an attribute of the female sex. The word designates indeed the fundamental human capacity to live for the other and because of the other.

Therefore, the promotion of women within society must be understood and desired as a humanization accomplished through those values, rediscovered thanks to women. Every outlook which presents itself as a conflict between the sexes is only an illusion and a danger: it would end in segregation and competition between men and women, and would promote a solipsism nourished by a false conception of freedom.

Without prejudice to the advancement of women's rights in society and the family, these observations seek to correct the perspective which views men as enemies to be overcome. The proper condition of the male-female relationship cannot be a kind of mistrustful and defensive opposition. Their relationship needs to be lived in peace and in the happiness of shared love.

On a more concrete level, if social policies – in the areas of education, work, family, access to services and civic participation – must combat all unjust sexual discrimination, they must also listen to the aspirations and identify the needs of all. The defence and promotion of equal dignity and common personal values must be harmonized with attentive recognition of the difference and reciprocity between the sexes where this is relevant to the realization of one's humanity, whether male or female.

IV. THE IMPORTANCE OF FEMININE VALUES IN THE LIFE OF THE CHURCH

15. In the Church, woman as "sign" is more than ever central and fruitful, following as it does from the very identity of the Church, as received from God and accepted in faith. It is this "mystical" identity, profound and essential, which needs to be kept in mind when reflecting on the respective roles of men and women in the Church.

From the beginning of Christianity, the Church has understood herself to be a community, brought into existence by Christ and joined to him by a relationship of love, of which the nuptial experience is the privileged expression. From this it follows that the Church's first task is to remain in the presence of this mystery of God's love, manifested in Jesus Christ, to contemplate and to celebrate it. In this regard, the figure of Mary constitutes the fundamental reference in the Church. One could say metaphorically that Mary is a mirror placed before the Church, in which the Church is invited to recognize her own identity as well as the dispositions of the heart, the attitudes and the actions which God expects from her.

The existence of Mary is an invitation to the Church to root her very being in listening and receiving the Word of God, because faith is not so much the search for God on the part of human beings, as the recognition by men and women that God comes to us; he visits us and speaks to us. This faith, which believes that "nothing is impossible for God" (cf. *Gn* 18:14; *Lk* 1:37), lives and becomes deeper through the humble and loving obedience by which the Church can say to the Father: "Let it be done to me according to your word" (*Lk* 1:38). Faith continually makes reference to Jesus: "Do whatever he tells you" (*Jn* 2:5) and accompanies Jesus on his way, even to the foot of the Cross. Mary, in the hour of darkness, perseveres courageously in faithfulness, with the sole certainty of trust in the Word of God.

It is from Mary that the Church always learns the intimacy of Christ. Mary, who carried the small child of Bethlehem in her arms, teaches us to recognize the infinite humility of God. She who received the broken body of Jesus from the Cross shows the Church how to receive all those in this world whose lives have been wounded by violence and sin. From Mary, the Church learns the meaning of the power of love, as revealed by God in the life of his beloved Son: "he has scattered the proud in the thoughts of their heart . . . he has lifted up the lowly" (*Lk* 1:51–52). From Mary, the disciples of Christ continually receive the sense and the delight of praise for the work of God's hands: "The Almighty has done great things for me" (*Lk* 1:49). They learn that they are in the world to preserve the memory of those "great things," and to keep vigil in expectation of the day of the Lord.

16. To look at Mary and imitate her does not mean, however, that the Church should adopt a passivity inspired by an outdated conception of femininity. Nor does it condemn the Church to a dangerous vulnerability in a world where what count above all are domination and power. In reality, the way of Christ is neither one of domination (cf. *Phil* 2:6) nor of power as understood by the world (cf. *Jn* 18:36). From the Son of God one learns that this "passivity" is in reality the way of love; it is a royal power which vanquishes all violence; it is "passion" which saves the world from sin and death and recreates humanity. In entrusting his

mother to the Apostle John, Jesus on the Cross invites his Church to learn from Mary the secret of the love that is victorious.

Far from giving the Church an identity based on an historically conditioned model of femininity, the reference to Mary, with her dispositions of listening, welcoming, humility, faithfulness, praise and waiting, places the Church in continuity with the spiritual history of Israel. In Jesus and through him, these attributes become the vocation of every baptized Christian. Regardless of conditions, states of life, different vocations with or without public responsibilities, they are an essential aspect of Christian life. While these traits should be characteristic of every baptized person, women in fact live them with particular intensity and naturalness. In this way, women play a role of maximum importance in the Church's life by recalling these dispositions to all the baptized and contributing in a unique way to showing the true face of the Church, spouse of Christ and mother of believers.

In this perspective one understands how the reservation of priestly ordination solely to men does not hamper in any way women's access to the heart of Christian life. Women are called to be unique examples and witnesses for all Christians of how the Bride is to respond in love to the love of the Bridegroom.

CONCLUSION

17. In Jesus Christ all things have been made new (cf. *Rev* 21:5). Renewal in grace, however, cannot take place without conversion of heart. Gazing at Jesus and confessing him as Lord means recognizing the path of love, triumphant over sin, which he sets out for his disciples.

In this way, man's relationship with woman is transformed, and the three-fold concupiscence described in the First Letter of John (*1 Jn* 2:16) ceases to have the upper hand. The witness of women's lives must be received with respect and appreciation, as revealing those values without which humanity would be closed in self-sufficiency, dreams of power and the drama of violence. Women too, for their part, need to follow the path of conversion and recognize the unique values and great capacity for loving others which their femininity bears. In both cases, it is a question of humanity's conversion to God, so that both men and women may come to know God as their "helper," as the Creator full of tenderness, as the Redeemer who "so loved the world that he gave his only begotten Son" (*Jn* 3:16).

Such a conversion cannot take place without humble prayer to God for that penetrating gaze which is able to recognize one's own sin and also the grace which heals it. In a particular way, we need to ask this of the Blessed Virgin Mary, the woman in accord with the heart of God, she who is "blessed among women" (cf. *Lk* 1:42), chosen to reveal to men and women the way of love. Only in this way, can the "image of God," the sacred likeness inscribed in every man and woman, emerge according to the specific grace received by each (cf. *Gn* 1:27). Only thus can the path of peace and wonderment be recovered, witnessed in the verses of the Song of Songs, where bodies and hearts celebrate the same jubilee.

The Church certainly knows the power of sin at work in individuals and in societies, which at times almost leads one to despair of the goodness of married couples. But through her faith in Jesus crucified and risen, the Church knows even more the power of forgiveness and self-giving in spite of any injury or injustice. The peace and wonderment which she trustfully proposes to men and women today are the peace and wonderment of the garden of the resurrection, which have enlightened our world and its history with the revelation that "God is love" (*1 Jn* 4:8, 16).

The Sovereign Pontiff John Paul II, in the Audience granted to the undersigned Cardinal Prefect, approved the present Letter, adopted in the Ordinary Session of this Congregation, and ordered its publication.

Rome, from the Offices of the Congregation for the Doctrine of the Faith, May 31, 2004, the Feast of the Visitation of the Blessed Virgin Mary.

INTERVENTION BY THE HOLY SEE AT THE 61ST SESSION OF THE GENERAL ASSEMBLY OF THE UNITED NATIONS ON THE PROMOTION OF GENDER EQUALITY AND THE EMPOWERMENT OF WOMEN

ADDRESS OF H. E. MSGR. CELESTINO MIGLIORE

NEW YORK
THURSDAY, 8 MARCH 2007

Madam President,

At the outset, my delegation thanks you for convening this *Informal Thematic Debate of the General Assembly on the Promotion of Gender Equality and the Empowerment of Women*, and its subsequent panel debates on *women in decision-making* and *empowerment of women* including microfinance. This timely debate is a significant contribution to the reflections on the issues of the dignity, rights and duties of women and to their role and achievements in the various sectors of society.

The legitimate quest for equality between men and women has achieved positive results in the area of equality of rights. This quest needs to be accompanied by the awareness that equality goes hand in hand with and does not endanger, much less contradict, the recognition of both the difference and complementarity between men and women. Without this recognition the struggle for equality would not be authentic.

It seems, in fact, that oftentimes the ideas on the equality of rights between men and women have been marked by an antagonistic approach which exalts opposition between them. This approach juxtaposes woman against man and vice-versa, while the identity and role of one is emphasized with the aim of merely diminishing that of the other. Success in the quest for equality and the empowerment of women can best be achieved when such antagonism gives way to mutual respect and recognition of the identity and the role of one towards the other.

A second tendency is to blur, if not entirely deny, the differences between men and women. In order to avoid the domination of one sex over the other, their differences tend to be obscured or viewed as mere effects of historical and cultural conditioning. Physical difference is often minimized, while the purely cultural dimension is maximized and held to be primary. This blurring of differences has impact on the stability of society and of families and, not least, on the quality of the relations between men and women. Equality between women and men and the empowerment of women will be attained when the differences of the sexes are recognized and highlighted as complementary and the cultural element of gender is understood in its proper context.

Empowerment of women refers to increasing their social, political, economic and spiritual strength, both individually and collectively, as well as to removing the obstacles that penalize women and prevent them from being fully integrated into the various sectors of society. Concretely, it means addressing discriminatory practices that exclude women from decision-making processes, oftentimes caused or aggravated by discrimination based on a woman's race, ethnicity, religion or social status. That women in society must be involved in decision-making is not only right for reasons of equality, but also for the specific insights that women bring to the process. This "feminine genius" will prove most valuable, as women increasingly play major roles in the solution of the serious challenges the world is facing. Empowerment of women also means equal pay for equal work, fairness in career advancement, and equality of spouses in family rights. Likewise, it means that women who choose to be wives and mothers are protected and not penalized.

With regard to empowering women through microfinance, my delegation takes pride in the fact that for decades some institutions and agencies of the Catholic Church have been active in microfinancing. Just to cite one example, Catholic Relief Services, which operates in 99 countries from all continents, began microfinance programmes in 1988 in five countries. Now programmes are operational in at least thirty countries, with more than 850,000 clients, of whom almost 75% are women. The programme focuses on the poor, especially poor women, in remote rural communities where there is no access to financial services. Moreover, in order to build managerial capacities and assure programme sustainability, the clients are directly involved in the management and administration of the services they receive.

Studies have shown how microfinance has led to a wide-ranging improvement of the status of women, from earning greater respect from men to being acknowledged as society's important contributors; from achieving better family health to greater awareness of the value of education; from greater self-esteem to taking a leading role in poverty reduction. These and other positive effects on the daily life of women tell us that microfinance is warmly to be supported. However, we must be aware that it is hardly a panacea for all the ills afflicting women in developing countries. Further, the system is not immune from abuse. It is, in fact, noted that in some circumstances and places, men ask their wives to get loans from microfinanciers, and then they take the loan and run the business themselves, or even, use the money for other purposes.

Hand in hand with the empowering benefits brought about by initiatives like microfinance, goes the need for education and awareness-raising, especially at the level of the local community. Education for women in particular remains the most vital tool in the promotion of equality between men and women and in the empowerment of women to contribute fully to society. The Holy See desires for its part to continue to educate boys and girls, men and women, to foster and uphold the dignity, role and rights of women. With tools such as these, women's empowerment can begin to take root and flourish in those places where it is still largely lacking.

Thank you, Madam President.

STATEMENT OF THE HOLY SEE DELEGATION TO THE ECONOMIC AND SOCIAL COUNCIL ON GENDER EQUALITY AND EMPOWERMENT OF WOMEN

STATEMENT BY H. E. MSGR. CELESTINO MIGLIORE APOSTOLIC NUNCIO

NEW YORK
THURSDAY, 1 JULY 2010

Mr. President,

This year's substantive session is particularly pertinent leading up to the long expected World Summit on the MDGs [Millennium Development Goals]. All women and girls who are affected by the MDGs look forward towards an increased recognition of their value and equality as well as their dignified role in development. Any deliberation on the matter will be incomplete without ensuring the advancement of women, who are dynamic agents of development in the family, society and the world.

Ever since world leaders committed their governments to the ambitious objective of attaining the MDGs, some remarkable progress has been achieved in mainstreaming women's perspectives in development both in multilateral and national policies. Even those countries lagging behind in many aspects of development are giving more prominence to the role of women in public life, especially in the political arena.

The empowerment of women presupposes universal human dignity and, thus, the dignity of each and every individual. The notion denotes complementarity between man and woman, which means equality in diversity: where equality and diversity are based on biological data, expressed traditionally by male and female sexuality, and on the primacy of the person. It concerns also roles to be held and functions to be performed in society. In that regard, equality is not sameness, and difference is not inequality.

Empowerment of women for development means also recognition of the gifts and talents of every woman and is affirmed through the provision of better health care, education and equal opportunities.

Empowering women and respecting their dignity mean also honoring their capacity to serve and devote themselves to society and to the family through motherhood which entails a self-giving love and care-giving. Altruism, dedication and service to others are healthy and contribute to personal dignity. If domesticity can be considered a particular gift of mothers in cultivating a genuine intrapersonal relationship in the family and society, then family-friendly working arrangements, shared family-care leave and redistribution of the burden of unpaid work will be given the attention they rightly deserve.

The Holy See notes with concern that inequalities between individuals and between countries thrive and various forms of discrimination, exploitation and oppression of women and girls persist, which must be addressed by the provision of adequate social protection measures for them, as appropriate to national contexts.

In the health sector there is a need to eliminate inequalities between men and women and increase the capacity of women to care for themselves principally by being afforded adequate health care. Scientific studies have shown remarkable improvement in the reduction of maternal and infant mortality, revealing the importance of complementary investing in other areas relevant to women and girls including nutrition, general health and education. The real advancement of women is not achieved by concentrating on a particular health issue to the neglect of others but by promoting their overall health which necessarily includes giving more attention to addressing women-specific diseases.

Women's economic empowerment is essential for the economic development of the family and of society. Access to land and property, credit facilities and equal opportunities for financial services for women will help ensure their economic stability. In this process, the whole household and community must support their entrepreneurship. The ethical dimension of their development and economic empowerment as well as their service to the family must not be overlooked.

Tragically, violence against women, especially in the home and work place, and discrimination in the professional field, even on the pay and pension scale, are growing concerns. Through adequate legal frameworks and national policies, perpetrators of violence must be brought to justice and women must be afforded rehabilitation. Women and girls must be guaranteed their full enjoyment of civil, political, economic, social and cultural rights including equal access to education and health.

My delegation supports the initiatives in favour of the rights in particular of women migrants and refugees and women with disabilities. Human rights learning campaigns especially for girls and women must be promoted, even from early school days and also through non-formal education. Civil society and NGOs, women's associations and faith-based organizations can contribute a great deal in human rights learning and in quality education.

In concluding, Mr. President, the more the dignity of women is protected and promoted, the more the family, the community and society will truly be fostered.

Thank you, Mr. President.

Conclusion

The goal of this book is to explain the Roman Catholic Church's theology of womanhood. Its production should be considered a historical event motivated by (and only sometimes agreeing with) feminism and other modern movements that struggle for freedom, equality, rights, and justice. Its origin can be traced to early feminist movements in the late 1800s and early decades of the 1900s in the United States and Europe. Yet, an actual theology of womanhood did not truly begin until at least 1960. With the dawn of the second-wave of feminism, the church undertook a more serious effort to define women's roles, position, and status in the world, always returning to the dignity and respect owed to women as well as their different yet complementary nature to men. It is this theology that will be summarized here.

We can trace four main themes within this theology of womanhood. They are (1) the definition of woman, (2) women and the creation of a family, (3) women within the church, and (4) women's interaction with the world. These categories interact and overlap. By examining these themes, this chapter hopes to address the theology of womanhood less from a chronological development and more as a whole body of doctrine. It is important to know what all of the documents explored within this book mean in a larger context.

The synthesis of the information within this book is important for understanding the Roman Catholic Church's theology of womanhood. In fact, moving from one decade to another offers the reader a good understanding of the development but does not necessarily paint the more practical picture of what womanhood means to the church today. With this in mind, this chapter answers the following questions in order for the reader to grasp this larger theological project within the Catholic Church:

- What does it mean to be a Roman Catholic woman according to the Roman Catholic Church?
- What significance should motherhood have in women's lives?
- How do women balance careers and family life?
- Should women work outside the home? What vocations are open to

women within the Roman Catholic Church? How do women find fulfillment?

- What do women contribute to the life and work of the church?

The answers to the questions are highly significant because the church understands this theology to be something true, based on the Holy Scriptures and on the life and death of Jesus Christ, and rooted in church tradition. It believes that these theological guidelines should be strived for on a daily basis by half the world's population. It also believes that women find fulfillment only by living out lives that are attuned with their nature as made by God.

WOMANHOOD DEFINED

As we have seen in church documents from the very beginning of the 1960s, women, as creations of God, are equal in dignity and respect to men. These documents also point out, as others do as well, that because of this dignity and respect owed to women, there should be no unjust discrimination, inequality, or oppression toward women. *Gaudium et spes* (1965) specifically states that women should have equal political, social, and economic rights. Unfortunately, they do not. *Familiaris consortio* (1981) acknowledges that women do not have these rights secured everywhere. They are the first to suffer in poverty, oppression, and lack of rights. Likewise, women often are not allowed to develop fully and actually become themselves. If they were allowed to do so, the world would be a better place.

Women are one of two gendered types of human beings created by God. According to *Persona humana* (1975) and "On the Collaboration" (2004), gender and sex are inseparable. All people are biological and psychologically gendered. Even the individual's soul is gendered. Sex and gender are not social constructions. Rather, women are naturally feminine and should cultivate their femininity, not detest it or try to imitate men or male models of domination. Their personalities are feminine, and their natural values and characteristics come from their femininity. One can see this as early as five years of age in little girls who want to play with dolls and play house (see "The Truth and Meaning of Human Sexuality" [1995]).

Femininity means living for the others. Women do this naturally. They are also better at relationships than men. Women are naturally tender, loving, caring, unselfish, humble, patient, generous, sensible, and understanding. Women also offer others the gift of themselves, have an innate respect for life, and operate out of love (what has been referred to as "an order of love"). Likewise, according to "On the Collaboration" (2004), women mature earlier, take on responsibility sooner, cherish the sacredness of life more, and are better at problem-solving than men. All of these gifts arise out of their natural feminine natures.

Women are biologically fulfilled and fulfilled in many others ways by motherhood. This motherhood can be biologically giving birth to children and raising them or a spiritual calling in which women "mother" others by caring for and loving them (*Mulieris dignitatem* [1988]). As physical mothers, women are the primary caregivers and educators of their children, especially in their first five years. Spiritual mothers care for the sick, hungry, poverty-stricken, and the like. Motherhood should be valued more by society, and women should take pride in their role as mothers. After all, the church has a great example of God's respect for women and women's dignity as God's creation: Jesus' mother Mary, who lived for others and offered herself as a gift.

WOMEN AND THE CREATION OF A FAMILY

As already mentioned, women have different roles than men do, and their most important role centers on the family. While *Gaudium et spes* (1965), *Familiaris consortio* (1981), and "On the Collaboration" (2004) mention that women and men should work as partners within a marriage, their roles are different within that context. Within marriage, women's primary role is that of mother and wife. Sexual relations are only permissible within the context of a marriage, the mutual commitment of one man and one woman to unite their lives together in love and in service. This commitment is permanent, according to *Persona humana* (1975).

Humanae vitae (1968) defines sex as the mutual physical self-giving of the two spouses. The sexual union must be open to procreation. The rhythm method may be used to space births, but the use of contraception is not permitted. Contraception does not allow full self-giving of the partners because it frustrates the finality of sex, which is procreation. Children are gifts from God and should be treated as such.

The use of contraception threatens a human's fundamental right to life, as explained in *Evangelium vitae* (1995). Likewise, women could be devalued and used only as sex objects if contraception is acceptable, according to *Humanae vitae* (1968). In addition, *Donum vitae* (1987) states that conception should be free of medical and other interventions and should happen naturally with a sexual union of a man and a woman.

The main purpose of marriage is the procreation of children, and they are best raised within the marriage context. Women have an innate biological connection to their children. By the actual physical act of growing children within their wombs, women affect their children's personalities, according to *Gratissimam sane* (1994). It is within the family and primarily through women that children learn about Jesus and are first educated in the Christian faith, according to *Familiaris consortio* (1981).

The institution of marriage itself has some prominent characteristics and responsibilities. Marriage and family life need to be protected through active engagement in politics that promotes the family. In marriage, hospitality is practiced not just between spouses but also offered to the rest of society. While the relationship between men and women has been affected through the Fall, since the coming of Jesus marriage can be fundamentally better, and husband and wife can become the partners they were meant to be when God created marriage.

WOMEN AND THE CHURCH

One of the most obvious positions of the church regarding women's roles is that women cannot be ordained to the priesthood. *Inter insigniores* (1976) says women cannot be priests because Jesus did not choose women and God was incarnated as a man. For these two reasons, the church has no power to ordain women.

The maleness of Jesus is highly significant. Woman cannot physically represent the male body of Jesus. The congregation would not recognize Jesus in a woman's body.

However, Jesus treated women well and therefore all of Jesus' choices regarding women and the priesthood are free of societal bias. Women were the first to see the empty tomb and witness the resurrection to the apostles. Likewise, *Ordinatio sacerdotalis* (1994) confirms Jesus' treatment of women with respect and dignity, which went against all societal expectations.

In addition, the male-only priesthood is part of the long tradition of the church. Women as priests could jeopardize salvation. The church declares that it has no authority to ordain women. This was first declared in *Inter insigniores* (1975), reaffirmed in *Ordinatio sacerdotalis* (1994), and declared an infallible doctrine in *Responsum ad propositum dubium* (1995).

Despite the fact that women cannot be priests, they still have an important function within the church. Women are members of the laity and should help spread Christianity. They are also part of the long history of faithful members of the church. Women should participate in church life to a greater capacity and should be allowed to reach their full potential. Women show the church and the larger world in general how to respond to the love of God as a bride responds to the love of the bridegroom. Women witness how to love and how to respond to love received, along with spreading the faith, and that is one of their primary roles within the church.

WOMEN AND THE WORLD

Women's role in the larger society is related to their role within the family and, at the same time, is separate from it. If women work outside the home, they should have jobs and responsibilities that suit their nature and allow them to prioritize their family life. *Gratissimam sane* (1994) says that women's work in the home needs to be valued the same as public sector work is, and women should be able to choose to stay home and raise a family if they wish to do so. Yet, women do not belong only in the home; to think this way is discriminatory toward women.

Apostolicam actuositatem (1965) says that women should work to make the world a better place. They do this by promoting peace, teaching men how to value life, teaching men how to live better, practicing justice according to *Evangelium vitae* (1995), fixing society, working for women's rights, and making society friendlier. They should change the culture of death that currently exists in society into a culture of life, according to *Evangelium vitae* (1995). Society should promote the order of love that women come by naturally, according to *Mulieris dignitatem* (1988).

Evangelium vitae (1995) argues that women should create a new kind of feminism that operates out of feminine genius. Out of their feminine qualities of caring, tenderness, love, and sensitivity, women should help bring about a world that operates out of love. They should help the world build better relationships and ways of relating. Their struggle for human rights should also promote human dignity, which frequently does not happen. Finally, women should teach all people how to be open to others. While women often face oppression, injustice, and discrimination, it is up to women to make the world a better place, one that fosters life, love, and human flourishing.

RECEPTION

One of the measures of the truth of church doctrine historically has been how it is received by the faithful. If the faithful, with their sense of faith given to them by God, do not accept something explained by the church as an article of faith or a part of church doctrine, then it cannot be understood to be such. Ecclesiologist Richard R Gaillardetz argues as much when he writes in *Teaching with Authority,* "A teaching that is not received is not efficacious; it has no transformative power within the community. In short, a nonreceived teaching becomes irrelevant to the life of the community."[1]

---

[1] Richard Gaillardetz, *Teaching with Authority: A Theology of the Magisterium in the Church* (Collegeville, MN: Liturgical Press, 1997), 235.

For Gaillardetz, reception is a historical process that can be seen only with the passing of decades, if not centuries. He suggests *Humanae vitae* may be an example of a church teaching that lacks reception, given the number of Catholic laity that ignore its teachings against contraception and abortion.[2]

At the same time, it is significant to note that different Vatican documents carry different weight. Anthony J. Figueiredo, in *The Magisterium-Theology Relationship*, addresses the theological debate that surrounded the release of *Ordinatio sacerdotalis*. As an apostolic letter, it is out of character for the pope to declare definitive teachings requiring consent. It showed a different kind of teaching authority not usually expressed by the pope: "a teaching of the *definitive* magisterium, even though it was formally an act of the *authentic* and *ordinary* magisterium of the Roman Pontiff. This was something new: that the pope in the framework of his ordinary magisterium should call for a definitive assent such as presupposes infallibility."[3] The choice of words and intent of the document affect its reception as does the theological debate that follows the promulgation of each Vatican document. For women and the theology of womanhood promulgated by the Vatican, this may be more important than the type of document issued.

For example, sometimes the debate is varied and questions authority almost to the point of its outright denial. Then the church may feel the need to clarify its position within a given document. *Ordinatio sacerdotalis* is a good example of this. Since the document is an apostolic letter, but the wording of the document disagrees with the teaching authority usually given this type of papal pronouncement, the Vatican clarifies this authority issue in *Responsum ad propositum dubium* (1995). According to Figueiredo, it does so when it grounds this theological position of the church—that it lacks the authority to ordain women—within the seemingly self-evident truth that is also confirmed in the Bible and supported by the long history of the church.

However, continually needing to declare a position infallible or correct seems to increase uncertainty concerning its validity. If most of the faithful find the doctrine faulty or untrue, then the church should recognize its lack of reception. In this regard, the church should heed the voice of the people rather than publish another document in an attempt to exercise its authority.

The Roman Catholic Church's theology of womanhood laid out within this book is a collection of teachings whose reception needs to be evaluated. There are many people who accept the church's understanding of wom-

---

[2] Ibid., 235.

[3] Anthony Figueiredo, *The Magisterium-Theology Relationship: Contemporary Theological Conceptions in Light of the Universal Church Teaching since 1835 and the Pronouncements of the Bishops of the United States* (Rome: Editrice Pontificia Università Gregoriana, 2001), 272.

anhood and try to live their lives accordingly. There are also theologians who represent this position. On the other hand, a large number of Catholics disagree with these church teachings. Theologians speak on this side of the issue as well. In regard to the reception of the church's theology of womanhood, it seems too soon to offer a judgment, yet one can examine the perspectives of those who agree with the church as well as those who disagree with the teachings.

Let us first look at the reception of this definition of womanhood from the side of those who agree with the Roman Catholic official teachings. There are too many writings to summarize here. With this in mind, this section explores three different authors and three different positions they take regarding the teachings.

Beatriz Vollmer Coles supports the union of gender and sex in her chapter entitled "New Feminism: A Sex-Gender Reunion," in *Women in Christ: Toward a New Feminism.*[4] In the same volume, Elizabeth Fox-Genovese supports gender complementarity in "Equality, Difference and the Practical Problems of a New Feminism," while at the same time she is highly critical of "traditional" or mainstream feminism. The final example is Manfred Hauke's *Women in the Priesthood? A Systematic Analysis in the Light of the Order of Creation and Redemption.*[5] This book explores the support of Jesus' maleness and its theological necessity. Of course, these are not the only arguments these authors make, but the discussion must be limited.

Coles is highly critical of "traditional" (mainstream) feminist arguments. She argues that traditional feminism in its separation of sex and gender has "fragment[ed] the dignity of women and men." Mainstream feminism has defined gender as the outward "intangible aspect of sexuality."[6] Coles agrees with this idea, but not as it is separated from one's gender. Rather, this is the transcendent part of women's sexuality (as well as all cultural and social influences) and selves that is rooted within the body and should be understood as such.[7] Therefore, one's immanence as a physical being (sex) and one's transcendent part (gender) come together to form the human being. A human being's fulfillment comes from operating as a gendered being.[8] Therefore, gender is a significant and inseparable part of being

---

[4] Beatriz Vollmer Coles, "New Feminism: A Sex-Gender Reunion," in *Women in Christ: Toward a New Feminism,* ed. Michele Schumacher (Grand Rapids, MI: Eerdmans Publishing Co., 2004).

[5] Trans. David Kipp (San Francisco: Ignatius Press, 1998).

[6] Here, sexuality is in line with traditional Roman Catholic definitions of it, and not contemporary definitions that understand sexuality to be one part of one's (political?) identity. Rather, sexuality is part of one's being, a dimension of existence.

[7] Coles, "New Feminism," 53.

[8] Ibid.

human just as the body and soul cannot be separated in the human being.[9] Human beings are embodied beings and all of their social interactions come from this gendered embodiment. Coles uses Aquinas's theology to bolster her argument.

Yet, the human being, even as it is gendered and its body is infused with a soul, is not born already made. Humans must develop physically, spiritually, morally, and psychologically. In other words, one must grow into a good human being. One of the ways this is accomplished is through actions. Citing Pope John Paul II, Coles argues that all human beings are fulfilled through their personal actions, not from liberating themselves from obligations or roles. What women must do is come together to figure out what this fulfillment, as specifically feminine beings, should look like.[10]

Another example of a "new feminist" position in line with the call of Pope John Paul II's *Evangelium vitae* is Elizabeth Fox-Genovese's "Equality, Difference and the Practical Problems of a New Feminism."[11] In general, Fox-Genovese is much more critical of and even quite polemical in dealing with mainstream feminism. She believes that the pope's call for a new feminism is necessary because the old version has failed humanity. She lays out seven specific reasons. First, its concern with free and uninhibited access to abortion hurts women across the globe whose problems are more immediate, like hunger, poverty, and disease.

The overemphasis on abortion is also problematic because it tries to imply that women should be able to have "no fault" sex like men can (or at least that problematic secular understandings of maleness believe should be true). Abortion and the larger feminist movement also devalue human life because they do not concern themselves more so with women's global situations. Likewise, abortion kills human life, which also devalues it. Mainstream feminism has also hurt the world because it fails to have an agreed-upon standard of justice, questions authority of all forms, devalues children, and treats persons as means to an end and not as ends in and of themselves. Feminism is also problematic because it is based in individualism and autonomy rather than in the Christian understanding of humans as relational beings. Likewise, feminism argues that women should act like men.[12]

Some Roman Catholic feminists are guilty of using this corrupted version of feminism in their critique of the church. According to Fox-Genovese, Rosemary Radford Ruether and Elisabeth Schüssler Fiorenza are

---

[9] Ibid., 63.

[10] Ibid., 63–66.

[11] Elizabeth Fox-Genovese, "Equality, Difference and the Practical Problems of a New Feminism," in Schumacher, *Women in Christ*, 297–311.

[12] Ibid., 302, 310–11.

"privileging the claims of feminism over those of Christianity by attempting to force Christianity to conform to feminist demands."[13] They also threaten to rid the Roman Catholic faith of all of its orthodoxy. These women are not faithful Christians. Rather, women who believe in gender difference, especially different roles, are the faithful Christians.

For Fox-Genovese, women are naturally grounded in connection, even if they do not have children. Women are also naturally connected to life. Sometimes, in order to honor their nature (based in connections) and the way women cherish life, women must surrender their autonomy for the needs of their children and some rights in accordance with the responsibilities of married life. They must also represent the authority of their children's needs and defer to their husband's authority.[14]

Fox-Genovese calls on women to be counter-cultural, as Jesus was in his time. Here, being counter-cultural is going against mainstream versions of feminism. In this counter-cultural mindset, women and men's differences should be honored. Women naturally care more for life and men are more naturally concerned with power and domination.[15] Women should develop themselves in ways that cherish life and support their family duties. Likewise, a new feminism should be more concerned with promoting life and helping women within developing countries.

The final argument explored here is Manfred Hauke's argument for the significance of Jesus' maleness in his book *Women in the Priesthood? A Systematic Analysis in the Light of the Order of Creation and Redemption*. Only one aspect of his argument in support of a male-only priesthood will be laid out here: the maleness of Jesus.

Jesus' maleness is significant for salvation and supports a male-only priesthood because only men can be priests, kings, and teachers. At first, Hauke explains this position as something other theologians have argued for and avoids taking a stand. He is somewhat tentative in his description of the argument in the beginning. However, he ends one of the sections by agreeing with Louis Bouyer, whom he cites as saying, "At the risk of provoking storms of righteous indignation, I shall state quite frankly: it would have been monstrous if the Son of God had appeared as a woman."[16]

Hauke lays out the argument that supports Jesus as a man. First, all of God's decisions are made out of divine wisdom, and it was God's decision

---

[13] Ibid., 301.

[14] She shies away from this somewhat and adds that if not for their husbands' authority then for their commitment to marriage.

[15] Fox-Genovese, "Equality, Difference and the Practical Problems of a New Feminism," 310.

[16] Hauke, *Women in the Priesthood?* 267. It seems women cannot do what men can, or at least are not as good as men at certain things.

to incarnate as a man.[17] God chose to incarnate as a man because God's relationship to the people of Israel has always been as a husband relates to his wife.[18] Likewise, as a man, Jesus is a better teacher. Men are naturally better at speaking in public because they are less emotional and are therefore better able to communicate, whereas women are better with children and in smaller groups. Jesus' maleness was also significant in his role of king and the power of a king. Men traditionally are the ones with authority and occupy authoritative roles more often than women. Finally, Jesus is the priest because he offers himself as a sacrifice to God and as God sacrificed for humanity. As a priest Jesus is submissive and a mediator, which are also roles of the priest.[19]

Hauke concludes that women represent creatureliness before God while men represent God before humanity as God is the bridegroom to the bride.[20] Men are bridegrooms too. Jesus' maleness is highly significant, but it is only one reason within the entire book why women cannot and should not be ordained priests. The other ones are historical and theological and can be found within the rest of the book.

Hauke's perspective is quite beyond how the Roman Catholic Church describes the differences between men and women. Yet, his theology, while more extreme than those of Fox-Genovese and Coles, is in line with Roman Catholic teaching regarding women's access to the priesthood. It also differs significantly. The church actually asks women to teach the world how to be better, how to listen more, how to care more, how to cherish life, and the like; it does not state that this can only take place within the family or within small gatherings of people. Likewise, the church would never describe God's incarnation within Jesus as monstrous if it took place in a woman. For the Roman Catholic Church, there is a difference between men and women that makes each excel at different roles because they have different but complementary natures.

On the other side of this debate are those religious feminists who disagree with some aspects of the Roman Catholic Church's theology of womanhood. Three examples of areas of contention are gender complementarity's idea of different roles for the sexes, the church's anti-abortion and anti-contraceptive stance, and its limiting of the priesthood to men only. In *In Memory of Her*, Elisabeth Schüssler Fiorenza argues for expanded leadership opportunities for women within the church. Benedictine Joan Chittister argues against limited roles for women. Finally, Rosemary Radford

---

[17] Ibid., 250.
[18] Ibid., 251.
[19] Ibid., 263.
[20] Ibid., 472.

Ruether speaks against church teaching regarding contraception and abortion, believing, instead, that women need to have control over their bodies.

According to Schüssler Fiorenza, the early church did have women in leadership roles because the first churches were house churches and women ran the households.[21] Women were apostles,[22] deaconesses with much authority,[23] and missionaries. For these reasons alone women should have more authority and leadership roles within the church. She writes, "Those who claim the authority of Andrew and Peter and argue against the teaching authority of women because of their hate for the female race distort the true Christian message."[24] At the same time, much historical evidence of the role of women in the early Christian community is lost due to androcentric text concerns and the patriarchal society out of which they came.[25] In this regard, Schüssler Fiorenza believes that the primary message of Jesus called for the end of patriarchy and the beginning of an egalitarian community, a "discipleship of equals."[26]

Benedictine Joan Chittister writes in *Job's Daughters* that "women need power to control resources, make laws, apply sanctions and shape ideas if this planet has any hope for salvation."[27] Yet, men have taken it upon themselves to define women,[28] and,that definition has always assumed that women were inferior to men in biology, in intellectual capacity, in decision-making abilities, and in morality. Women have been taught that self-sacrifice and service for others, rather than care for themselves and their own development, are divine.[29] In some sense women have internalized the official church teaching and the societal ideal of women. For this reason, Chittister writes:

> We talk about God's will for us and a woman's role and woman's lot in life. We tell our intelligent daughters that intelligence is something they should pursue on the side, and we tell our athletic daughters that athletics is a pastime, not a life for them, and we tell our assertive

---

[21] Elisabeth Schüssler Fiorenza, *In Memory of Her: A Feminist Theological Reconstruction of Christian Origins* (New York: Crossroad, 1994), 183.

[22] Ibid., 172.

[23] Ibid., 170.

[24] Ibid., 306.

[25] Ibid., 60.

[26] Ibid., 140.

[27] Joan Chittister, O.S.B., *Job's Daughters: Women and Power* (New York: Paulist Press, 1990), 76.

[28] Ibid., 1; Joan Chittister, O.S.B., *WomanStrength: Modern Church, Modern Women* (Kansas City, MO: Sheed and Ward, 1990), 2–3.

[29] Joan Chittister, O.S.B., *The Way We Were: A Story of Conversion and Renewal* (Maryknoll, NY: Orbis Books, 2005), 39.

daughters that management is a man's task but that housekeeping is their task.[30]

She continues, "To say that there are some Christian ministries that are limited by sex (i.e., the priesthood) is to say that no one is obliged to the whole Gospel. Some demands of the Gospel are male, some female."[31] "[Women] are beginning to wonder whether or not those who do not have the full rights of baptism do or do not have its responsibilities either."[32] In the same vein, obedience and fidelity are not measures of an adult spirituality and never can be.[33]

Ruether, in *Disputed Questions,* declares the church denial of the ability of women to control their reproductive capacity through contraception and abortion "irrational."[34] She also denies the official church position that one's salvation hinges on whether or not one follows church teaching regarding contraception and abortion. Ruether labels the ban against birth control and abortion a "public crime" because of the emotional, physical, and societal effects of this policy on millions of women around the globe.[35] In addition, "the Vatican's denial of reproductive agency to women is one of the most egregious forms of violence against women and children."[36] The denial of contraceptive practices is one of those laws/regulations that support sexism in society because it denies women control over their own bodies.[37] So strong is her opinion about the church's teachings on abortion and contraception that she judges the leadership of the Catholic Church responsible for fostering situations that force women to have abortions. She states, "The Vatican's contradictory religious ethic denies women effective birth control and disparages women's moral agency, making the Catholic Church a major force in the world that caused some women to need abortions."[38] With this in mind, as well as the church leadership's own

---

[30] Joan Chittister, O.S.B., *Beyond Beijing: The Next Step for Women* (Kansas City, MO: Sheed and Ward, 1996), 5; Chittister, *The Way We Were*, 19.

[31] Chittister, *Women, Ministry and the Church* (New York: Paulist Press, 1983), 48.

[32] Ibid., 72.

33   Joan Chittister, O.S.B., *Heart of Flesh: A Feminist Spirituality for Men and Women* (Grand Rapids, MI: Eerdmans Publishing Co., 1998), 64; Chittister, *The Way We Were*, 67.

[34] Rosemary Radford Ruether, *Disputed Questions: On Being a Christian* (Maryknoll, NY: Orbis Books, 1989), 115.

[35] Ibid., 117–18.

[36] Ruether, *Catholic Does Not Equal the Vatican: A Vision for Progressive Catholicism* (New York: The New Press, 2008), 59.

[37] Rosemary Radford Ruether, *Sexism and God-Talk: Toward a Feminist Theology* (Boston: Beacon Press, 1993), 175.

[38] Ruether, *Catholic Does Not Equal the Vatican*, 57.

approval of slavery and serfdom well after many in society had seen the evil in those institutions, Ruether deems that the church is not a credible moral teacher. Since sexuality, contraception, abortion, and even some aspects of women's roles are moral issues, Ruether denies the authority of church pronouncements on these subjects.

ROCK-HARD DOCTRINE OR MALLEABLE TEACHINGS?

In November 2010, Ignatius Press published *Pope Benedict XVI: Light of the World*, a compilation of interviews between Peter Seewald and the pope. One of the most discussed interviews was the section on condom usage based on the pope's trip to Africa in 2009. The pope ends his answer by saying:

> There may be a basis in the case of some individuals, as perhaps when a male prostitute uses a condom, where this can be a first step in the direction of a moralization, a first assumption of responsibility, on the way toward recovering an awareness that not everything is allowed and that one cannot do whatever one wants. But it is not really the way to deal with the evil of HIV infection. That can really lie only in a humanization of sexuality.[39]

He goes on to say that it is important for sexuality to become something more human and more connected to humanity and human lives rather than seen as a strictly biological action or function, an outward act with little to no real human significance or relationship to human community.

In the days that followed publication of the book, confusion reigned about how this idea affected church teachings on condom use, with many church leaders in Africa welcoming the idea and many conservative Catholics disagreeing.[40] Vatican officials made a point of explaining that condom use as a lesser evil does not change the church's stance on contraception, illicit sex, and other sinful acts. Chastity and abstinence are still better methods to prevent disease. Likewise, the church must continue to invest time and resources in caring for the sick, providing education, and advocating an understanding of sexuality that emphasizes its humanity.

---

[39] Ignatius Press, "Excerpts from *Light of the World*," available on the ignatius.com website.

[40] John Harper, "Catholic Church Tries to Clear Confusion over Condom Use," *Guardian News and Media* 2011, available on the guardian.co.uk website.

While the statement by no means changes church teachings on condom use,[41] it definitely opens the door to more theological discussion concerning church teachings on sexuality, ethics, and morality. It points to the fact that much church doctrine is theological discussion. The church used to think that condom use was inherently evil, but through an experience of human suffering and a fuller understanding of human responsibility, it is now seeing that in some situations the use of condoms could actually be more moral than not using them. It could save lives.

Church teachings on women are also part of a theological discussion. In fact, it is easy to see how much a part of a discussion they are since women's ordination is specifically declared a topic *not* up for discussion. This means that the rest of the church's teachings on women—women's roles, definitions of femininity, how women find fulfillment, and women's contribution to the church and the world—are all theological matters open for discussion. Feminist theologians, middle-of-the-road theologians, liberal theologians, conservative theologians, laity, and clergy all have the responsibility to read church documents, to contemplate them, and to pray on them.

The theological discussion of what it means to be a woman continues. This book offers a summary of its key characteristics up to this point in time. However, something seems to be missing from this official discussion. In the future, it seems that official Vatican teachings need to include more women's voices. After all, women are the topic of discussion, and it makes sense that they become a central part of that discussion as well as recognized in a more official capacity. The church calls for more expanded roles within the church for women in many of the documents examined in this book; this would be an excellent way to add a more formal and official level to women's participation, mission, and ministry within the church. In fact, women's voices from all parts of life, ages, vocations, and locations should be a required part of their own theological self-definition. This is another way to make the world more just and more human. If women have much to teach the world, the church has an excellent opportunity to let their voices be heard, empower them, and show them respect and dignity. Who knows how the Roman Catholic Church's theology of womanhood would evolve when women are empowered to speak for and about themselves?

---

[41] For an explanation of the traditional stance of the church regarding contraception, see Chapters 1 and 2 in this book.

Bibliography

Brownmiller, Susan. *In Our Time: Memoir of a Revolution*. New York: The Dial Press, 1990.

Butler, Judith. *Gender Trouble: Feminism and the Subversion of Identity*. New York: Routledge 1990.

Catechism of Christian Doctrine, no. 1–4. Philadelphia: J. J. McVey, 1922.

Chittister, O.S.B., Joan. "Coming Soon: 'An Effective and Intelligent Campaign,'" *The National Catholic Reporter*. http://www.nationalcatholicreporter.org/fwis/fw101403.htm

———. *Beyond Beijing: The Next Step for Women*. Kansas City, MO: Sheed and Ward, 1996.

———. *Heart of Flesh: A Feminist Spirituality for Women and Men*. Grand Rapids, MI: William B. Eerdmans Publishing Co., 1998.

———. *Job's Daughters: Women and Power*. New York: Paulist Press, 1990.

———. *The Way We Were: A Story of Conversion and Renewal*, Maryknoll, NY: Orbis Books, 2005.

———. *WomanStrength: Modern Church, Modern Women*. Kansas City, MO: Sheed and Ward, 1990.

———. *Women, Ministry and the Church*. New York: Paulist Press, 1983.

Connell, Francis. *Outlines of Moral Theology*. Milwaukee: Bruce Publishing Co., 1958.

Curd, Ann E., and Robin O. Andreasen, eds. *Feminist Theory: A Philosophical Anthology*. Oxford: Blackwell Publishing, 2005.

Daly, Mary. *Gyn/ecology: The Meta-ethics of Radical Feminism*. Boston: Beacon Press, 1978.

Donovan, J., trans. *Catechism of the Council of Trent*. New York: Catholic Publication Society, 1890.

Fausto-Sterling, Anne. *Sexing the Body: Gender Politics and the Construction of Sexuality*. New York: BasicBooks, 2000.

Figueiredo, Anthony. *The Magisterium-Theology Relationship: Contemporary Theological Conceptions in Light of the Universal Church Teaching since 1835 and the Pronouncements of the Bishops of the United States*. Rome: Editrice Pontificia Università Gregoriana, 2001.

Forster, Margaret. *Significant Sisters: The Grassroots of Active Feminism 1839-1939*. New York: Alfred A. Knopf, 1985.

Freedman, Estelle B. *No Turning Back: The History of Feminism and the Future of Women*. New York: Ballantine Books, 2002.

Gaillardetz, Richard. *Teaching with Authority: A Theology of the Magisterium in the Church*. Collegeville, MN: Liturgical Press, 1997.

Gruenbaum, Ellen. "Feminist Activism for the Abolition of FGC in Sudan." *Journal of Middle East Women's Studies* 1, no. 2 (April 1, 2005): 89-111 and 165.

Harper, John. "Catholic Church Tries to Clear Confusion over Condom Use." Guardian News and Media 2011. http://www.guardian.co.uk/world/2010/nov/23/catholic-church-condom-use

Hauke, Manfred. *Women in the Priesthood?: A Systematic Analysis in the Light of the Order of Creation and Redemption*. Translated by David Kipp. San Francisco: Ignatius Press, 1988.

Ignatius Press. "Excerpts from *Light of the World*." http://www.ignatius.com/promotions/light-of-the-world/excerpt.htm

International Humanist and Ethical Union. "International Women's Year, 1975," IHEU Congress, 1974. http://www.iheu.org/node/2127

Jaggar, Allison M. *Feminist Politics and Human Nature*. Savage, MD: Rowman and Littlefield Publishers, 1988.

Mansbridge, Jane J. *Why We Lost the ERA*. Chicago: University of Chicago Press, 1986.

Mohanty, Chandra Talpade, Ann Russo, and Lourdes Torres, eds. *Third World Women and the Politics of Feminism*. Bloomington: University of Indiana Press, 1991.

Narayan, Uma. *Dislocating Cultures: Identities, Traditions and Third World Feminisms*. New York: Routledge, 1997.

Ruether, Rosemary Radford. *Catholic Does Not Equal the Vatican: A Vision for Progressive Catholicism*. New York: The New Press, 2008.

———. *Contemporary Roman Catholicism Crises and Challenges*. Kansas City, MO: Sheed and Ward, 1987.

———. *Disputed Questions: On Being a Christian*. Nashville, TN: Abingdon, 1982.

———. *Sexism and God-Talk: Toward a Feminist Theology*. Boston: Beacon Press, 1993.

Roberts, Dorothy. *Killing the Black Body: Race, Reproduction, and the Meaning of Liberty*. New York: Pantheon Books, 1997.

Schumacher, Michele, ed. *Women in Christ: Toward a New Feminism*. Grand Rapids, MI: William B. Eerdmans Publishing Co., 2004.

Schüssler Fiorenza, Elisabeth. *In Memory of Her: A Feminist Theological Reconstruction of Christian Origins*. New York: Crossroad, 1994.

SUGGESTIONS FOR FURTHER READING

Support for the Official Theology of Womanhood

Benkovic, Johnnette. *Full of Grace: Women and the Abundant Life*. Cincinnati: OH: St. Anthony Messenger Press, 2004.

Kineke, Genevieve. *The Authentic Catholic Woman*. Cincinnati, OH: St. Anthony Messenger Press, 2006.

Pope John Paul II. *The Genius of Women*. Washington DC: U.S. Catholic Conference, 1997.

Von Hildebrand, Alice. *The Privilege of Being a Woman*. Ypsilanti, MI: Veritas Press of Ave Maria College, 2002.

Against the Official Theology of Womanhood

Cahill, Lisa Sowle. *Sex, Gender and Christian Ethics*. New York: Cambridge University Press, 2005.

Farley, Margaret. *Just Love: A Framework for Christian Sexual Ethics*. New York: Continuum Publishing, 2006.

Ruether, Rosemary Radford. *Christianity and the Making of the Modern Family*. Boston: Beacon Press, 2000.

Torjesen, Karen Jo. *When Women Were Priests: Women's Leadership in the Early Church and the Scandal of their Subordination in the Rise of Christianity*. New York: HarperCollins Publishers, 1995.

Index

255